RAF
Airborne Forces Manual

This series is published in association with
The RAF Museum, Hendon, London

RAF
Airborne Forces
Manual

The Official Air Publications for RAF Paratroop Aircraft
and Gliders, 1942-1946

RAF Museum Series: Volume 8
General Editor: John Tanner, Director,
RAF Museum, Hendon

LONDON: ARMS AND ARMOUR PRESS
NEW YORK: HIPPOCRENE BOOKS, INC.

Published in Great Britain, 1979,
by Arms and Armour Press,
2-6 Hampstead High Street,
London NW3 1QQ

Published in the United States, 1979,
by Hippocrene Books, Inc.,
171 Madison Avenue, New York,
N.Y. 10016

ISBN 0-85368-163-5

ISBN 0-88254-485-3
Library of Congress Catalog Card
Number: 7 -84780

RAF Airborne Forces Manual is Crown Copyright and published by permission of the Controller of Her Majesty's Stationery Office. The material contained in this volume originally appeared under the Air Publication references 2453 (*Airborne Forces Manual*), 2453A (*Carriage and Dropping of Paratroops and Equipment*) and 2453D (*Carriage of Equipment*). The original Air Publications were produced for official use and internal purposes by the Air Ministry. The quality of both the type and illustrations in the originals used in the production of this volume fall short of the high standards normally expected in a modern book; they have, of necessity, been reproduced to complete this facsimile edition.

Printed by Kingprint Limited, Richmond, Surrey.
Bound by Kemp Hall Bindery, Oxford.

Contents

Foreword

by J. M. Bruce
Keeper of Aircraft and Research Studies,
Royal Air Force Museum, Hendon

"We ought to have a corps of at least five thousand parachute troops . . . I hear something is being done already to form such a corps but only, I believe, on a very small scale. Advantage must be taken of the summer to train these forces, who can none the less play their part meanwhile as shock troops in home defence. Pray let me have a note from the War Office on the subject."

Thus wrote the Prime Minister, Winston Churchill, on 22 June 1940. Action to create Britain's airborne forces began within forty-eight hours, scarcely a moment too soon. Even then, Britain was some years behind Germany, and even further behind Russia, which had pioneered the creation of parachute troops in the early 1930s. The efficacy of such airborne forces was first demonstrated in war by the Germans, nowhere more effectively than in their capture of Crete.

In the beginning, the evolution of British aircraft and equipment was somewhat empirical and was based on what was available, however marginal its suitability might be. Nevertheless, the pressures of war and British ingenuity soon produced a body of fully-trained paratroops. On 10/11 February 1941, a handful of parachutists went into action against the Monte Vulture aqueduct in Southern Italy, and, on 12 November 1942, the 3rd Battalion of the 1st Parachute Brigade dropped from C.47 aircraft of No. 60 Group, USAAF, to capture Bône airfield in North Africa.

British airborne forces then went on to successes in Sicily, Italy and elsewhere in war-ravaged Europe. As their numbers grew and their effectiveness increased, so did the range and variety of their equipment and the means of its delivery. This is reflected in the pages of these reprints of Air Publications 2453, 2453A and 2453D, which describe aircraft conversions, parachute troop installations, flying and emergency procedures, and the uses of the transport gliders.

What they cannot describe is the gallantry and skill of the men who went to war in this unique way. Perhaps the reading of this book may convey something of that special courage that was marked by the red beret: let it never be forgotten.

1

Conversion of Bomber Aircraft for Paratroop Operations, 1942/3

WHITLEY V
CONVERSION FOR PARATROOPS

REMOVE	**ADD**
BALLAST WEIGHT CRADLE	WINDSHIELD FOR APERTURE
DESERT EQUIPMENT LOCKER	TAIL WHEEL SPAT
FORWARD FLARE RACK	TWO STRONG POINTS
OXYGEN BOTTLE MOUNTINGS	FOUR PANELS
SPARE AMMUNITION RACKS	TEN STROPS
MAINTENANCE LADDER	CONTAINER RELEASE SWITCH
	SIGNAL LIGHT
	LOCKING BAR FOR SELECTOR SWITCH

This page issued with A.L. No. 1
October, 1942

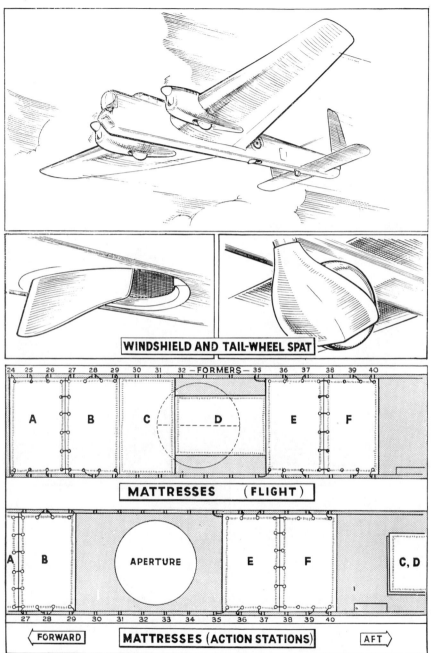

WINDSHIELD AND TAIL-WHEEL SPAT

MATTRESSES (FLIGHT)

MATTRESSES (ACTION STATIONS)

FORWARD

AFT

FIG.1. **WHITLEY V.** PARATROOP MODIFICATIONS

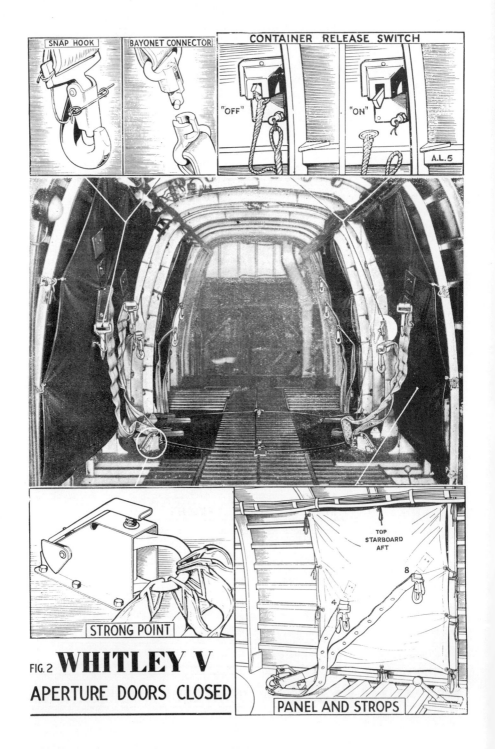

SNAP HOOK

BAYONET CONNECTOR

CONTAINER RELEASE SWITCH

"OFF"

"ON"

A.L.5

STRONG POINT

TOP STARBOARD AFT

PANEL AND STROPS

FIG. 2 **WHITLEY V**
APERTURE DOORS CLOSED

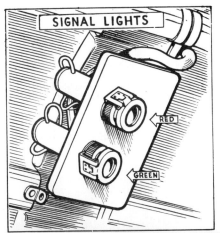

SIGNAL LIGHTS

RED

GREEN

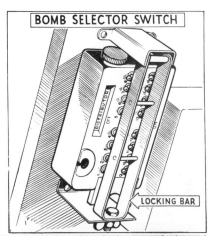

BOMB SELECTOR SWITCH

LOCKING BAR

FIG.3 **WHITLEY V** APERTURE DOORS OPEN

Whitley V

Floor aperture (*see* figs. 2 and 3)

6.   The Whitley V has a floor aperture occupying the hole originally provided for a bottom turret which is not fitted.   This aperture is an oval hole 36 inches wide, by 40 inches long, and provides the means by which the paratroops leave the aircraft.   The aperture is covered by two doors hinged to the floor of the aircraft.   These doors are semi-circular in shape and are secured, during flight, by means of two sliding bolts engaging with fitments on the floor of the fuselage.   For action by paratroops each door is opened and hitched to one of the fuselage frames by means of a strap and press stud.

7.   A canvas cover may be fitted over the aperture on the underside of the fuselage if the aircraft is to be flown extensively between paratroop operations.   Ref. Whitley Mod. 238, para. 2 (xii).

Windshield (*see* fig. 1)

8.   The forward edge of the aperture, on the underside of the aircraft, is protected by a metal windshield.   The purpose of this is to divert the air-flow at the mouth of the aperture and assist the paratroops to make a safe exit.   The Mod. sheet referred to below indicates a backward slope on the windshield; this has been changed to a forward slope by the insertion of welded fillets in the sides of the original windshields.   The rear edge of the aperture is fitted with a wooden rear bend to prevent chafing of the trailing strops.   Ref. Whitley Mod. 238, para. 2 (viii) Drg. L 219.

Tail wheel spat (*see* fig. 1)

9.   A streamlined tail wheel spat is fitted to prevent the parachutes and static lines becoming entangled with the tail wheel.   Ref. Whitley Mod. 238, para. 2 (x), Drg. L 217.

Strong points (*see* fig. 2)

10.   Two strong points are fitted, one on each side of a fuselage cross member, just aft of the aperture.   Each comprises a bracket, mounted on the flooring, and carrying a removable pin and shackle to which five strops are attached.   The pin is integral with a top lever which must be depressed and rotated through 90° before it can be withdrawn to release the shackle for attachment or jettisoning of strops.   Two quadrant-shaped hinged plates, mounted one on each side of the lever, act as a safety catch to prevent inadvertent release of the shackle.   Ref. Whitley Mod. 238, para. 2 (ix), Drg. L 218.

Panels (*see* fig. 2)

11.   Four khaki duck panels are secured by tapes to the frames of the fuselage interior.   One port and one starboard panel are fitted forward of the aperture, and one port and one starboard panel are fitted aft of the aperture.   The panels are stencilled to indicate which position each is to occupy, and also to indicate the numbers of the strops which each panel is intended to carry.   Ref. Whitley Mod. 238, para. 2 (xi).

Strops (*see* fig.2)

12.   Ten strops are fitted, leading from the two strong points to the four panels.   The distribution of the strops is as follows :—

Strop No.	Panel position		Length		Strong point
1	Starboard	Forward	5 ft.	6 in.	Starboard
2	Port	Aft	3 ft.	3 in.	Port
3	Port	Forward	5 ft.	6 in.	Port
4	Starboard	Aft	3 ft.	3 in.	Starboard
5	Starboard	Forward	6 ft.	9 in.	Starboard
6	Port	Aft	4 ft.	0 in.	Port
7	Port	Forward	6 ft.	9 in.	Port
8	Starboard	Aft	4 ft.	0 in.	Starboard
9	Starboard	Forward	7 ft.	10 in.	Starboard
10	Port	Aft	4 ft.	9 in.	Port

13.   The strops are made of $1\frac{3}{4}$ inch wide heavy, white, double webbing, and are equipped with press studs for attachment to the panels.   One end of each strop carries a D ring for attachment to a strong point, and the other end is fitted either with a snap hook or a bayonet connector for attachment to the parachute static lines.   Number 5 strop carries, in addition, a tab for holding the cord which operates the container release switch.

Snap hook (*see* fig. 2)

14. The snap hook is a standard fitting for connecting static lines to strops. It comprises a rectangular eye for the strop and a hook having a spring latch and safety-pin fastening.

Bayonet connector (*see* fig. 2)

15. The bayonet connector is an alternative means of attaching the strop to the static line. It comprises a male part with a rectangular eye for the strop, and a female part with a rectangular eye for the static line. Spring catches prevent the parts being disengaged except with the aid of a special tool.

Container release switch (*see* fig. 2)

16. A type "B" single unit switch, Stores Ref. 5C/543, is fitted to a frame at the starboard side of the fuselage and opposite the floor aperture. This switch is electrically connected to the bomb selector, and, when operated by a cord attached to strop number 5, releases the containers from the bomb cradles. The operating cord terminates in a ring which is passed over the switch lever when this is in the ON position, and is trapped under a slotted shroud when the switch is OFF. Thus, when number 5 strop is pulled and the switch actuated, the release of the cord and ring from the switch lever is assured. Ref. Whitley Mod. 238, para. 2 (XV on corrigenda sheet 1).

17. A piece of No. 18 linen thread is whipped to the operating cord and tied through a stringer cut-away just above the switch so as to leave a four inch loop of cord. In this way a safeguard is provided against operation of the switch by an accidental pull on the number 5 strop, since the force so applied will be dissipated in breaking the thread.

Signal lights (*see* fig. 3)

18. A two-colour signal light is mounted inside the fuselage above the port aperture door. The signal light is wired to switches under the control of the pilot and the observer. When the red light is switched on, the paratroops take up "action stations"; when the green light appears, the paratroops leave the aircraft.

Locking bar for bomb selector switches (*see* fig. 3)

19. The bomb selector, mounted on the bomb aimer's panel, is fitted with a locking bar which prevents accidental movement of the selected switches. Release of the containers from the bomb cradles is effected by the container release switch described above. Ref. Whitley Mod. 238, para. 2 (xiv on corrigenda sheet 1) Drg. L 287.

Setting of bomb distributor for release of containers

20. The bomb distributor should be set to give an interval of 0·05 secs. between the release of successive containers.

Accessories

21. The following accessories may be required in Whitley aircraft used for paratroop operations:—

    (i) One intercomm. helmet

    (ii) One thermos flask

    (iii) Two rubber urine bottles

    (iv) A supply of paper "sick" bags.

Container strong points

22. The four bomb stations in the fuselage, and the inner three bomb stations on each wing are equipped with container strong points which comprise lugs to which the static lines of the container parachutes may be tied. It should be noted that the wing stations are not suitable for carrying 500 lb. loads.

Mattresses (*see* fig. 1)

23. Six "Numna" mattresses, each measuring 5 ft. by 3 ft., are supplied for use on the floor of the Whitley for paratroop operations. Two mattresses are fastened by cords to formers forward of the aperture and two are fastened to formers aft of the aperture. The remaining two mattresses are laid loosely over the aperture doors during flight and are stowed at the rear of the side entrance to the fuselage when the paratroops take up action stations.

Whitley Modification Numbers

24. The following Whitley Modification Sheets refer to paratroop operations:—

    (i) Fixed Mods. Nos. 237, 408, and 489.

    (ii) Removable Mods. Nos. 238 and 480.

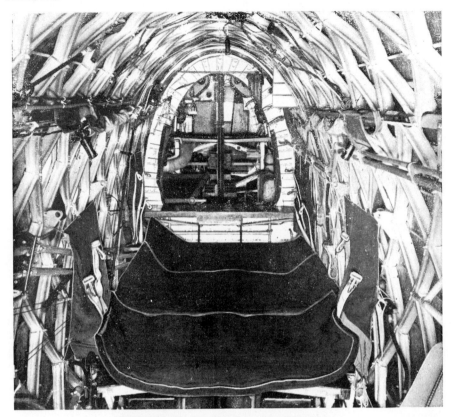

WELLINGTON

CONVERSION FOR PARATROOPS

REMOVE	ADD
BEAM GUNS	WINDSHIELD AND REAR BEND
BEAM GUN AMMUNITION RACKS	DIM LIGHTING SET
BEAM GUNNERS' SEATS	WOODEN SEAT, BATTENS AND FLOORING
FLARE CHUTE INSTALLATION	TWO STRONG POINTS
MIDSHIPS ARMOURED BULKHEAD	FOUR PANELS
OXYGEN BOTTLES AND RACKS	TEN STROPS AND SNAP HOOKS
SEA-MARKER STOWAGE AT STARBOARD	CONTAINER RELEASE SWITCH
	SIGNAL LIGHTS
	MASK FOR SELECTOR SWITCHES

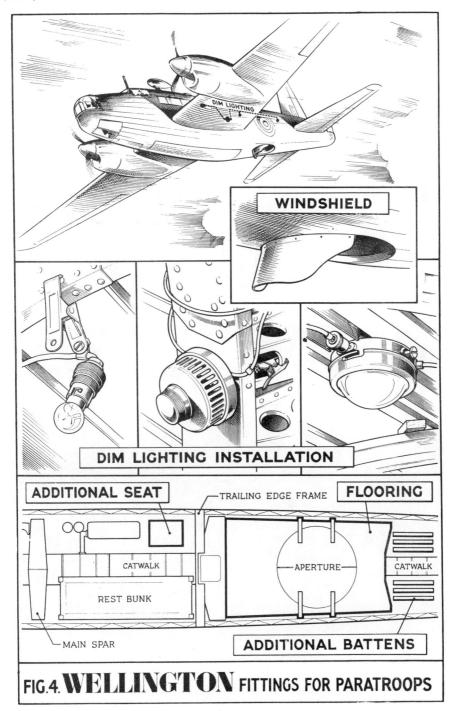

FIG. 4. **WELLINGTON** FITTINGS FOR PARATROOPS

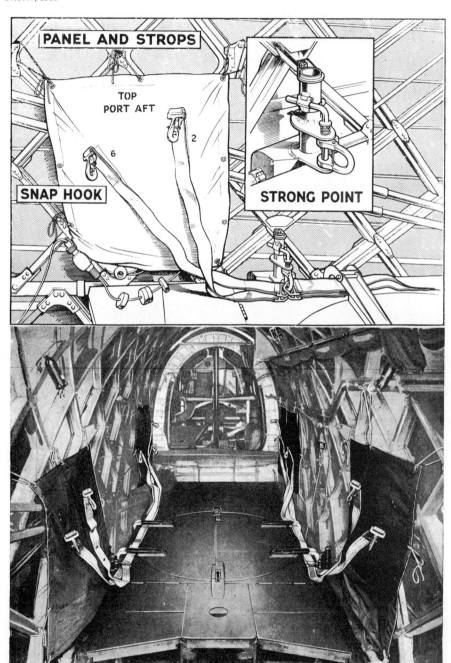

FIG. 5 **WELLINGTON** APERTURE DOORS CLOSED

This page issued with A.L. No. 1
October, 1942

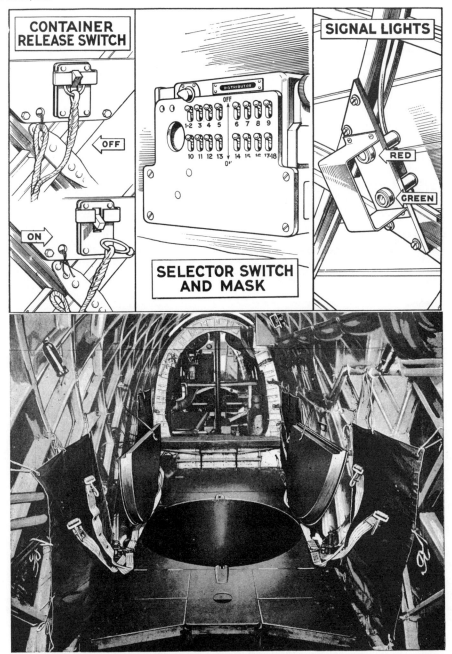

CONTAINER RELEASE SWITCH

OFF

ON

SELECTOR SWITCH AND MASK

SIGNAL LIGHTS

RED

GREEN

FIG. 6 **WELLINGTON** APERTURE DOORS OPEN

Wellington Ic, II, III, IV and X

Alterations and removal of equipment

25. The modifications to Wellington aircraft for the carriage of paratroops are covered by Alterations Nos. P.1019 and P.1449. The following equipment is removed from the aircraft:—
    (i) Flare chute installation. The flare chute aperture is blanked off.
    (ii) Beam guns, beam gun ammunition racks and the rack supports.
    (iii) Beam gunners' seats.
    (iv) Midships armoured bulkhead.
    (v) Oxygen bottles and racks.
    (vi) The sea-marker stowage on the starboard side, just forward of the trailing edge frame.

(A.L.8)

Floor aperture

26. The floor aperture, through which the paratroops drop, is approximately forty-six inches in diameter and is covered by two semicircular hinged doors. During take-off and flight to target the doors are secured by bolts to the floor of the aircraft; for action by paratroops each door is opened and hitched to the geodetic structure by means of a strap and a press stud.

Windshield (*see* fig. 4)

27. The forward edge of the aperture, on the underside of the aircraft, is protected by a metal windshield. The purpose of this is to divert the air-flow at the mouth of the aperture and assist the paratroops to make a safe exit. The rear edge of the aperture is fitted with a wooden rear bend to prevent chafing of the trailing strops.

Tail wheel

28. The tail wheel is retractable and does not therefore require a spat to prevent fouling of strops and static lines.

Dim lighting installation (*see* fig. 4)

29. A standard dim lighting installation designed for paratroop operations is provided for the Wellington. The set comprises two 6-watt lamps attached to the fuselage roof forward and aft of the aperture, a resistance mounted on the port side of the fuselage to enable the lights to be dimmed some minutes before the paratroops leave the aircraft, and a plug to energise the circuit from one of the normal roof lighting fitments. Clips are provided for attaching the wiring.

30. The purpose of the dim lighting installation is to accustom the eyes of the paratroops to a dim light before action takes place during the hours of darkness.

Seating accommodation (*see* fig. 4)

31. A wooden strut is fitted at the aft end of the rest bunk to replace the steel cable support and allow Number 9 paratroop to move freely to the aperture.

32. A removable ply-wood seat is fitted on the starboard side immediately forward of the trailing frame. This forms the travelling station for Number 10 paratroop.

Extension of cat-walk battens (*see* fig. 4)

33. The battens on each side of the cat-walk just aft of the step are extended to give Numbers 6 and 8 paratroops a better foothold at action stations. These battens are also made of heavier section material than standard.

Alteration to flooring (*see* fig. 4)

34. Provision is made, by means of altered flooring, to accommodate the paratroops at action stations and to guard the control cables and CO_2 flotation tubes running along the lower part of the fuselage.

Stowage of handrail

35. The rope handrail on the port side of the fuselage, just forward of the aperture, is disconnected at one end and coiled up for paratroop operations to prevent interference with Number 7 paratroop at his action station.

Strong points (see fig. 5)

36. Two strong points are fitted, one on each side of the fuselage, just aft of the aperture. Each comprises a bracket, mounted on the geodetic structure, and carrying a removable pin and shackle to which five strops are attached. The pin is integral with a top lever which must be rotated through 90° before it can be withdrawn to release the shackle for the attachment or jettisoning of strops.

Panels (see fig. 5)

37. Four khaki duck panels are secured by tapes to the fuselage geodetic structure. One port and one starboard panel, each equipped for three strops, are fitted forward of the aperture and one port and one starboard panel, each equipped for two strops, are fitted aft of the aperture. The panels are stencilled to indicate which position each is to occupy, and also to indicate the numbers of the strops which each panel is intended to carry.

Strops (see fig. 5)

38. Ten strops are fitted, leading from the two strong points to the four panels. The distribution of the strops is as follows:—

Strop No.	Panel position		Length of strop	Strong point
1	Starboard	Forward	5 ft. 6 in.	Starboard
2	Port	Aft	3 ft. 0 in.	Port
3	Port	Forward	5 ft. 6 in.	Port
4	Starboard	Aft	3 ft. 0 in.	Starboard
5	Starboard	Forward	6 ft. 9 in.	Starboard
6	Port	Aft	3 ft. 0 in.	Port
7	Port	Forward	6 ft. 9 in.	Port
8	Starboard	Aft	3 ft. 0 in.	Starboard
9	Port	Forward	7 ft. 10 in.	Port
10	Starboard	Forward	7 ft. 10 in.	Starboard

39. The strops are made of 1¾ inch wide, heavy, white, double webbing, and are equipped with press studs for attachment to the panels. One end of each strop carries a D ring for attachment to a strong point, and the other end is fitted with a snap hook for attachment to the parachute static lines. Number 5 strop carries, in addition, a tab for holding the cord which operates the container release switch.

Snap hook (see fig. 5)

40. The snap hook is a standard fitting for connecting static lines to strops. It comprises a rectangular eye for the strop and a hook having a spring latch and safety pin fastening.

Container release switch (see fig. 6)

41. A type "B" single unit switch, Stores Ref. 5D/534, is fitted to a bracket at the starboard side of the fuselage and opposite the floor aperture. This switch is electrically connected to the bomb selector, and, when operated by a cord attached to a Number 5 strop, releases the containers from the bomb cradles. The operating cord terminates in a ring which is passed over the switch lever when this is in the ON position, and is trapped under a divided bridge piece when the switch is OFF. Thus, when Number 5 strop is pulled and the switch actuated, the release of the cord and ring from the switch lever is certain.

42. A piece of No. 18 linen thread is whipped to a loop in the operating cord and tied to a fixed point in such a way that an accidental pull on the operating cord will stress or break the thread without actuating the switch.

Signal lights (see fig. 6)

43. A two-colour signal light is mounted inside the fuselage above the starboard door of the aperture. The signal light is wired to a switch in the pilot's cockpit. When the red light is switched on the paratroops take up "Action stations"; when the green light appears the paratroops leave the aircraft. A shield is fitted over the signal lights to prevent their being seen from the ground when the aperture doors are open.

Mask for bomb selector switches (*see* fig. 6)

44.   A mask is fitted across the bomb selector switchbox to enable the sixteen selector switches to operate on the eighteen bomb stations provided on the Wellington.   By means of the mask, switch number 1 releases bombs numbers 1 and 2, switch number 2 releases bomb number 3, and so on up to switch number 16 which releases bombs numbers 17 and 18.   For the purpose of container release during paratroop operations, only top, outside stations are used and therefore only the corresponding switches will need to be selected (*see* Chapter 5, Section 2 of this Manual).

Setting of bomb distributor for release of containers

45.   The bomb distributor should be set to give an interval of 0·15 secs. between the release of successive containers.   It should be noted that, since only top stations are employed, the first eight studs of the distributor will be inoperative.

Accessories

46.   The following accessories may be required in Wellington aircraft used for paratroop operations:—

    (i)   One intercomm. helmet

   (ii)   One thermos flask

  (iii)   Two rubber urine bottles

  (iv)   A supply of paper "sick" bags.

Mattresses (*see* **Wellington frontispiece**)

47.   Three "Numna" mattresses, each measuring 5 ft. by 3 ft., are used in the Wellington for paratroop operations.   During flight to target the mattresses are laid transversely across the wooden flooring and aperture doors; at action stations the mattresses are stacked on, and in line with, the cat-walk to the rear of the aperture.

HALIFAX
CONVERSION FOR PARATROOPS

REMOVE	ADD
LOWER BRACKET FOR RECONNAISSANCE FLARES	WINDSHIELD AND REAR BEND
	SIX MATTRESSES
	TWO STRONG POINTS
	THREE PANELS
WIRE ESCAPE LADDER	TEN STROPS AND SNAP HOOKS
	CONTAINER RELEASE SWITCH
	SIGNAL LIGHTS
FLAME FLOAT BRACKET	DIM LIGHTING SET

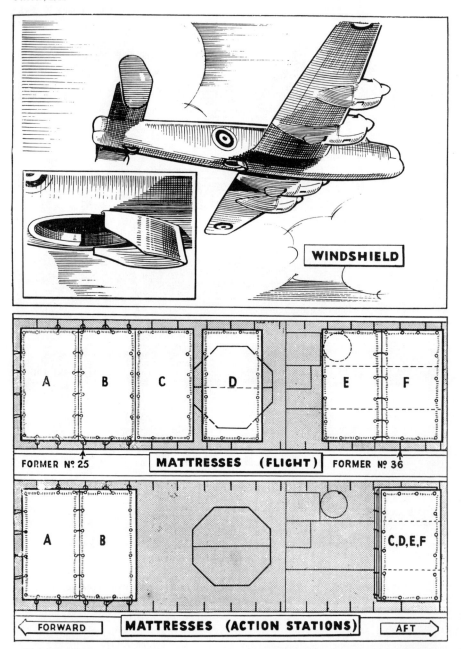

FIG. 7 **HALIFAX** WINDSHIELD AND MATTRESSES

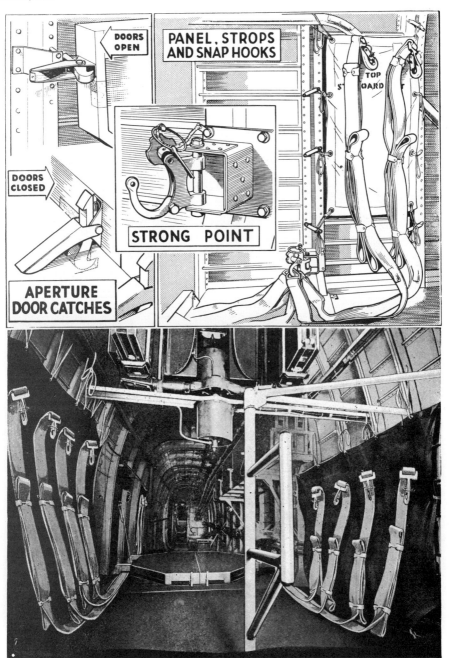

FIG. 8 **HALIFAX II** APERTURE DOORS CLOSED

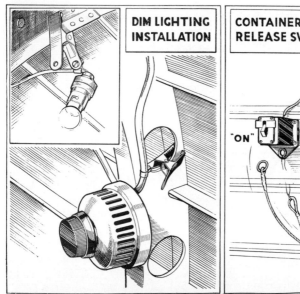

DIM LIGHTING INSTALLATION

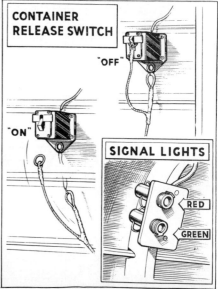

CONTAINER RELEASE SWITCH

"OFF"

"ON"

SIGNAL LIGHTS

RED

GREEN

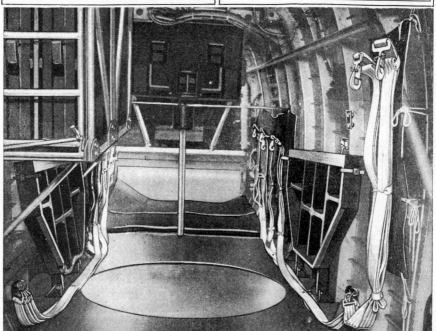

FIG. 9 **HALIFAX II** APERTURE DOORS OPEN

Halifax II and V

Modifications to Halifax II and V

48. Halifax Modifications Nos. 22, 286, 287 and 356 contain details of the alterations and additions referred to in the following paragraphs.

Removal of equipment

49. The following equipment is removed from the aircraft for paratroop operations:—

(i) Lower bracket for reconnaissance flares

(ii) Wire escape ladder

(iii) Flame float bracket on floor immediately forward of paratroop aperture.

(iv) Part of rear turret ammunition (ammunition is limited to 700 rounds per gun).

Floor aperture

50. The floor aperture, through which the paratroops drop, is an enlarged version of the existing hole provided for a bottom turret and measures approximately forty inches in diameter. During take-off and flight to target the aperture is covered by two polygonal hinged doors; these are opened and latched against the side of the fuselage when the paratroops are ready to make their exit.

Door catches (*see* fig. 8)

51. The door catches are of a double-acting pattern, providing a self-locking attachment for the aperture doors when these are in the open and closed positions. Two catches are fitted to each door.

Windshield (*see* fig. 7)

52. The forward edge of the aperture, on the underside of the aircraft, is protected by a metal windshield. This is approximately eleven inches deep and is secured by means of bolts and Simmonds nuts located inside the aircraft skin. The rear edge of the aperture is fitted with a wooden rear bend to prevent chafing of the trailing strops.

Tail wheel

53. The Halifax tail wheel is not retractable. It has been proved that the sixteen-foot strops used in this aircraft are long enough to trail the static lines clear of the tail wheel. No fouling of static lines occurs and therefore no spat is fitted to the tail wheel.

Rear turret accumulator tray

54. The rear turret accumulators are repositioned on the port bunk of the main rest station, and a revised pattern of tray is provided to accommodate them.

Mid-upper turret

55. The horizontal support for the mid-upper turret mounting is replaced by a vertical structure in order to prevent interference with the paratroops attached to the port forward panel. A removable ladder for the mid-upper turret gunner replaces the hinged ladder previously supplied.

Rear gunner's ammunition rack

56. The position of the rear gunner's ammunition rack on the port side of the fuselage prevents the use of a panel and strops for paratroops at the port, aft station.

Guard for controls

57. A simple metal guard is fitted to prevent interference between the aircraft control rods and paratroops or their equipment.

Mattresses (*see* fig. 7)

58. Six "Numna" mattresses measuring 5 ft. by 3 ft. are laid across the floor of the aircraft. Two of these are laced together and tied to clips and holes provided immediately aft of the rear spar (*i.e.* well forward of the aperture); the purpose of these is to enable the paratroops to move rapidly on the rough floor. The remaining four mattresses are laid loosely on the floor for the comfort of the paratroops while travelling to the target, and are arranged as follows:—

(i) One mattress adjacent to the fixed ones and immediately forward of the aperture.

(ii) One mattress across the closed aperture doors.

(iii) Two mattresses, preferably laced together, placed aft of the aperture, the forward mattress partially covering the main entrance door when this is shut.

59. When the paratroops take up action stations, the rearmost mattresses are folded together and the remaining two loose ones are piled on top so that all the loose mattresses occupy a space 5 ft. by 3 ft. aft of the main entrance door.

Strong points (*see* fig. 8)

60. The port and starboard strong points are similar except for the carriages bolted to the fuselage members. These carriages are drilled to opposite hands. Each carriage is fitted with a swivelling lug and hinged shackle. Each shackle is secured at its upper end by means of a threaded shackle pin with handwheel and locking pin. As a result of the similarity of the port and starboard fitting, the handwheel on the starboard strong point lies against the fuselage skin to avoid fouling the starboard strops, whereas the handwheel on the port strong point projects outwards. Since there is no rear panel on the port side of the fuselage this handwheel causes no interference with strops.

Panels (*see* fig. 8)

61. Three khaki duck panels are secured by tapes to brackets on the fuselage frames. One port and one starboard panel, each equipped for four strops, are fitted forward of the aperture, and one starboard panel only, equipped for two strops, is fitted aft of the aperture.

Strops (*see* fig. 8)

62. Ten strops are fitted, leading from the two strong points to the three panels. The strops are made of 1¾ in. wide, heavy, white, double webbing, and are equipped with press studs for attachment to the panels. One end of each strop carries a D ring for attachment to a strong point, and the other end is fitted with a snap hook for attachment to the parachute static lines. Number 5 strop carries, in addition, a tab for the cord which operates the container release switch. The distribution of the strops is as follows:—

Strop No.	Panel position		Length of strop	Strong point
1	Starboard	Aft	16 ft. 0 in.	Starboard
2	Starboard	Aft	16 ft. 0 in.	Starboard
3	Starboard	Forward	16 ft. 0 in.	Starboard
4	Port	Forward	16 ft. 0 in.	Port
5	Starboard	Forward	16 ft. 0 in.	Starboard
6	Port	Forward	16 ft. 0 in.	Port
7	Starboard	Forward	16 ft. 0 in.	Starboard
8	Port	Forward	16 ft. 0 in.	Port
9	Starboard	Forward	16 ft. 0 in.	Starboard
10	Port	Forward	16 ft. 0 in	Port

63. The strops attached to the forward panel on the starboard side are grouped one above the other to pass under the starboard aperture door hinges. The strops attached to the forward panel on the port side are laid side by side under the port aperture door, the wooden blocks under this door being replaced by sponge rubber for this purpose. The reason for this arrangement is that the port hinges are too short to accommodate the strops.

64. All the strops are 16 ft. in length to ensure deployment of the parachutes approximately 2 ft. aft of the tail wheel. For attachment to the panels the strops are folded and tied with webbing tabs having eyelets through which a doubled thread of No. 18 linen thread is looped and knotted.

65. Owing to the length of the strops it is necessary that these should be withdrawn or, in an emergency, jettisoned before landing. Two men working together can withdraw the strops and static lines by hand at flying speeds up to 200 m.p.h. The strops can be jettisoned by withdrawing the split pin from each of the strong point shackle pins and unscrewing the handwheels.

Snap hook (*see* fig. 8)

66. The snap hook is a standard fitting for connecting static lines to strops. It comprises a rectangular eye for the strop and a hook having a spring latch and a safety pin fastening.

Container release switch (*see* fig. 9)

67. A type "B" single unit switch, Stores Ref. 5D/534, is fitted to a bracket on the starboard side of the fuselage and opposite the floor aperture. This switch is electrically connected to the bomb selector, and, when operated by a cord attached to Number 5 strop, releases the containers from the bomb carriers. The operating cord terminates in a ring which is passed over the switch lever when this is in the ON position, and is trapped under a divided bridge piece when the switch is OFF. Thus, when Number 5 strop is pulled and the switch actuated, the release of the cord and ring from the switch lever is certain.

68. A piece of No. 18 linen thread is whipped to a loop in the operating cord and tied to a fixed point in such a way that an accidental pull on the strop will stress or break the thread without actuating the switch.

Signal lights (*see* fig. 9)

69. A two-colour signal light is mounted inside the fuselage above the starboard aperture door. The red and green lights are wired to a switch in the pilot's cockpit and indicate "action station" and "drop" respectively.

Bomb selector and distributor

70. No special modification is required for the bomb selecting and distributing circuits when these are used for the purpose of releasing containers. A pre-selector, which is a standard fitting wired between the selector switchbox and the bomb release mechanism, enables each bomb station to be controlled by any one of the sixteen selector switches. It is thus a simple matter to drop the containers in any order required. The necessary interval on the bomb distributor is $0 \cdot 13$ secs. between successive containers.

Dim lighting installation (*see* fig. 9)

71. A standard dim-lighting installation is provided on the Halifax. It comprises two 6-watt lamps attached to the fuselage roof, one forward and one aft of the aperture, a resistance mounted on the port side of the fuselage, and a plug for insertion in one of the normal roof lighting fitments. The wiring is attached throughout by means of Bulldog clips.

72. The purpose of the dim-lighting installation is to accustom the eyes of the paratroops to a gradual reduction in illumination, preparatory to their leaving the aircraft during the hours of darkness.

Container strong points

73. Strong points, for the static lines of supplies dropping parachutes, are provided for use at each bomb station. The brackets comprising the strong points are not normally fitted to the aircraft but the holes are ready drilled and bolts and Simmonds nuts are provided for securing them to the frames.

Accessories

74. The following accessories may be required in Halifax aircraft used for paratroop operations:–

(i) One intercomm. helmet

(ii) One thermos flask

(iii) Two rubber urine bottles

(iv) A supply of paper "sick" bags.

Albemarle I and II

General

98. The aft position of the aperture in Albemarle aircraft modified for paratroop operations makes it necessary that all the ten paratroops carried travel forward of the aperture. They all make their exit from the forward edge. For this reason it is not practicable to employ fixed strong points, panels and strops as described earlier in this chapter for other aircraft types.

99. (*See* fig. 16). Instead, a static line cable on the port side and a static line rail on the starboard side of the fuselage are employed. A special jumping technique has been developed for use with this installation.

Modifications to the Albemarle

100. Albemarle modifications Nos. A.542 (airframe structure), A.543 (fixed electric) and A.544 (removeable parts) contain details of the alterations and additions referred to in the following paragraphs.

Removal of equipment

101. The following equipment is removed from the Albemarle aircraft used for paratroop operations:—

   (i)   Diagonal member across the fuselage forward of the under turret aperture.

   (ii)   Reconnaissance flares and racks.

   (iii) Flare tube and stowage.

   (iv) Sea crash gear.

   (v)   Access ladder and stowage.

   (vi) Spare ammunition boxes and stowage racks

   (vii) Sea marker and flame float racks.

 (viii) Vacuum flask and stowage aft of turret.

   (ix) Oxygen cylinders (9) and portable oxygen equipment.

   (x)   Heating system duct (starboard side of step).

Items repositioned

102. The following items are moved to the new positions described:—

   (i)   Gunner's parachute and stowage. Repositioned forward of gun turret, port side.

   (ii)   Fire extinguisher. Repositioned as near to port side of step as possible.

   (iii) Starboard sanitary bag clips. Turned through a right angle to face forward.

   (iv) Interior lamp switch. (Starboard side of fuselage above escape hatch.) Turned through right angle to face forward.

   (v)   R.3003 and stowage. Repositioned on starboard side aft of aperture.

Floor aperture (*see* figs. 13 and 15)

103. An extension of the under turret aperture gives an elongated hole situated approximately six feet aft of the step. It is unnecessary to fit a windshield to the aperture because its length gives ample clearance when the paratroops jump and they all make their exit facing aft.

Aperture doors (*see* figs. 13 and 15)

104. The floor aperture is covered during flight to target by two doors, each hinged at the side of the fuselage. The starboard door is flanged along the underside of its straight edge and held down by the port door which is fastened to the floor by a bolt at either end. Each door, when open, is secured to the side of the fuselage by means of a strap carrying a metal plate in which is cut an elongated slot. This slot is passed over the head of a turnbutton attached to the underside of each door. It is important that the doors are held securely open as the paratroops may hold the open edges for support immediately prior to jumping.

Mattresses (*see* fig. 14)

105. Four Numna mattresses, each measuring 5 ft. × 3 ft. are laid across the floor of the aircraft, two forward and two aft of the step. They are tied at the edges to fuselage members, and to each other in pairs, by lengths of 16 oz. cord, and are not moved during a paratroop operation.

Static line cable (*see* fig. 16)

106. A length of 60 cwt. steel cable forms the attachment for the port static lines and is secured at each end near to the roof along the port side of the aircraft fuselage. The strops for paratroops Nos. 2, 4, 6, 8 and 10 are attached to the static line cable by means of "D" rings.

Static line rail (*see* fig. 16)

107. To provide a positive means of actuating the container release switch, a rail is used on the starboard side of the fuselage instead of a cable. The rail is of inverted "T" section and is secured by tubular struts to fuselage members. A spring catch at the forward end of the rail allows the roller carriages for paratroop strops Nos. 1, 3, 5, 7 and 9 to be threaded on the rail and prevents them riding off. A fibre stop at the aft end of the rail prevents the disengagement of the carriages after the paratroops have left the aircraft

Strops (*see* fig. 16)

108. Ten strops are fitted, five to the port static line cable and five to the starboard static line rail. They are all 72 in. long and made of 1¾ in. wide, heavy white double webbing. Those on the cable differ from those on the rail in their means of attachment only.

   (i)   The port strop attachment is by means of a "D" ring—a triangular piece of metal supporting the strop attached to a slot at its base. The cable runs through the triangle at its apex.

   (ii)   The starboard strop attachment is by means of a carriage which rides the inverted "T" rail on four rollers.

Plunger for the operation of the container release switch (*see* fig. 15)

109. A spring-loaded plunger attached to strop carriage No. 5 actuates the container release switch. The plunger, which faces starboard, is retained (against its spring) by means of a pin which is attached to a tab on the strop by a lanyard which takes the support of the strop off the carriage. When the paratroop jumps the carriage is opposite the container release switch and the tension on the strop pulls out the plunger retaining pin. A breaking tie of No. 8 linen thread prevents the premature withdrawal of the pin.

Container release switch (*see* fig. 15)

110. The container release switch comprises a fixed plate carrying six contact studs held apart by three springs from a movable plate carrying six corresponding studs. The plates are horizontally mounted on the inside of the starboard static line rail and near to the floor aperture. When the spring-loaded plunger mounted on No. 5 strop carriage is released by the withdrawal of the retaining pin it engages the spring-mounted plate causing one or more of the six pairs of contact studs to meet. The continued travel of the carriage along the rail causes the plunger to ride out of engagement with the switch plate, with the result that the firing circuit is broken and the distributor cannot overheat.

Signal lights (*see* fig. 15)

111. Two coloured signal lights are mounted inside the fuselage on the roof above the aperture. The red and green lights are wired to switches under the control of the pilot and the navigator. The red indicates "action stations" and the green indicates "that paratroops may leave the aircraft".

Bomb distributor circuit (*see* fig. 19)

112. The bomb distributing circuit comprises an auto-distributor, a selector switchbox and a series of numbered sockets in the bomb cells to which the cables from the bomb carrier E.M. units are plugged. The circuit is arranged so that stud No. 1 of the distributor corresponds to switch No. 1 of the selector and socket No. 1 in the bomb cell and so on. For the safe release of containers it is necessary to release container No. 7 before container No. 4. Extension leads are used to connect bomb carriers Nos. 4 and 7 to sockets Nos. 7 and 4 respectively. This changes the firing order of the bomb stations carrying items from 1, 2, 4, 6, 7, 9 to 1, 2, 7, 6, 4, 9. Section 2, Chapter 5 of this manual gives the loading of containers and other items.

Setting of bomb distributor

113. A distributor interval of 0·15 secs. is necessary for the safe release of containers or other items. Further details concerning the operation of the container release circuit are given in Section 2, Chapter 7 of this manual.

FIG.13 **ALBEMARLE** CONVERSION FOR PARATROOPS VIEW LOOKING FORWARD

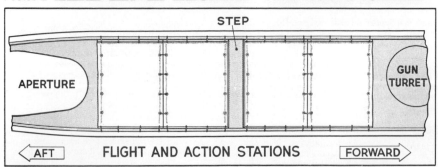

FIG.14 POSITION OF TROOP MATTRESSES

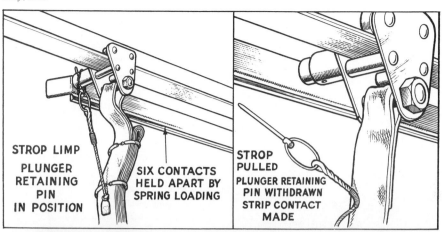

STROP LIMP

PLUNGER RETAINING PIN IN POSITION

SIX CONTACTS HELD APART BY SPRING LOADING

STROP PULLED

PLUNGER RETAINING PIN WITHDRAWN STRIP CONTACT MADE

SPECIAL CARRIAGE (No.5) FOR OPERATING STROP SWITCH

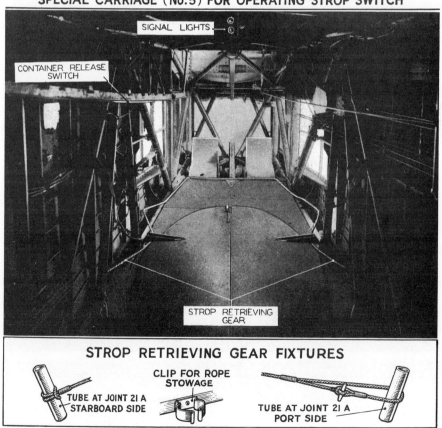

SIGNAL LIGHTS

CONTAINER RELEASE SWITCH

STROP RETRIEVING GEAR

STROP RETRIEVING GEAR FIXTURES

CLIP FOR ROPE STOWAGE

TUBE AT JOINT 21 A STARBOARD SIDE

TUBE AT JOINT 21 A PORT SIDE

FIG.15 ALBEMARLE **PARATROOP INSTALLATIONS LOOKING AFT**

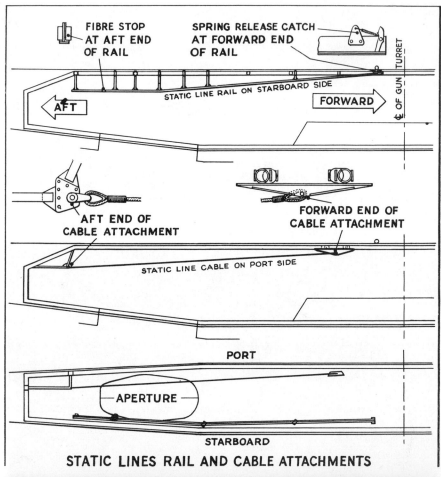

FIBRE STOP AT AFT END OF RAIL

SPRING RELEASE CATCH AT FORWARD END OF RAIL

℄ OF GUN TURRET

STATIC LINE RAIL ON STARBOARD SIDE

AFT

FORWARD

AFT END OF CABLE ATTACHMENT

FORWARD END OF CABLE ATTACHMENT

STATIC LINE CABLE ON PORT SIDE

PORT

APERTURE

STARBOARD

STATIC LINES RAIL AND CABLE ATTACHMENTS

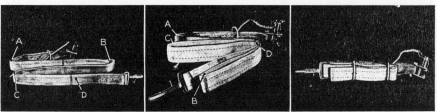

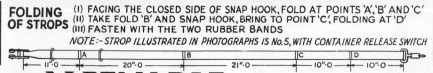

FOLDING OF STROPS

(I) FACING THE CLOSED SIDE OF SNAP HOOK, FOLD AT POINTS 'A','B' AND 'C'
(II) TAKE FOLD 'B' AND SNAP HOOK, BRING TO POINT 'C', FOLDING AT 'D'
(III) FASTEN WITH THE TWO RUBBER BANDS

NOTE:- STROP ILLUSTRATED IN PHOTOGRAPHS IS No.5, WITH CONTAINER RELEASE SWITCH

A | B | C | D
11".0 — 20".0 — 21".0 — 10".0 — 10".0

FIG.16 ALBEMARLE STATIC LINE INSTALLATION

This page issued with A.L. No. 7
May, 1943

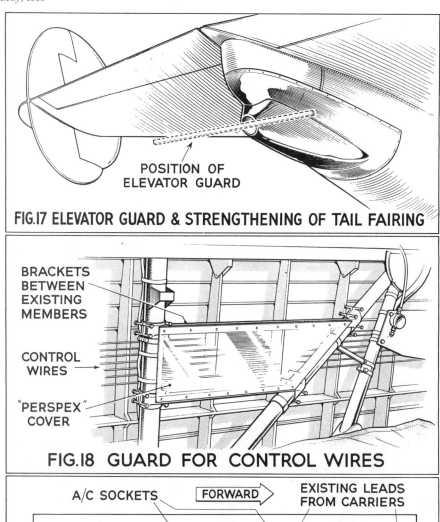

POSITION OF
ELEVATOR GUARD

FIG.17 ELEVATOR GUARD & STRENGTHENING OF TAIL FAIRING

BRACKETS
BETWEEN
EXISTING
MEMBERS

CONTROL
WIRES

"PERSPEX"
COVER

FIG.18 GUARD FOR CONTROL WIRES

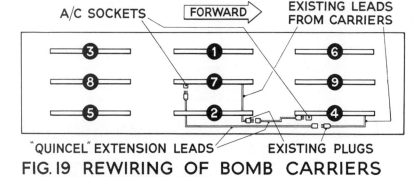

A/C SOCKETS

FORWARD

EXISTING LEADS
FROM CARRIERS

3 1 6

8 7 9

5 2 4

"QUINCEL" EXTENSION LEADS

EXISTING PLUGS

FIG.19 REWIRING OF BOMB CARRIERS

ALBEMARLE PARATROOP MODIFICATIONS

Dakota I (C47)

General (*see* fig. 20)

121.   The adaptation of the Dakota I for paratroop operations involves the fitting of a static cable, the masking of certain protrusions on the outside of the fuselage and the fitting of six external bomb racks for container carrying.   Numna mattresses are used to prevent the paratroops slipping when making their way to the exit door.

122.   The following information is based upon installations and tests on C47 aircraft which were found to vary one from another in details.   These instructions are published pending official Mod. procedure for Dakota aircraft which may also include similar variations of type.

123.   Special nomenclature is in use for loading calculations on American aircraft and for an explanation of the terms used *see* Sect. 5, Chap. 4, paras. 9 to 12 of this manual.

Static line cable (*see* figs. 22, 23 and 24)

124.   The length of the static line cable is 24 ft. $6\frac{3}{4}$ in.   It is made of 60 cwt. steel cable spliced to a thimble at each end.   When fitted, the static cable must not be taut as this puts an undue strain on the strong points.   It should assume a slight curve as indicated in fig. 24.

125.   Twenty D-rings with snap-hooks should be threaded on the static cable before the cable is attached to the strong points (*see* para. 133).

Forward strong point (*see* fig. 22)

126.   The forward strong point is an L-shaped bracket with a lug for the attachment of the static cable.   It is located against and bolted to the forward face of transverse former No. $195\frac{1}{2}$ on the starboard side of the aircraft with two 2 B.A. bolts and Simmonds elastic stop nuts.   It is also bolted to the main longitudinal stringer by means of six 2 B.A. bolts and Simmonds elastic stop nuts.

127.   On some aircraft the vent pipes for the overload fuel tanks interfere slightly with the correct placing of the forward strong point.   In these cases it is permissible to cut a semi-circular notch of a maximum diameter of 1 in. in the lug.

128.   Where a fuel pipe-line is located just aft of the forward strong point the pipe-line must be well taped to prevent it being chafed by the static cable.

Aft strong point, Dakota I, with a 70 in. cargo door (*see* fig. 23)

129.   These aircraft are fitted with an idler pulley and bracket on the floor at the starboard side between the transverse frames at fuselage stations 479 and 492.   The bracket is used as the aft strong point by removing the pin holding the pulley bracket and replacing it by a longer bolt and nut carrying a shackle which is threaded through the thimble at the aft end of the static cable.

Aft strong point, Dakota I, with 84 in. cargo door (*see* fig. 24)

130.   The bracket holding the idler pulley on these aircraft is too far forward to be used as the aft strong point for the static cable.   Instead, a rear attachment bracket is fitted.

131.   The rear attachment consists of a strong point which can be moved along the length of a 1 in. tube.   The tube, 13 in. long, is attached by brackets to frames at fuselage stations 479 and 492 as near as possible to the floor.   Six holes are drilled with a No. 12 drill in each of the two frames to take the 2 B.A. bolts for attaching the brackets.   When the correct position for the strong point is decided the two clamping bolts are tightened.   A hole is then drilled through the tube with a No. 12 drill and a $1\frac{3}{8}$ in. 2 B.A. bolt used to secure the sliding strong point to the tube.

Attaching the static cable to the strong points

132.   The forward end of the static cable is attached to the forward strong point by means of a shackle, a shackle pin and a split pin or cotter.   The head of the shackle pin should be uppermost and the split pin should be well spread.   The aft end of the static cable is attached to the aft strong point by means of a shackle and an eye bolt.   The eye bolt is locked with wire which is threaded through the eye and the shackle and the ends twisted together.   Where the idler pulley bracket is used as the aft strong point, a bolt and a Simmonds elastic stop nut may be used to secure the shackle as described in para. 129.

Fitting of D-rings and snap-hooks

133. The means of attachment between the parachute static lines and the static cable comprise 20 D-rings each bolted to a snap-hook by two bolts with washers and Simmonds elastic stop nuts, and a two-holed backing plate between the nuts and the D-ring. The D-rings are threaded on the static cable and are so mounted that the tongues of the snap-hooks face forward. This disposition is of the greatest importance as, otherwise, there would be a danger of the tongues striking some obstacle and tending to open while the snap-hooks were sliding down the static cable.

134. Before fitting a snap-hook and D-ring to the static cable the safety pin should be fastened in position and the movement of the tongue tested to ensure that there is no possibility of its opening and releasing the parachute static line.

135. Instead of the combined D-rings and snap-hooks 20 strops, 9 ft. 9 in. in length, may be used.

Masking (*see* fig. 25)

136. The object of masking is to cover all projections or sharp edges on the aircraft which might cut the static line or interfere with its free movement.

137. For masking purposes a 2 in. wide adhesive masking tape should be used. Projections such as the axle bobbins on the tail wheel assembly will require padding with rag or paper before taping.

138. In addition to the masking of projections, certain obstructions may have to be removed.

139. The main points requiring masking are illustrated in fig. 25 and are as follows:—

(i) Door handles. A guard is provided for the external door handles on the Dakota I; this guard must not be taped.
(ii) Aft door hinges.
(iii) Lower outside edge of door frame.
(iv) The fire extinguisher bracket inside the cabin near the door.
(v) The joint between the root fairing and de-icing equipment on the leading edge of the tail plane.
(vi) Both axle bobbins on the tail wheel
(vii) Front main through-bolt on the tail wheel assembly.
(viii) The forward end of the glider towing attachment if the bridle type is fitted.

140. In addition a careful inspection should be made both inside and outside the aircraft and all sharp edges or obstructions where it is possible that the static lines might suffer damage or interference should be carefully masked. Particular care should be exercised where a glider towing bridle is fitted.

141. If a venturi is used for the lavatory drain this should be removed. If a metal tube is used this should be pushed up inside the aircraft or cut short. Rubber tubes may be safely left. The rear mooring eye should be removed.

Door handle guard (*see* fig. 25)

142. For paratroop purposes the rear half of the door remains closed and a guard is fitted over the external door handles to allow the static lines to slide easily down to the floor of the aircraft. The guard should be positioned $\frac{1}{2}$ in. back from the forward edge of the dividing frame to enable the key to be inserted in the upper handle.

Installation of container carrying equipment (*see* fig. 26)

143. The adaptation of the Dakota I aircraft to carry C.L.E. Mark I and Mark III containers involves the fitting of six universal bomb carriers which are attached to chassis bolted to existing strong points on the aircraft. These chassis are standard for all six positions.

Fitting the forward pair of universal bomb carriers

144. The procedure when fitting the forward pair of bomb carriers and chassis is as follows:—

(i) Fit the front pair of carrier chassis to the existing strong points on the aircraft, using the $\frac{3}{8}$ in. S.A.E. bolts from the existing attachment. Alternative holes are drilled in the rear end of the chassis to accommodate individual variations in different aircraft. Four wedge washers are supplied with each chassis. They are intended for use on the front pair only; they adjust the flat of the carrier chassis to the curvature of the underside of the aircraft.

(ii)   Remove the nuts and bolts from the three suspension points on each of two No. 2 universal bomb carriers. The front and rear bolts screw out from the crutch brackets.

(iii)   See that the release hook on the carrier is pointing forward and raise the carrier to the carrier chassis. Fit the bolt through the centre suspension point of the carrier and the centre strong point in the "T" member of the chassis. Fit the bolts to the front and rear crutch brackets. Finally tighten and lock all bolts and nuts.

(iv)   Adjust the four eye bolts which retain the crutches so that they face the correct way to take the bracing stays.

(v)   Attach the bracing stays to the eye bolts and to the bomb carrier chassis and tighten up. The bomb carrier should be quite rigid.

(vi)   The single electrical lead from the junction box is then inserted into No. 2 position in the appropriate socket in the aircraft fuselage. This is the positive lead from the electro-magnetic release unit to the release switchbox mounted beside the aircraft door. If a 3-pin cannon plug is available the lead is connected to the positive terminal of the plug which is then inserted in the 3-pin socket on the aircraft in the usual way. Any surplus cable should be secured to the carrier beam.

(vii)   Ensure that all pins and nuts are locked with split pins or cotters.

(viii)   Test the carriers as detailed in the daily inspection.

      Note.—When the universal bomb carriers are to be used exclusively for container dropping from the Dakota I the fusing units, five-pin plug and wiring are to be removed.

Fitting the centre and rear universal bomb carriers *(see* fig. 26)

145.   The method of fitting the centre and rear universal bomb carriers is similar to that described for the front carriers with the exception of the attachment of the chassis to the aircraft. The wedge washers mentioned in para. 144 (i) are not used. The length of the bolts necessitates the use of four tubular collars on the underside of each chassis.

Loading containers on to aircraft

146.   Before commencing to load, ensure that all daily inspections have been completed and proceed as detailed in A.P.1180A, Vol. I. On the Dakota aircraft, due to the exposed position of the containers, it is imperative that the No. 8 cord breaking ties anchoring the static lines to the outside of the parachute packs and the safety ties of the flap retaining pins are correctly fitted and inspected prior to flight.

Items thrown from the aircraft door

147.   When throwing bicycles or other loose items of equipment from the door of the aircraft, a 10 ft. rope extension must be attached to a static cable fitted along the aircraft roof and to the static line of the parachute of the item.

148.   A $\frac{3}{4}$ in. rope (approximately $\frac{1}{4}$ in. diameter) is used for this purpose, and must be capable of bearing a snatch load of 400 lb. An eye is spliced at one end of the rope and this end is connected to the static line. A snap-hook is spliced to the other end and this snap-hook is attached to the overhead static cable.

149.   Because of the differences in the deployment of the American and the British X type parachutes, it is considered dangerous to use the latter on the American overhead static cable.

Mattresses *(see* fig. 21)

150.   Two Numna mattresses, the main one 15 ft. long and 4 ft. 2 in. wide and one at the aircraft door 4 ft. 6 in. long and 3 ft. wide, are placed as indicated in fig. 21. It is important that there are no wrinkles in the mats when they are in position.

Stores Reference numbers

151.   When an aircraft is grounded or held back from operation through lack of a spare part, the demand for that part should be marked "A.O.G." in order that it shall receive priority.

152. Stores reference numbers of items of paratroop equipment for the Dakota I are as follows:—

Chassis, universal for attaching universal bomb carriers... ...	126JQ/PC/100
Static cable fittings:—	
Bracket	126JQ/PC/30
Cable	126JQ/PC/31
Snap-hooks	126JQ/PC/32
Shackle, A.G.S.690/F	126JQ/PC/33
Shackle, A.G.S.914/C	126JQ/PC/34
Pins, safety locking spring type (1·15 in.)	28B/5413
Rear attachment bracket	126JQ/PC/110
Bundles of six supply cables and six earthing cables for universal carriers	126JQ/PC/70
Door handle guard	126JQ/PC/80
"Numna" floor mat, 15 ft. by 4 ft. 2 in.	126JQ/PC/90
"Numna" floor mat, 4 ft. 6 in. by 3 ft.	126JQ/PC/91
Pins for bracing stays (pins, shackle, steel, $\frac{3}{16}$ in. dia., 0·6 in. long) ...	28B/834
Universal bomb carrier No. 1 (2 per aircraft)	11A/520
or alternatively	11A/598
Universal bomb carrier No. 2 (4 per aircraft)	11A/533
or alternatively	11A/607
Electro-magnetic release unit, type C, Mark II	11A/466

      Note.—Electro-magnetic release units, type C, Mark II or Mark III are both suitable with 12 or 24 volt supply.

Junction box, type C	5D/579
Crutch lever assembly, comprising:—	
Buttons, adjusting screw	11A/1124
Shoes	11A/1126
Keep pins, adjusting screw	11A/1324
Screw, adjusting, ball ended	11A/1325
Rings, crutch pad retaining	11A/1871
Nuts, for adjusting screws, M.S., $\frac{3}{8}$ in. B.S.F.	28/760
Release slip, Mark I...	11A/487
Cannon plug, 3 pin (RWK)	105X/857
2 oz. reel of No. 18 thread (10 lb. breaking strain) for container static lines	32B/451

Guard for tail fairing (*see* fig. 17)

114.   A metal shield of 20 gauge duralumin is fitted over the lower part of the transparent tail fairing to prevent damage being caused by the impact of parachute bags.

Elevator guard (*see* fig. 17)

115.   An 8 ft. bar is fitted in a transverse position below the tail plane to prevent the parachute static lines and bags from fouling the elevators.

Strop retrieving gear (*see* fig. 15)

116.   To enable the trailing strops and parachute bags to be withdrawn through the aperture into the fuselage, after the paratroops have jumped, a strop retrieving gear has been devised.   A rope is secured at floor level on the tube at joint 21A on the starboard side, passed underneath the door hinges, across to the port side, well aft of the aperture, and back along the port side, under the door hinges and fastened to the tube at joint 21A, port side.   The rope is held in position by ten spring clips distributed along its length screwed to wooden longerons at floor level.   One, or preferably two, members of the aircraft crew can retrieve the strops by pulling on one end of the retrieving gear which then comes away from its retaining clips forming a loop round the ten strops. It is important that during retrieval the bags must not be allowed to slip back as they would then pass over the elevator guard and foul the elevators.

Control cable guard (*see* fig. 18)

117.   A perspex panel and frame is fitted inside the fuselage on the port side just aft of the upper turret over the control wires to prevent interference from paratroops seated in this position.

Dim lighting installation

118.   A standard dim lighting installation is provided.   It comprises two 6-watt lamps attached to the fuselage roof by bulldog clips, a dimmer switch and a plug for insertion in an existing ceiling light.   The forward light is positioned on the former adjacent to the gun turret bulkhead, the aft lamp is positioned on the former adjacent to the dinghy container, and the dimmer is clipped to gusset plates on joint No. 20.

119.   The purpose of the dim lighting installation is to accustom the eyes of the paratroops to a gradual reduction in illumination prior to leaving the aircraft during the hours of darkness.

Accessories

120.   The following accessories may be required in aircraft used for paratroop operations:—

(i)   One intercomm. helmet

(ii)   One thermos flask

(iii)   Two rubber urine bottles

(iv)   A supply of paper "sick" bags.

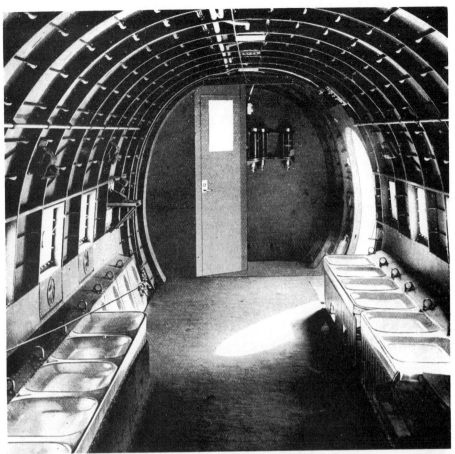

FIG. 20. DAKOTA I
CONVERSION FOR PARATROOPS
VIEW LOOKING AFT

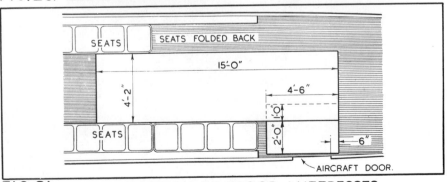

FIG. 21. POSITION OF TROOP MATTRESSES

This page issued with A.L. No. 10
July, 1943

FIG.22. DAKOTA I. FORWARD STRONG POINT FOR STATIC CABLE.

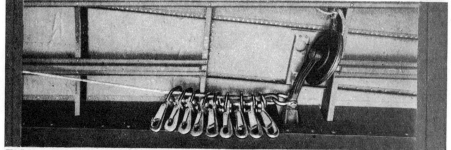

FIG.23. DAKOTA I. WITH 70 IN. DOORS. AFT STRONG POINT.

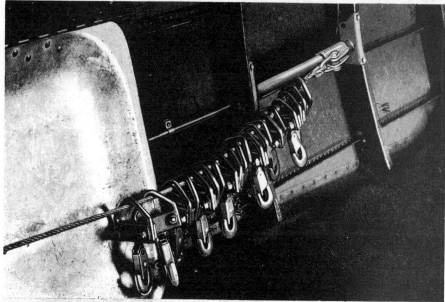

FIG.24. DAKOTA I. WITH 84 IN. DOORS. AFT STRONG POINT.

DAKOTA I   DOOR HANDLE GUARD

FIG. 25   DAKOTA I   ITEMS WHICH REQUIRE MASKING

This page issued with A.L. No. 10
July, 1943

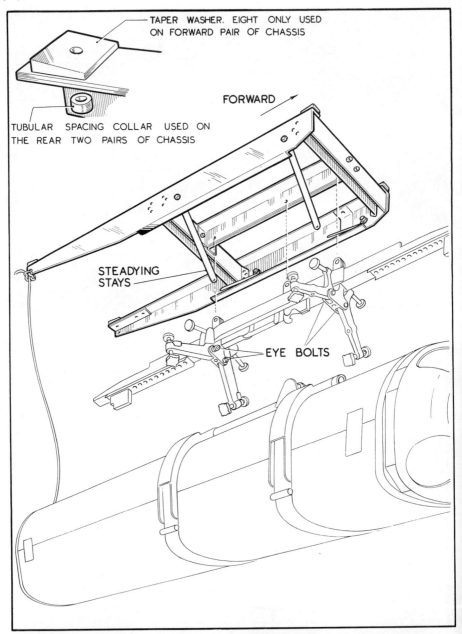

TAPER WASHER. EIGHT ONLY USED ON FORWARD PAIR OF CHASSIS

TUBULAR SPACING COLLAR USED ON THE REAR TWO PAIRS OF CHASSIS

FORWARD

STEADYING STAYS

EYE BOLTS

FIG. 26. CHASSIS, BOMB CARRIER AND CONTAINER.

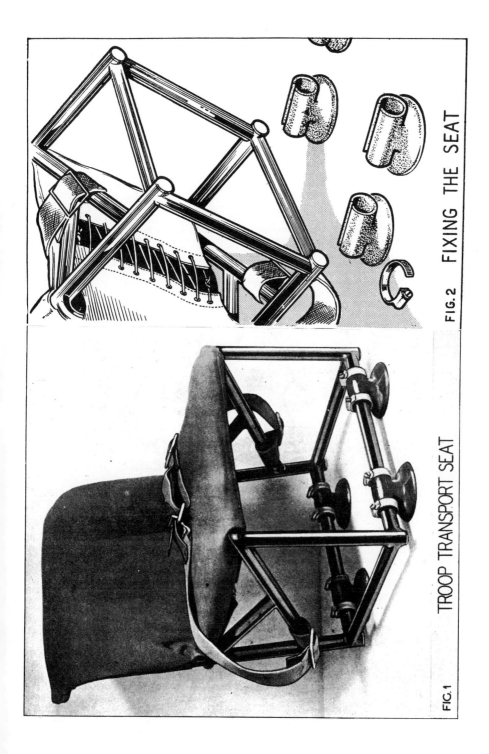

FIG. 2   FIXING THE SEAT

TROOP TRANSPORT SEAT

FIG. 1

43

CHAPTER 5

AIRCRAFT CAPACITY AND LOADING

General

1. In order to compile C.G. and loading schedules for individual aircraft taking part in paratroop operations reference should be made to Sect. 4 of the relevant aeroplane handbook for the procedure to be adopted. The loading schedules given in the following pages are typical examples only, and care should be taken to establish accurate figures for the Aeroplane Tare (*see* Sect. 2, Chap. 2 of this manual for items included and omitted) and Military Load (excluding Airborne Forces load) for each aircraft.

2. To simplify the C.G. calculations the mean "x-arm" figures for the C.G. of paratroops at take-off, flight and action stations are included in the diagrams detailing the positions of paratroops.

3. The following considerations affect the loading and C.G. conditions of paratroop-carrying aircraft:—

    (i) The radius of operation, determining the minimum amount of fuel and oil to be carried.

    (ii) The weight of ammunition carried in the rear turret.

    (iii) The weight of the paratroops with their personal equipment.

    (iv) The weight of containers or other loads carried on the bomb racks.

    (v) The fore and aft movement of the C.G. occasioned by the consumption of fuel, the release of paratroops and containers and the expenditure of ammunition (especially at the rear turret).

Radius of operation

4. A practical radius of 250 miles is at present envisaged for paratroop operations. This practical radius is 75% of the "still-air" value, the safety margin being intended to allow for reasonable errors of pilotage, a reasonable time over the target, the effect of moderate wind and any other minor deviations from optimum flying conditions. **All figures for radius (or range) which are quoted in subsequent loading statements are "practical" values.**

5. The fuel carried for the practical radius of 250 miles has therefore to be determined on the following basis:—

    (i) 335 miles flight with paratroops on board, plus

    (ii) 335 miles flight without paratroops (i.e. return journey), plus

    (iii) Fuel for taxying and take-off, plus

    (iv) Fuel used on climb in excess of that required for level flight.

Ammunition for rear turret

6. The aft condition of the C.G. in certain paratroop-carrying aircraft is compensated for to some extent by limiting the rear turret ammunition. Such limitations are detailed on the individual aircraft loading statements contained in this chapter.

Weight of paratroops

7. A unit of ten paratroops and personal equipment, at an average weight of 237 lbs. per head, is the standard paratroop loading for Whitley, Wellington, Halifax, Manchester and Lancaster aircraft.

Weight of containers

8 The number of containers or other items carried in the bomb racks has been scheduled by A.F.E.E. The maximum weight of a loaded Mk. I C.L.E. container is 350 lbs., but at some bomb stations a lower limit is imposed. It is important, both for the stability of an aircraft and the safety of the paratroops and supplies, that the recommendations laid down for each aircraft should be closely followed.

Movement of the C.G. of a paratroop aircraft

9. In order to keep the C.G. of an aircraft within safe limits during take-off and flight to target the paratroops take up pre-arranged stations. These movements, together with the gradual eduction of fuel during flight, the release of paratroops and containers and the possible expenditure of rear turret ammunition, produce wide changes in the C.G. position. Except where these changes are negligible, as in certain of the larger aircraft, diagrams are included in this chapter to depict these movements of the C.G. and to draw attention to any violation of the permissible limits.

Whitley V

Fuel and oil

10. The wing tanks are filled giving a total of 550 gallons of fuel. 50 gallons of oil are carried.

Paratroop positions (*see* fig. 1)

11. All ten paratroops are bunched forward of the aperture for take-off; an easier distribution is permitted during flight to target. At action stations No. 1 paratroop sits with his legs over the open aperture. For paratroop drill refer to Sect. 2, Chap. 7 of this manual and to the series of Air Diagrams Nos. 3900–6.

12. Should an emergency landing be necessary with paratroops and containers still on board, the paratroops will, at the discretion of the pilot, take up the positions indicated for take-off. It may also be necessary for two paratroops to move forward into the wireless compartment and for the rear gunner to move forward to a position just aft of the aperture as indicated in fig. 1.

Containers and supplies carried (*see* fig. 2)

13. Bomb stations on the Whitley V may be used as follows for the carriage of containers and other items, but all the items listed cannot necessarily be carried at the same time.

Station Nos.	Position	Item carried
8 and 10	Front fuselage	Mk. I or Mk. III C.L.E. container.
7 and 9	Rear fuselage	Mk. I or Mk. III C.L.E. container.
5 and 6	Wings (innermost)	Mk. I or Mk. III C.L.E. container.
1, 2, 3 and 4	Wings	Small items only, such as folding trolleys, due to restricted space.

Container release equipment (*see* fig. 2)

14. The containers and other items should be auto-distributed at a distributor setting of 0·05 secs.

15. Fixed wiring is installed on Whitley V's between the selector switchbox and the bomb release mechanism. It is important to check the relationship between the numbering of the bomb stations and that of the corresponding selector switches as indicated in fig. 2.

C.G. conditions (*see* figs. 3, 4, and 5)

16. The accompanying diagrams represent typical examples of C.G. conditions on the Whitley V during a paratroop operation. Each diagram differs only in respect of the containers and supplies carried. Loads "A" and "B" include four containers and four other items, but arranged differently at the bomb stations. Load "C" includes six containers and four other items. It will be noticed that, for an emergency landing with troops and containers still on board, a C.G. position aft of the permissible limit for landing is given for loads "A" and "C". This can be corrected (and also improved for load "B") by the transfer of the rear gunner from his turret to the position indicated in fig. 1.

17. The all-up weight of the Whitley V must not exceed 32,000 lbs.

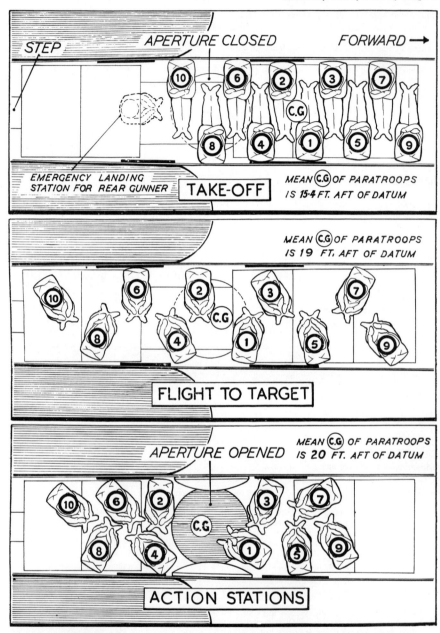

STEP

APERTURE CLOSED

FORWARD →

C.G

EMERGENCY LANDING
STATION FOR REAR GUNNER

TAKE-OFF

MEAN C.G OF PARATROOPS
IS 15·4 FT. AFT OF DATUM

MEAN C.G OF PARATROOPS
IS 19 FT. AFT OF DATUM

C.G

FLIGHT TO TARGET

APERTURE OPENED

MEAN C.G OF PARATROOPS
IS 20 FT. AFT OF DATUM

C.G

ACTION STATIONS

FIG. 1. **WHITLEY V.** PARATROOP POSITIONS

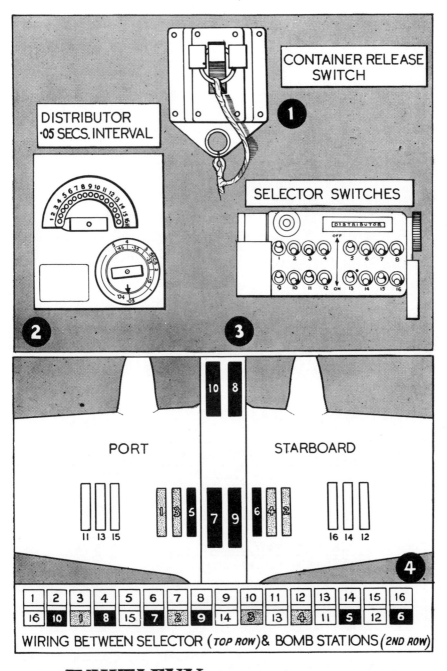

CONTAINER RELEASE SWITCH

1

DISTRIBUTOR
·05 SECS. INTERVAL

2

SELECTOR SWITCHES

DISTRIBUTOR

3

PORT STARBOARD

10 8

11 13 15   1 13 5   7 9   6 4 2   16 14 12

4

1	2	3	4	5	6	7	8	9	10	11	12	13	14	15	16
16	10	1	8	15	7	2	9	14	3	13	4	11	5	12	6

WIRING BETWEEN SELECTOR *(TOP ROW)* & BOMB STATIONS *(2ND ROW)*

FIG.2 **WHITLEY V.** CONTAINER RELEASE EQUIP.

DIAGRAM SHOWING MOVEMENT OF C.G.

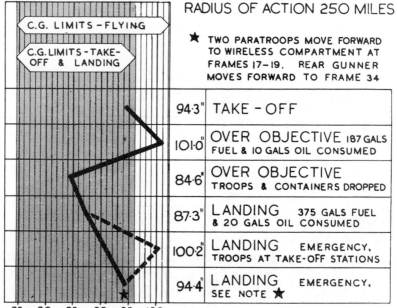

INCHES AFT OF DATUM

74·5   95·9 102·0

RADIUS OF ACTION 250 MILES

C.G. LIMITS – FLYING

C.G. LIMITS – TAKE-OFF & LANDING

★ TWO PARATROOPS MOVE FORWARD TO WIRELESS COMPARTMENT AT FRAMES 17–19. REAR GUNNER MOVES FORWARD TO FRAME 34

94·3" TAKE – OFF

101·0" OVER OBJECTIVE 187 GALS FUEL & 10 GALS OIL CONSUMED

84·6" OVER OBJECTIVE TROOPS & CONTAINERS DROPPED

87·3" LANDING 375 GALS FUEL & 20 GALS OIL CONSUMED

100·2" LANDING EMERGENCY, TROOPS AT TAKE-OFF STATIONS

94·4" LANDING EMERGENCY, SEE NOTE ★

75 80 85 90 95 100

INCHES AFT OF DATUM

LOAD 'A'	WEIGHT IN LBS
A/C TARE AND MILITARY LOAD	21,168
CREW (5) WITH PARACHUTES	1,000
FUEL 550 GALLONS IN WING TANKS	3,960
OIL 50 GALLONS	450
PARATROOPS (10) AT 237 LBS EACH	2,370
CONTAINERS (2) AT 350 LBS – STATIONS 7 & 9	700
CONTAINERS (2) AT 350 LBS – STATIONS 5 & 6	700
ITEMS (4) AT 100 LBS – STATIONS 1,2,3 & 4	400
WEIGHT AT TAKE – OFF	30,748 LBS

FIG.3. **WHITLEY V** LOADING AND C.G. CONDITIONS FOR PARATROOPS & CONTAINERS

DIAGRAM SHOWING MOVEMENT OF C.G.

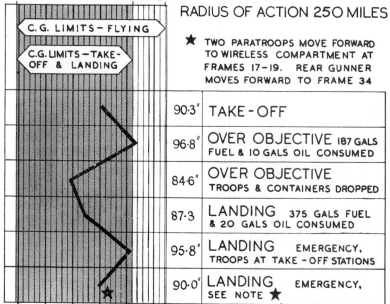

INCHES AFT OF DATUM
74.5   95.9 102.0

C.G. LIMITS – FLYING

C.G. LIMITS – TAKE-OFF & LANDING

RADIUS OF ACTION 250 MILES

★ TWO PARATROOPS MOVE FORWARD TO WIRELESS COMPARTMENT AT FRAMES 17–19. REAR GUNNER MOVES FORWARD TO FRAME 34

90·3″	TAKE - OFF
96·8″	OVER OBJECTIVE 187 GALS FUEL & 10 GALS OIL CONSUMED
84·6″	OVER OBJECTIVE TROOPS & CONTAINERS DROPPED
87·3	LANDING 375 GALS FUEL & 20 GALS OIL CONSUMED
95·8″	LANDING EMERGENCY, TROOPS AT TAKE - OFF STATIONS
90·0″	LANDING EMERGENCY, SEE NOTE ★

75   80   85   90   95   100
INCHES AFT OF DATUM

LOAD 'B'	WEIGHT IN LBS
A/C TARE AND MILITARY LOAD	21,168
CREW (5) WITH PARACHUTES	1,000
FUEL 550 GALLONS IN WING TANKS	3,960
OIL 50 GALLONS	450
PARATROOPS (10) AT 237 LBS EACH	2,370
CONTAINERS (2) AT 350 LBS - STATIONS 8 & 10	700
CONTAINERS (2) AT 350 LBS - STATIONS 5 & 6	700
	–
ITEMS (4) AT 100 LBS – STATIONS 1,2,3 & 4	400
WEIGHT AT TAKE - OFF	30,748 LBS

FIG. 4 **WHITLEY V** LOADING AND C.G. CONDITIONS FOR PARATROOPS & CONTAINERS

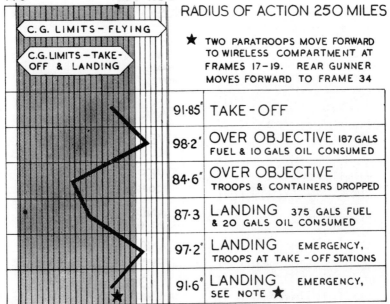

DIAGRAM SHOWING MOVEMENT OF C.G.

INCHES AFT OF DATUM
74.5   95.9 102.0

RADIUS OF ACTION 250 MILES

★ TWO PARATROOPS MOVE FORWARD TO WIRELESS COMPARTMENT AT FRAMES 17–19. REAR GUNNER MOVES FORWARD TO FRAME 34

C.G. LIMITS – FLYING

C.G. LIMITS – TAKE-OFF & LANDING

91·85″ TAKE-OFF

98·2″ OVER OBJECTIVE 187 GALS FUEL & 10 GALS OIL CONSUMED

84·6″ OVER OBJECTIVE TROOPS & CONTAINERS DROPPED

87·3 LANDING 375 GALS FUEL & 20 GALS OIL CONSUMED

97·2″ LANDING EMERGENCY, TROOPS AT TAKE-OFF STATIONS

91·6″ LANDING EMERGENCY, SEE NOTE ★

75 80 85 90 95 100
INCHES AFT OF DATUM

LOAD 'C'	WEIGHT IN LBS
A/C TARE AND MILITARY LOAD	21168
CREW (5) WITH PARACHUTES	1000
FUEL 550 GALLONS IN WING TANKS	3960
OIL 50 GALLONS	450
PARATROOPS (10) AT 237 LBS EACH	2370
CONTAINERS (2) AT 350 LBS - STATIONS 8 & 10	700
CONTAINERS (2) AT 350 LBS - STATIONS 5 & 6	700
CONTAINERS (2) AT 350 LBS - STATIONS 7 & 9	700
ITEMS (4) AT 100 LBS - STATIONS 1,2,3 & 4	400
WEIGHT AT TAKE-OFF	31,448 LBS

FIG. 5 **WHITLEY V** LOADING AND C.G. CONDITIONS FOR PARATROOPS & CONTAINERS

Fuel and oil

18. Fuel should be carried in the nacelles and front wing tanks only, a total of 416 gallons being required on all Marks. 32 gallons of oil are carried except on the Mk. IV which carries 24 gallons.

Paratroop positions (*see* fig. 6)

19. For take-off the paratroops are grouped between the wireless operator's cabin and the trailing-edge frame. For flight to target use is made of the rest seats and the mattresses laid across the floor and aperture doors. At action stations paratroops Nos. 6 and 8 take up standing positions on battens at either side of the cat-walk immediately aft of the step. Paratroop No. 1 sits with his legs over the open aperture. For paratroop drill refer to Sect. 2, Chap. 7 of this manual and to the series of Air Diagrams Nos. 3900–6.

Containers and supplies carried (*see* fig. 7)

20. Only the outer bomb stations in the top tier (Nos. 10, 11, 12, 16, 17 and 18) may be used on Wellington aircraft for the carriage of containers or other supplies. Containers Mk. I C.L.E., Mk. II C.L.E., No. 11 W/T, No. 18 W/T, or items such as the folding trolley may be carried at any of these stations with the reservation that containers at stations 11 and 17 must be restricted in weight to 200 lbs. The reason for this restriction is that, in order to provide clearance with other containers, the cradles at stations 11 and 17 have to be moved forward until the lugs are $27\frac{1}{2}$ in. from the percussion heads, thus introducing a twisting moment at the point of suspension.

Container release equipment (*see* fig. 7)

21. The containers and other items should be auto-distributed at a distributor setting of 0·15 secs.

22. The distributor arm should be set to start at No. 9 contact (*see* fig. 7) in order that the first container is released immediately the strop switch is fired.

23. Fixed wiring is installed on Wellington aircraft between the selector switchbox and the bomb release mechanism. A No. 3 mask is plugged into the selector switchbox.

C.G. conditions (*see* figs. 8, 9, 10, 11 and 12)

24. The accompanying diagrams represent typical examples of C.G. conditions for Wellington Ic, II, III, IV and X aircraft during a paratroop operation. It will be noticed that for Wellingtons Ic, II, IV and X, when troops and containers have been dropped and the rear turret ammunition used, a landing condition occurs in which the C.G. is forward of the permissible landing limit. This can be corrected, at the pilot's discretion, by the transfer of the nose gunner from his action station to the Elsan, this transfer having no ill effect on the C.G. even if the rear ammunition has not been used.

Nose ballast

25. In order to bring the C.G. sufficiently far forward to avoid restrictions on container loading for Wellingtons Ic and IV it is advisable for these aircraft to carry nose ballast. This can be done by loading a 250 lb. bomb, real or dummy, at station No. 4 and another at station No. 13. The 250 lb. dummy bomb is as follows:—

Bomb, Aircraft, H.E., Dummy weighted, 250 lbs. G.P., Mk. IV, Ref. 12B/222.

26. Alternatively a single 500 lb. bomb may be carried, as follows:—

Bomb, Aircraft, H.E., Dummy weighted, 500 lbs. G.P., Mk. IV, Ref. 12B/231.

27. If real bombs are carried, suitable precautions should be taken to prevent their release when the containers are dropped.

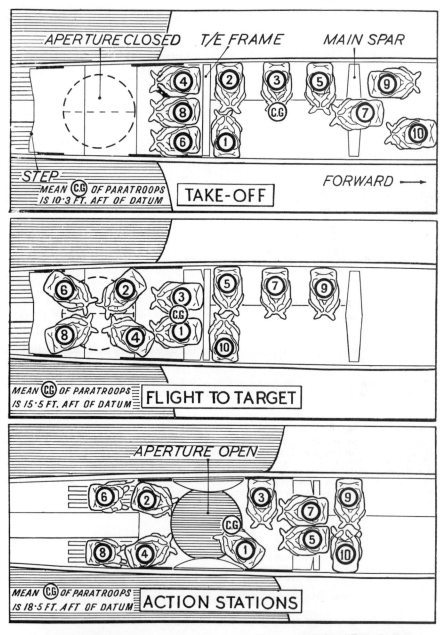

FIG.6 **WELLINGTON** PARATROOP POSITIONS

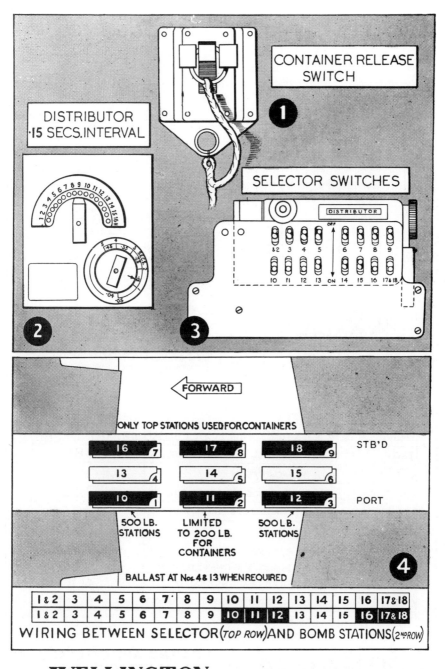

CONTAINER RELEASE SWITCH

1

DISTRIBUTOR
·15 SECS. INTERVAL

2

SELECTOR SWITCHES

DISTRIBUTOR

OFF

1&2 3 4 5 6 7 8 9

10 11 12 13 ON 14 15 16 17&18

3

FORWARD

ONLY TOP STATIONS USED FOR CONTAINERS

16 7	17 8	18 9	STB'D
13 4	14 5	15 6	
10 1	11 2	12 3	PORT

500 LB.
STATIONS

LIMITED
TO 200 LB.
FOR
CONTAINERS

500 LB.
STATIONS

4

BALLAST AT Nos. 4 & 13 WHEN REQUIRED

1&2	3	4	5	6	7	8	9	10	11	12	13	14	15	16	17&18
1&2	3	4	5	6	7	8	9	10	11	12	13	14	15	16	17&18

WIRING BETWEEN SELECTOR (TOP ROW) AND BOMB STATIONS (2ND ROW)

FIG. 7. WELLINGTON CONTAINER RELEASE EQUIPT

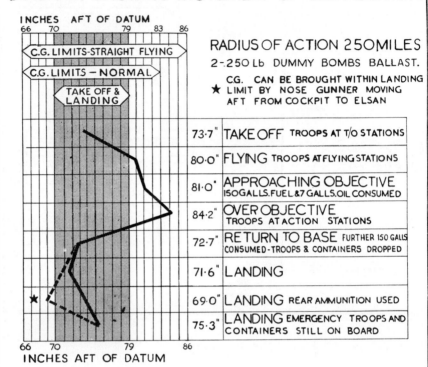

DIAGRAM SHOWING MOVEMENT OF C.G. POSITION

INCHES AFT OF DATUM
66 70   79   83   86

C.G. LIMITS-STRAIGHT FLYING

C.G. LIMITS — NORMAL

TAKE OFF & LANDING

RADIUS OF ACTION 250 MILES
2-250 Lb DUMMY BOMBS BALLAST.

★ C.G. CAN BE BROUGHT WITHIN LANDING LIMIT BY NOSE GUNNER MOVING AFT FROM COCKPIT TO ELSAN

73.7"	TAKE OFF TROOPS AT T/O STATIONS
80.0"	FLYING TROOPS AT FLYING STATIONS
81.0"	APPROACHING OBJECTIVE 150 GALLS. FUEL & 7 GALLS. OIL CONSUMED
84.2"	OVER OBJECTIVE TROOPS AT ACTION STATIONS
72.7"	RETURN TO BASE FURTHER 150 GALLS CONSUMED-TROOPS & CONTAINERS DROPPED
71.6"	LANDING
69.0"	LANDING REAR AMMUNITION USED
75.3"	LANDING EMERGENCY TROOPS AND CONTAINERS STILL ON BOARD

66   70   79   86
INCHES AFT OF DATUM

ITEMS OF SERVICE & AIRBORNE FORCES LOAD	WEIGHT IN LBS.
TARE (STANDARD MK Ic A/c FOR PARATROOPS)	18,986
CREW (5) WITH PARACHUTES	1,000
MILITARY LOAD (2000 ROUNDS AMM. AT REAR TURRET)	1,022
FUEL 416 GALLONS IN NACELLES & FRONT WING	2,995
OIL 32 GALLONS IN NACELLES	288
PARATROOPS (10) AT 237 LBS. EACH	2,370
CONTAINERS (4) AT 350 LBS. STATIONS 10, 12, 16, 18.	1,400
CONTAINERS (2) AT 200 LBS. STATIONS 11 AND 17	400
BALLAST 2-250 LB. DUMMY BOMBS STATIONS 4 AND 13	500
WEIGHT AT TAKE-OFF	28,961

FIG. 8 **WELLINGTON Ic** LOADING AND C.G. CONDITIONS FOR PARATROOPS AND CONTAINERS

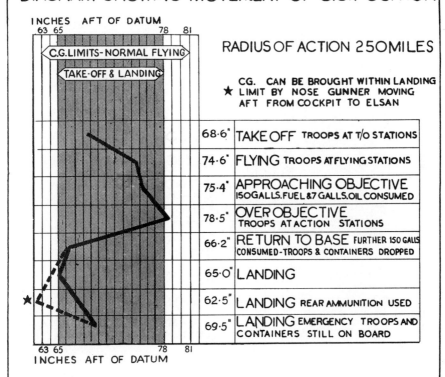

DIAGRAM SHOWING MOVEMENT OF C.G. POSITION

INCHES AFT OF DATUM
63 65   78   81

C.G. LIMITS - NORMAL FLYING
TAKE-OFF & LANDING

RADIUS OF ACTION 250 MILES

★ CG. CAN BE BROUGHT WITHIN LANDING
LIMIT BY NOSE GUNNER MOVING
AFT FROM COCKPIT TO ELSAN

68·6"	TAKE OFF TROOPS AT T/O STATIONS
74·6"	FLYING TROOPS AT FLYING STATIONS
75·4"	APPROACHING OBJECTIVE 150 GALLS. FUEL & 7 GALLS. OIL CONSUMED
78·5"	OVER OBJECTIVE TROOPS AT ACTION STATIONS
66·2"	RETURN TO BASE FURTHER 150 GALLS CONSUMED - TROOPS & CONTAINERS DROPPED
65·0"	LANDING
62·5"	LANDING REAR AMMUNITION USED
69·5"	LANDING EMERGENCY TROOPS AND CONTAINERS STILL ON BOARD

63 65   78   81
INCHES AFT OF DATUM

ITEMS OF SERVICE & AIRBORNE FORCES LOAD	WEIGHT IN LBS.
TARE (STANDARD MK II A/C FOR PARATROOPS)	20,456
CREW (5) WITH PARACHUTES	1,000
MILITARY LOAD (2000 ROUNDS AMM. AT REAR TURRET)	1,022
FUEL 416 GALLONS IN NACELLES & FRONT WING	2,995
OIL 32 GALLONS IN NACELLES	288
PARATROOPS (10) AT 237 LBS. EACH	2,370
CONTAINERS (4) AT 350 LBS. STATIONS 10,12, 16, 18.	1,400
CONTAINERS (2) AT 200 LBS. STATIONS 11 AND 17	400
BALLAST	—
WEIGHT AT TAKE-OFF	29,931

FIG. 9 **WELLINGTON II** LOADING AND C.G. CONDITIONS FOR PARATROOPS AND CONTAINERS

DIAGRAM SHOWING MOVEMENT OF C.G.POSITION

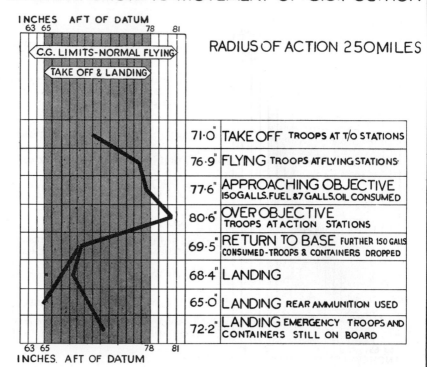

INCHES AFT OF DATUM
63 65   78   81

C.G. LIMITS-NORMAL FLYING

TAKE OFF & LANDING

RADIUS OF ACTION 250 MILES

71·0″	TAKE OFF TROOPS AT T/O STATIONS
76·9″	FLYING TROOPS AT FLYING STATIONS
77·6″	APPROACHING OBJECTIVE 150 GALLS. FUEL & 7 GALLS. OIL CONSUMED
80·6″	OVER OBJECTIVE TROOPS AT ACTION STATIONS
69·5″	RETURN TO BASE FURTHER 150 GALLS CONSUMED-TROOPS & CONTAINERS DROPPED
68·4″	LANDING
65·0″	LANDING REAR AMMUNITION USED
72·2″	LANDING EMERGENCY TROOPS AND CONTAINERS STILL ON BOARD

63 65   78 81
INCHES. AFT OF DATUM

ITEMS OF SERVICE & AIRBORNE FORCES LOAD	WEIGHT IN LBS.
TARE (STANDARD MK III A/C FOR PARATROOPS)	21,231
CREW (5) WITH PARACHUTES	1,000
MILITARY LOAD (2000 ROUNDS AMM.AT REAR TURRET)	1,481
FUEL 416 GALLONS IN NACELLES & FRONT WING	2,995
OIL 32 GALLONS IN NACELLES	288
PARATROOPS (10) AT 237 LBS. EACH	2,370
CONTAINERS (4) AT 350 LBS. STATIONS 10,12, 16, 18.	1,400
CONTAINERS (2) AT 200 LBS. STATIONS 11 AND 17	400
BALLAST	—
WEIGHT AT TAKE-OFF	31,165

FIG.10 **WELLINGTON III** LOADING AND C.G.CONDITIONS FOR PARATROOPS AND CONTAINERS

DIAGRAM SHOWING MOVEMENT OF C.G. POSITION

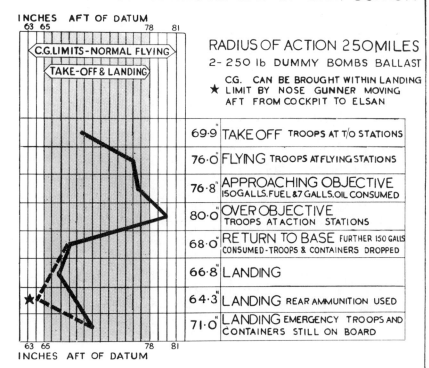

INCHES AFT OF DATUM
63 65   78   81

C.G. LIMITS - NORMAL FLYING

TAKE-OFF & LANDING

RADIUS OF ACTION 250 MILES
2- 250 lb DUMMY BOMBS BALLAST

★ CG. CAN BE BROUGHT WITHIN LANDING LIMIT BY NOSE GUNNER MOVING AFT FROM COCKPIT TO ELSAN

69·9" TAKE OFF TROOPS AT T/O STATIONS

76·0" FLYING TROOPS AT FLYING STATIONS

76·8" APPROACHING OBJECTIVE 150 GALLS. FUEL & 7 GALLS. OIL CONSUMED

80·0" OVER OBJECTIVE TROOPS AT ACTION STATIONS

68·0" RETURN TO BASE FURTHER 150 GALLS CONSUMED - TROOPS & CONTAINERS DROPPED

66·8" LANDING

64·3" LANDING REAR AMMUNITION USED

71·0" LANDING EMERGENCY TROOPS AND CONTAINERS STILL ON BOARD

63 65   78   81
INCHES AFT OF DATUM

ITEMS OF SERVICE & AIRBORNE FORCES LOAD	WEIGHT IN LBS.
TARE (STANDARD MKIV A/c FOR PARATROOPS)	20,022
CREW (5) WITH PARACHUTES	1,000
MILITARY LOAD (2000 ROUNDS AMM. AT REAR TURRET)	1,022
FUEL 416 GALLONS IN NACELLES & FRONT WING	2,995
OIL 24 GALLONS IN NACELLES	216
PARATROOPS (10) AT 237 LBS. EACH	2,370
CONTAINERS (4) AT 350 LBS. STATIONS 10, 12, 16, 18.	1,400
CONTAINERS (2) AT 200 LBS. STATIONS 11 AND 17	400
BALLAST 2-250 LB. DUMMY BOMBS STATIONS 4 AND 13	500
WEIGHT AT TAKE - OFF	29,925

FIG.11 **WELLINGTON IV** LOADING AND C.G. CONDITIONS FOR PARATROOPS AND CONTAINERS

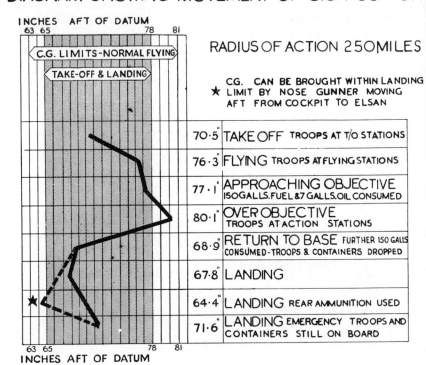

DIAGRAM SHOWING MOVEMENT OF C.G. POSITION

INCHES AFT OF DATUM
63 65   78   81

C.G. LIMITS - NORMAL FLYING
TAKE-OFF & LANDING

RADIUS OF ACTION 250 MILES

★ CG. CAN BE BROUGHT WITHIN LANDING
LIMIT BY NOSE GUNNER MOVING
AFT FROM COCKPIT TO ELSAN

70·5"	TAKE OFF TROOPS AT T/O STATIONS
76·3"	FLYING TROOPS AT FLYING STATIONS
77·1"	APPROACHING OBJECTIVE 150 GALLS. FUEL & 7 GALLS. OIL CONSUMED
80·1"	OVER OBJECTIVE TROOPS AT ACTION STATIONS
68·9"	RETURN TO BASE FURTHER 150 GALLS CONSUMED - TROOPS & CONTAINERS DROPPED
67·8"	LANDING
64·4"	LANDING REAR AMMUNITION USED
71·6"	LANDING EMERGENCY TROOPS AND CONTAINERS STILL ON BOARD

63 65   78   81
INCHES AFT OF DATUM

ITEMS OF SERVICE & AIRBORNE FORCES LOAD	WEIGHT IN LBS.
TARE (STANDARD MK X A/C FOR PARATROOPS)	21,420
CREW (5) WITH PARACHUTES	1,000
MILITARY LOAD (4000 ROUNDS AMM. AT REAR TURRET)	1,607
FUEL 416 GALLONS IN NACELLES & FRONT WING	2,995
OIL 32 GALLONS IN NACELLES	288
PARATROOPS (10) AT 237 LBS. EACH	2,370
CONTAINERS (4) AT 350 LBS. STATIONS 10, 12, 16, 18.	1,400
CONTAINERS (2) AT 200 LBS. STATIONS 11 AND 17	400
BALLAST	–
WEIGHT AT TAKE-OFF	31,480

FIG.12 **WELLINGTON X** LOADING AND C.G. CONDITIONS FOR PARATROOPS AND CONTAINERS

Fuel and oil

28. 1,192 gallons of fuel are carried in Nos. 1, 3 and 4 tanks, collectively, and 200 gallons in No. 2 tank. No. 5 fuel tank cocks should be shut off. 132 gallons of oil are carried.

Paratroop positions (see fig. 13)

29. The diagrams in fig. 13 indicate the positions for each paratroop at take-off and at action stations. During flight to target the paratroops are allowed freedom of movement between the front spar and the forward edge of the aperture; these boundaries keep the mean C.G. of the paratroops within the permissible limits of from 2 ft. 9 in. to 17 ft. 9 in. aft of the datum point. At action stations paratroops Nos. 1 and 2 sit with their legs over the open aperture. For paratroop drill refer to Sect. 2, Chap. 7 of this manual and to the series of Air Diagrams Nos 3900–6.

Containers and supplies carried (see fig. 14)

30. There is no restriction on loading up to 350 lbs. at any of the fifteen bomb stations on Halifax aircraft. For the safe dropping of supplies, however, the heavier items such as Mk. I and Mk. III C.L.E. containers should be loaded at the fuselage stations and the lighter items such as Nos. 11 or 18 W/T containers, or the folding trolley, loaded at the wing stations. A typical arrangement of seven items is given in fig. 14.

31. The following is an alternative arrangement for the release of nine items:—

Station Nos.	Position	Item carried
2, 3, 4, 6, 8 and 9	Fuselage	Mk. I or Mk. III C.L.E. containers
11, 14 and 15	Wings	Nos. 11 or 18 W/T containers or folding trolley.

Container release equipment (see fig. 14)

32. The containers and other items should be auto-distributed at a distributor setting of 0·3 secs.

Pre-selector

33. Halifax container release equipment includes a pre-selector in circuit between the selector switchbox and the bomb release mechanism. The pre-selector enables any selector switch to be set to operate the bomb release mechanism at any station. It is thus a simple matter to arrange for the safe release of heavy and light items and to ensure the least interference with the stability of the aircraft while the various items are being dropped. The setting of the pre-selector indicated in fig. 14 should be regarded as typical only.

C.G. conditions

34. The change in the C.G. conditions of the Halifax II and V caused by the consumption of fuel and the release of men and containers is very slight. The following is a statement of typical loading conditions for Halifax II and V aircraft equipped for a paratroop operation:—

Items of Load	Weight (Mark II)	(Mark V)
Aircraft Tare (see para. 35)	35942 lbs.	36500 lbs
Typical Service Load (see para. 35)	3285 lbs.	3285 lbs.
Fuel, 1192 gallons, Nos. 1, 3 and 4 tanks	8582 lbs.	8582 lbs.
Fuel, 200 gallons, No. 2 tank	1440 lbs.	1440 lbs.
Oil, 132 gallons	1188 lbs.	1188 lbs.
Paratroops (10) at 237 lbs. each	2370 lbs.	2370 lbs.
Containers (2) at 350 lbs.—stations 4 and 6	700 lbs.	700 lbs
Container (1) at 350 lbs.—station 8	350 lbs.	350 lbs.
Container (1) at 350 lbs.—station 2	350 lbs.	350 lbs.
Items (3) at 100 lbs.—stations 10, 12 and 13	300 lbs.	300 lbs.
Weight at take-off	54507 lbs.	55065 lbs.

35. The Tare weight and Typical Service Load referred to above cover the following conditions:—

(i) Rear turret ammunition, 700 rounds per gun.
(ii) Reconnaissance flares removed.
(iii) Flame floats removed.
(iv) Rear turret accumulators moved forward 7 ft.

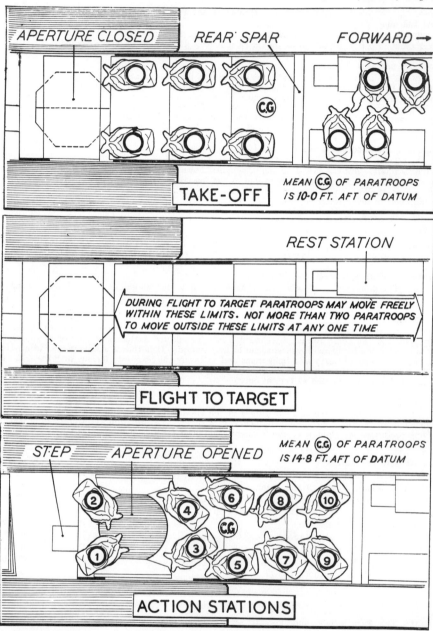

APERTURE CLOSED   REAR SPAR   FORWARD →

C.G

TAKE-OFF   MEAN C.G OF PARATROOPS
IS 10·0 FT. AFT OF DATUM

REST STATION

DURING FLIGHT TO TARGET PARATROOPS MAY MOVE FREELY
WITHIN THESE LIMITS. NOT MORE THAN TWO PARATROOPS
TO MOVE OUTSIDE THESE LIMITS AT ANY ONE TIME

FLIGHT TO TARGET

STEP   APERTURE OPENED   MEAN C.G OF PARATROOPS
IS 14·8 FT. AFT OF DATUM

C.G

ACTION STATIONS

FIG.13 **HALIFAX II & V** PARATROOP POSITIONS

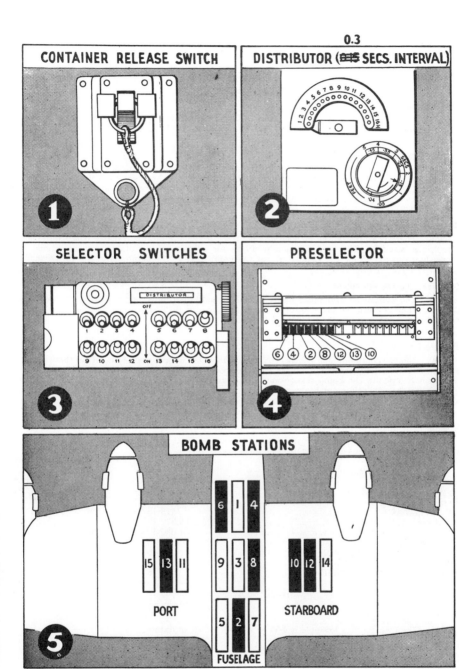

Fig. 14 **HALIFAX** CONTAINER RELEASE EQUIPMENT

Manchester I

Fuel and oil

36. For a radius of action of 250 miles, 750 gallons of fuel are carried and 57 gallons of oil. The full tankage of 1,160 gallons of fuel may be carried if required.

Paratroop positions (*see* fig. 15)

37. For take-off the position of each paratroop in a Manchester aircraft is indicated by the inset diagram at the top of fig. 15. For flight and action stations the positions of the paratroops are generally similar to those indicated for the Lancaster. For paratroop drill refer to Sect. 2, Chap. 7 of this manual and to the series of Air Diagrams Nos. 3900–6.

Containers and supplies carried

38. There is no restriction on loading up to 350 lb. at any of the available bomb stations on Manchester aircraft. The recommended positions for containers and other items are similar to those shown in fig. 16 for the Lancaster, but the numbering of the bomb stations is different.

Container release equipment

39. The containers and other items should be auto-distributed at a distributor interval of 0·3 secs. when consecutive pre-selector contacts are used, or 0·15 secs. when alternate pre-selector contacts are used. *See* Sect. 2, Chap. 7 of this manual.

Pre-selector

40. Manchester container release equipment includes a pre-selector in circuit between the selector switchbox and the bomb release mechanism. The pre-selector enables any selector switch to be set to operate the bomb release mechanism at any station. It is thus a simple matter to arrange for the safe release of heavy and light items and to ensure the least interference with the stability of the aircraft while the various items are being dropped.

Loading statement

41. The following statement refers to a Manchester I at take-off condition for a paratroop operation with a radius of action of 250 miles:—

Items of load	Weight	Moment (lb. ft.) Forward	Aft
Aircraft Tare	29,716 lb.		126,685
Typical Service Load	2,175 lb.		22,354
Fuel, 750 gallons	5,400 lb.		26,568
Oil, 57 gallons	513 lb.		2,220
Paratroops (10) at 237 lb. each	2,370 lb.		23,650
Containers (3) at 350 lb.—stations 1, 3 and 5 ...	1,050 lb.	9,366	
Container (1) at 350 lb.—station 7	350 lb.	889	
Item (1) at 63 lb.—station 9	63 lb.	160	
Item (1) at 86 lb.—station 11	86 lb.	218	
Item (1) at 86 lb.—station 13	86 lb.		329
Weight at take-off	41,809 lb.	Total moment	191,173

The C.G. for this example is 4·57 ft. or 54·8 in. aft of datum.

The C.G. limits for the Manchester I are from 49 in. to 66·5 in. aft of the datum point.

42. The change in the C.G. conditions of Manchester aircraft caused by the consumption of fuel and the release of men and containers for a typical paratroop operation does not cause any infringement of the permissible C.G. limits.

Albemarle I and II

Fuel and oil

51.   Practical radius of 525 miles.   A full tankage of 769 gallons of fuel and $59\frac{1}{4}$ gallons of oil is sufficient for a practical radius of 525 miles or a practical extreme range of 1,000 miles.   When paratroops are at action stations the C.G. is aft of the extended aft limit unless 220 gallons of fuel remain in the wing tanks.   Therefore paratroops may not be dropped between ranges of 759 to 1,000 miles but must be landed and deplaned.   Sufficient fuel will then remain for a flight of 247 miles without paratroops.   *Note.*—With all tanks filled, fuel must first be drawn from the fuselage tanks simultaneously and then from the wing tanks.

Paratroop positions *(see* fig. 17)

52.   The diagrams in fig. 17 indicate the positions of each paratroop at take-off, flight, and action stations.   For paratroop drill refer to Sect. 2, Chap. 7, para. 24 of this manual.

Containers and supplies carried *(see* fig. 18)

53.   Only four bomb stations Nos. 4, 6, 7 and 9 may be used on the Albemarle aircraft for the carriage of containers Mark I or Mark III, each loaded to a maximum of 350 lb.   Bomb stations 1 and 2 may be utilized for lighter articles, such as folding trolleys, each of a maximum weight of 100 lb.

Modified container cradles

54.   To enable three containers to be carried abreast the cradles have to be modified to decrease the overall width.   This is achieved by shortening forks of the cradles and lengthening the metal supporting straps so that the fastening points come above the horizontal centre-line of the container *(see* Sect. 2, Chap. 4 of this volume).

Influence of the gun turret on the C.G.

55.   When paratroops are carried the containers must also be in position to keep the C.G. within safe limits.   If the containers are not carried the removal of the gun turret will compensate for their absence by decreasing the positive moment.

Container release equipment *(see* fig. 18)

56.   The containers and other items should be auto-distributed at a distributor setting of 0·15 secs. in the order 1, 2, 7, 6, 4 and 9 *(see* Chap. 2, para. 112, and Chap. 7, para. 25).

Loading statements

57.   The following statements refer to the Albemarle I at take-off, flight to target, and action stations for paratroop operations with a radius of 525 miles:—

		Moment (*lb. in.*)	
Items of load	*Weight (lb.)*	*Forward.*	*Aft*
4 Browning guns	92		15,820
Ammunition in turret	159		27,820
Avro bomb carriers, forward	70	940	
Avro bomb carriers, centre	70		6,100
Avro bomb carriers, rear	70		13,390
Bomb distributor	8	1,110	
Electrical equipment	9	400	
Navigational equipment	101·5		12,330
Dinghy	60		18,120
Miscellaneous	44		12,140
Power units for T.1154 and R.1155	56·5		1,020
T.1154/R.1155	88·5		1,240
TR.9F	52		2,240
Intercommunication	24		380
R.1124A/R.1125A	42		500
R.3003	31		14,200
Pilot and parachute	200	5,600	
Navigator	180	15,170	
Navigator's parachute	20	1,360	
W/T operator and parachute	200		1,800
Gunner	180		28,080
Gunner's parachute	20		2,920
Tare weight	22,350		1,615,905
	24,128		1,749,425

Items of load	Weight (lb.)	Moment (lb. in.) Forward	Aft
ADD:—			
Tail guard	30		15,600
Paratroop modifications	50		15,100
Troop mattresses	100		24,200
	24,308		1,804,325
LESS:—			
Sea crash gear	25		6,680
Reserve ammunition boxes etc.	65		15,080
Basic load	24,218	Total moment	1,782,565

Take-off condition:—

Items of load	Weight (lb.)	Moment (lb. in.) Forward	Aft
Basic load	24,218		1,782,565
Fuel front fuselage tank 204 gallons	1,469		77,860
Fuel rear fuselage tank 165 gallons	1,188		127,120
Fuel in wing tanks 400 gallons	2,880		161,280
Oil 59¼ gallons	533		30,916
3 containers on forward racks	1,050	14,070	
One container and two items (100 lb. each) ...	550		47,960
Paratroops, ten fully equipped	2,370		545,100
Weight at take-off	34,258	Total moment	2,758,731

The C.G. in the case of take-off is 80·5 in. aft of datum.
The C.G. limits for the Albemarle I are from 69·5 in. to 84 in. aft of datum.

Flight to target condition:—

Items of load	Weight (lb.)	Moment (lb. in.) Forward	Aft
Basic load	24,218		1,782,565
Fuel, front fuselage tank, 179 gallons	1,288		68,318
Fuel, rear fuselage tank, 140 gallons	1,008		107,859
Fuel, in wing tanks, 400 gallons	2,880		161,280
Oil, 59¼ gallons	533		30,916
3 containers on forward racks	1,050	14,070	
1 container and 2 items (100 lb. each)	550		47,960
Paratroops, 10 fully equipped	2,370		594,870
Total weight at flight to target	33,897	Total moment	2,779,698

The C.G. in the case of flight to target is 82 in. aft of datum.
The C.G. limits for the Albemarle I are from 69·5 in. to 84 in. aft of datum.

Action stations condition:—

Items of load	Weight (lb.)	Moment (lb. in.) Forward	Aft
Basic load	24,218		1,782,565
Fuel, in wing tanks, 385 gallons	2,272		127,232
Oil, 59¼ gallons	533		30,916
3 containers forward racks...	1,050	14,070	
1 container and 2 items (100 lb. each)	550		47,960
Paratroops, 10 fully equipped	2,370		618,570
Total weight at action station	30,993	Total moment	2,593,173

The C.G. in the case of action stations is 83·7 in. aft of datum.
The C.G. limits for the Albemarle I are from 69·5 in. to 84 in. aft of datum.

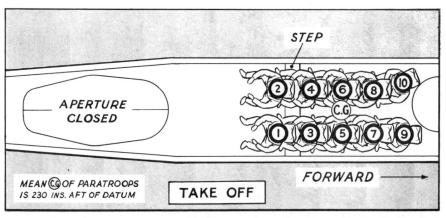

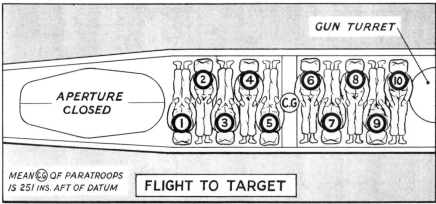

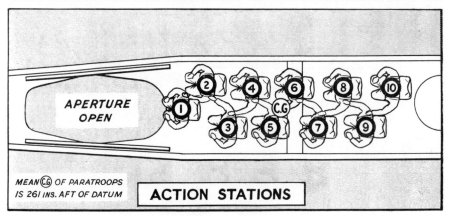

FIG.17 **ALBEMARLE** PARATROOP POSITIONS

This page issued with A.L. No. 7
May, 1943

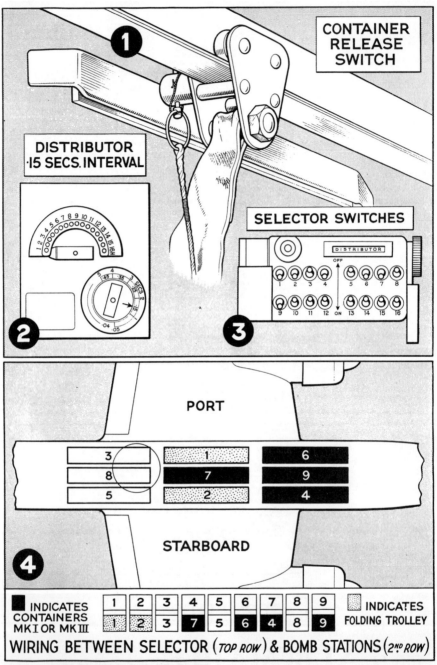

CONTAINER RELEASE SWITCH

DISTRIBUTOR ·15 SECS. INTERVAL

SELECTOR SWITCHES

DISTRIBUTOR
OFF
ON

PORT

3
8
5
1
7
2
6
9
4

STARBOARD

■ INDICATES CONTAINERS MK I OR MK III

▨ INDICATES FOLDING TROLLEY

1	2	3	4	5	6	7	8	9
2	2	3	7	5	6	4	8	9

WIRING BETWEEN SELECTOR (*TOP ROW*) & BOMB STATIONS (*2ND ROW*)

FIG.18 ALBEMARLE CONTAINER RELEASE EQUIP.T

Dakota I (C47)

Fuel and oil

58. With full fuel capacity of 822 U.S. gallons (684 Imperial gallons) and 58 U.S. gallons (48 Imperial gallons) of oil, the Dakota I has an estimated practical range of 850 miles or radius of action of 425 miles for paratroop operations when loaded as detailed in para. 60. An allowance of 25 U.S. gallons is made for run-up and take-off, and a further 60 U.S. gallons for a climb to 8,000 ft.

Paratroop positions

59. Twenty paratroops can be comfortably accommodated on the seats provided. As this load with the containers carried is not unusual for the Dakota I, there are no special provisions made for "take-off", "flight to target" or "action" stations provided the paratroops remain reasonably well spaced down the aircraft. For paratroop drill refer to Sect. 2, Chap. 7, paras. 30 to 32 of this manual.

Containers and supplies carried (*see* fig. 20)

60. The procedure adopted for fitting bomb carriers to the Dakota I aircraft is detailed in Sect 2, Chap. 2 of this manual. At stations 3 and 4 short universal bomb carriers must be fitted, such as the No. 1 Mark I and II or the Mark III. This is to minimise interference with the flaps. At stations 1, 2, 5 and 6, bomb carriers No. 2 may be fitted.

61. Six C.L.E. Mark I or Mark III containers, each loaded to a maximum weight of 350 lb., may be carried. , The containers at bomb stations 3 and 4 make it necessary that the flap movement be restricted by 50 per cent. This restriction is obviated for landing purposes if the containers are dropped before landing.

62. Folding bicycles, replacing an equivalent weight in paratroops, may be carried inside the fuselage and dropped from the aircraft door immediately prior to the paratroops jumping.

Container release equipment (*see* fig. 19)

63. There is a separate dropping switch for each container mounted on a panel forward of the exit door. First switch on the circuit breaker switch; this will illuminate the red warning light. Immediately before container dropping is to commence operate the master switch; this will extinguish the red warning light showing that the circuit is live. Then operate each container release switch in turn, taking approximately two seconds to complete the operation. The green warning lights do not operate since the 0·25 amp. required to light the filaments is more than can be passed through the safety armature on the British E.M. unit. A bomb firing switch will be found connected to No. 1 container release switch; it should be disregarded, as should the manually operated salvo release wire situated below the switchbox.

C.G. conditions

64. The C.G. conditions of the Dakota I is satisfactory carrying 20 paratroops and six containers under all conditions involved in a paratroop operation.

Loading statement

65. The all up weight of a typical C.47 loaded as in the previous paragraph was 30,842 lb., made up as follows:—

Tare weight (including filters, alcohol, flooring, etc.)	16,900
Two long-range tanks, complete	325
Numna mattresses	80
Static line and D-rings	20
Containers, racks and beams	210
Kennedy kit	100
Crew of five and parachutes	1,000
20 paratroops (237 lb. each maximum)	4,740
6 containers at 350 lb.	2,100
Fuel, 822 U.S. gallons	4,932
Oil, 58 U.S. gallons	435
	30,842 lb.

66. This load is approximately 160 lb below the maximum all up weight of 31,000 lb. It should be noted that 26,000 lb. is the maximum recommended weight at which the aircraft may land, so that if the aircraft has to land without dropping the paratroops the weight must be reduced either by consuming fuel or by releasing the containers.

This page issued with A.L. No. 10
July, 1943

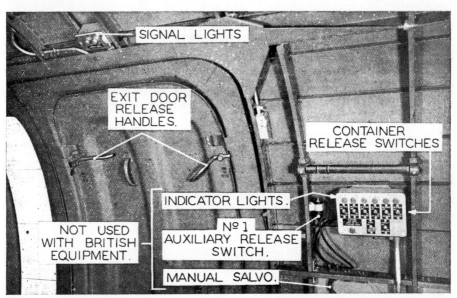

FIG.19. PARATROOP'S SIGNAL LIGHTS AND CONTAINER RELEASE SWITCHES

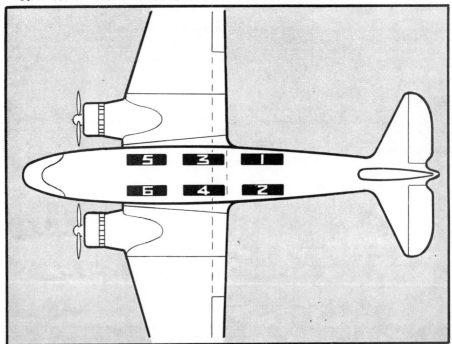

FIG.20. **DAKOTA I** LOCATION OF CONTAINERS

CHAPTER 6

SAFETY OF AIRCRAFT IN FLIGHT

LIST OF CONTENTS

General

1. Serious accidents may occur to a paratroop-carrying aircraft and its personnel if paratroops, either inadvertently or through curiosity, interfere with aircraft fitments before or during flight. For this reason precautions similar to those outlined in subsequent paragraphs should be taken to ensure that no interference occurs.

Authority of the Captain of the aircraft

2. The Captain of the aircraft is in absolute control of all personnel in the aircraft. He will issue orders to paratroops through the Section Commander of the paratroops. Prior to an operation the Captain of the aircraft should ensure that the Section Commander is familiar with the exact location of any aircraft fittings which it may be necessary for him to use, such as the intercomm. sockets, lighting switches, dim-lighting control, and hot air controls. No other controls should be touched.

Instructions to paratroops

3. The Captain of the aircraft might usefully address a few remarks to the paratroops before take-off. The following is a suggestion for the substance of such remarks:—

   (i)   All troops will carry out the orders given by the Captain of the aircraft.

   (ii) Paratroops will stow equipment carefully in aircraft, ensuring that it does not interfere with control wires or cables. Paratroops will ensure that any sleeping bags, rugs, etc., are safely stowed in the aircraft before jumping.

   (iii) In the event of any small item of equipment (personal or otherwise) being dropped in an aircraft by a paratroop, such an item *must be recovered* as its presence might cause serious interference with controls.

   (iv) There will be no smoking in the aircraft.

   (v)   Paratroops will adhere to the specified take-off positions (*see* Sect. 2, Chap. 5) until ordered to move by the Captain of the aircraft.

   (vi) There must be no undue movement of troops from their specified positions during flight.

   (vii) No aircraft fittings must be touched by paratroops other than those agreed on between the Captain of the aircraft and the paratroop Section Commander, and these should only be used on the orders of, or in agreement with, the Captain of the aircraft.

   (viii) Wellington and Warwick aircraft have a fabric skin which is particularly vulnerable to damage by heavy boots, rifles, etc. Paratroops travelling in these aircraft should be warned to keep to the catwalks when getting aboard and when taking up action stations.

   (ix) In the event of an emergency the paratroops should be prepared to take up action stations and to jump in their normal rotation if the Captain gives the order to abandon aircraft.

CHAPTER 7

TECHNICAL PROCEDURE IN FLYING

General

1. The handling of an aircraft for all operational requirements is detailed in the Pilot's Notes for the relevant aircraft. A summary of the specialised technique required on the part of the captain and crew of a paratroop-carrying aircraft is given in the following paragraphs. Such details as flying speeds and flap angles to be observed over the dropping zone are listed separately for each aircraft under the aircraft type name.

Use of intercomm.

2. The following example of air drill for the crew of a paratroop-carrying aircraft includes the use of intercomm. between the captain of the aircraft and the stick commander. Where intercomm. is not available the red and green signal lights will be the only direct means of communication.

Typical air drill

3. The special duties of the aircrew during a paratroop operation are as follows:—

(i) *Before taxying out for take-off.* Captain of A/C re-tests intercomm. with stick commander.

(ii) *Before take-off.* Captain of A/C orders: 'Take-off positions'. The paratroops having complied with the order, the stick commander replies: 'O.K. Take-off positions'.

(iii) *Approximately five minutes after take-off.* The captain of A/C orders: 'Travelling positions'. Positions assumed by paratroops.

(iv) *20 minutes before dropping time.* Captain of A/C orders: 'Prepare for action'. Paratroops take up dropping positions and attach the static lines of their parachutes to the appropriate strops. When paratroops have attached their static lines the W/Operator goes aft and checks that the container release switch is up, with ring attached and cord free, and reports to navigator. Navigator then selects the container switches (*see* Chap. 5).

(v) *Five minutes before dropping time.* Captain of A/C orders: 'Action stations'. The paratroops switch out or dim the fuselage interior lights and then open the aperture doors. The stick commander removes his intercomm. helmet and replaces it with his steel helmet, but he holds the intercomm. helmet to his ear so as to maintain intercomm. with the captain of the A/C until the red signal light is switched on. The W/Operator takes up a position from which he can watch the paratroops make their exit. The navigator opens the bomb doors.

(vi) *Five seconds before the drop.* Navigator switches on the red signal light, No. 1 of the stick of paratroops puts his feet in the aperture. It is important who leaves the aircraft facing aft should sit on the centre line of the aperture to avoid a twisting effect as he enters the slipstream.

(vii) *One second before reaching the dropping zone.* Navigator switches on the green signal light. Paratroops leave the A/C. There is a pause between the dropping of paratroops Nos. 5 and 6 to allow for the containers to fall clear. The necessary time allowance for this purpose is stated in subsequent paragraphs under the aircraft type names.

(viii) The W/Operator watches the paratroops leave the A/C and reports: 'All gone'. Navigator pulls the bomb jettison toggle.

(ix) Captain of A/C closes the bomb doors, increases the flying speed, raises flaps and raises the undercarriage if this has been lowered.

(x) Two of the crew (e.g. the W/Operator and the navigator) go aft to withdraw or jettison the strops and to close the aperture doors. The strop switch should be returned to the up position, otherwise the distributor is liable to overheat.

Whitley V

Selector and distributor setting

4. The selector switches are set in accordance with the information given in Chap. 5. When set, they are locked in position by means of the locking bar described in Chap. 2. The automatic distributor is set to operate at an interval of 0·05 secs.

Container dropping time

5. Approximately 2 secs. are required for the release of containers between the dropping of paratroops No. 5 and 6. The time is made up as follows:—

(i)	Between No. 5 paratroop and release of first container	0·5 sec.
(ii)	Travel of distributor arm	0·7 sec.
(iii)	For last container to fall clear	0·5 sec.

Flying speed over dropping zone

6. The aircraft is to be flown straight and level at 95–100 m.p.h. I.A.S. with flap applied at about 15°.

C.G. conditions

7. The C.G. conditions of the Whitley V during a paratroop operation are described in Chap. 5. When making an emergency landing with paratroops and containers still on board it is necessary to bring the rear gunner forward to Frame 34, just aft of the aperture, and to bring two paratroops forward to Frames 17–19, in the wireless compartment.

Length of stick of paratroops

8. The length of stick for ten paratroops and seven containers or other items when dropped from 500 ft. is approximately 700 yds.

Wellington IC, II, III, IV and X

Selector and distributor setting

9. A No. 3 mask is plugged onto the selector switchbox, and the top station switches only are selected. The automatic distributor is set to operate at an interval of 0·15 sec. and to start at contact No. 9.

Container dropping time

10. Approximately 2 secs. are required for the release of containers between the dropping of paratroops Nos. 5 and 6. The time is made up as follows:—

(i)	Between No. 5 paratroop and release of first container	0·5 sec.
(ii)	Travel of distributor arm	1·05 sec.
(iii)	For last container to fall clear	0·5 sec.

Precaution for paratroops Nos. 9 and 10

10a. The static line for paratroop No. 9 should pass over his right shoulder to the strop. The static line for paratroop No. 10 should pass over his left shoulder to the strop. This arrangement reduces the delay made instinctively by paratroop No. 10 to avoid the possibility of catching his legs in the large loop of static line trailed by No. 9 as he makes his exit.

Flying speed over dropping zone

11. The aircraft is to be flown straight and level at 105 m.p.h. I.A.S. with flap applied at about 20°. The undercarriage should be retracted to prevent the fouling of strops.

C.G. conditions

12. The C.G. conditions of the various Marks of Wellingtons used for paratroop operations are described in Chap. 5. In certain instances, when making an emergency landing with paratroops and containers still on board and the rear turret ammunition used, it is necessary to send the nose gunner back to the Elsan to keep the C.G. of the aircraft within the safe landing limits.

Length of stick of paratroops

13. The length of stick for ten paratroops and six containers or other items when dropped from 500 ft. is 700–800 yds.

Halifax II and V

Selector and distributor setting

14. Owing to the provision of a pre-selector in the bomb release circuit of the Halifax, the following alternative methods may be used for the release of containers:—

(i) *Using the pre-selector in the normal way.* Set the automatic distributor to operate at an interval of 0·3 sec. Set the first seven contacts of the pre-selector to correspond to the numbers of the seven loaded bomb racks and to initiate the required order of release. Select the first seven selector switches (*see* Chap. 5, fig. 14).

(ii) *Using the pre-selector for spacing only* Set the automatic distributor to operate at an interval of 0·15 sec., and to start at the stud corresponding to the first loaded rack, i.e., stud 2 for the loading shown in Chap. 5, fig. 14. Set the pre-selector contacts in numerical order: 1, 2, 3, 4, etc. Select the selector switches numbered to correspond to the loaded bomb racks. Since the loaded racks shown in fig. 14 are Nos. 2, 4, 6, 8 etc., the distributor will traverse one ineffective contact between each effective one, giving a 0·3 sec. interval between successive containers, the one permissible exception being the 0·15 sec. interval between racks Nos. 12 and 13. It should be noted that the order of release of the containers in this instance can only be the numerical order of their bomb rack numbers.

Container dropping time

15. Owing to the great length of the strops used on the Halifax, 4½ secs. are required for the release of containers between the dropping of paratroops Nos. 5 and 6. The time is made up as follows:—

(i)	Between No. 5 paratroop and release of first container	1·3 sec.
(ii)	Travel of distributor arm (either 0·3 × 6, or 0·15 × 12)	2·0 sec.
(iii)	For last container to fall clear	1·0 sec.

Flying speed over dropping zone

16. The aircraft is to be flown straight and level at 130 m.p.h. I.A.S. The undercarriage should be lowered and flap applied at about 30°.

C.G. conditions

17. The Halifax is not sensitive to small changes in position of paratroop load. Providing the paratroops keep within the limits outlined in Chap. 5, no special precautions are necessary.

Length of stick of paratroops

18. The length of stick for ten paratroops and seven containers or other items when dropped from 500 ft. is 700–800 yds.

Manchester I (*see* Lancaster)

Lancaster I and II

Selector and distributor setting

19. Owing to the provision of a pre-selector in the bomb release circuit of the Lancaster, the following alternative methods may be used for the release of containers:—

(i) *Using the pre-selector in the normal way.* Set the automatic distributor to operate at an interval of 0·3 sec. Set the first seven contacts of the pre-selector to correspond to the numbers of the seven loaded bomb racks and to initiate the required order of release. Select the first seven selector switches, (*see* Chap. 5, fig. 16).

(ii) *Using the pre-selector for spacing only.* Set the automatic distributor to operate at an interval of 0·15 sec., and to start at the stud corresponding to the first loaded rack, i.e., stud 2 for the loading shown in Chap. 5, fig. 16. Set the pre-selector contacts in numerical order, 1, 2, 3, 4, etc. Select the selector switches numbered to correspond to the loaded bomb racks. Since the loaded racks shown in fig. 16 are Nos. 2, 4, 6, 8, etc., the distributor will traverse one ineffective contact between each effective one, giving a 0·3 sec. interval between successive containers. It should be noted that the order of release of the containers in this instance can only be the numerical order of their bomb rack numbers.

Container dropping time

20. Approximately 3½ secs. are required for the release of containers between the dropping of paratroops Nos. 5 and 6. The time is made up as follows:—

(i)	Between No. 5 paratroop and release of first container	0·75 to 1·0 sec.
(ii)	Travel of distributor arm (either 0·3 × 6, or 0·15 × 12)	approx. 2·0 sec.
(iii)	For last container to fall clear	0·5 sec.

Flying speed over dropping zone

21. The aircraft is to be flown straight and level at 125–130 m.p.h. I.A.S. Flap should be applied at about 15°.

C.G. conditions

22. The Lancaster is not sensitive to small changes in the position of its paratroop load. Providing the paratroops keep to the positions outlined in Chap. 5, no special precautions are necessary.

Length of stick of paratroops

23. The length of stick for ten paratroops and seven containers or other items when dropped from 500 ft. is 700–800 yds.

Albemarle I and II

Special air drill (*see* fig. 1)

24. The notes in Typical air drill, para. 3 of this chapter, apply in the case of the Albemarle except for the following amendments to the indicated sub-paragraphs:—

  (i) Replacing para. 3 (iv). *20 minutes before dropping time* Captain of A/C orders: "Prepare for action". Paratroops take up dropping positions and attach the static lines of their parachutes to the appropriate strops. The navigator then selects the container switches.

  (ii) Replacing para. 3 (vi). *Five seconds before the drop.* Navigator switches on the red signal light. No. 1 of the stick of paratroops *takes up a knees bend position with feet at the edge of the aperture, head back looking at the signal lights, and steadying himself by holding the doors. The other paratroops, crouched similarly, place alternate hands on the preceding man's shoulder. They all make their exit from the centre of the forward edge of aperture facing aft* (*see* Sect. 2, Chap. 5, fig. 17).

Fig. 1.—ALBEMARLE I and II.   Correct paratroop jumping attitude

  (iii) Replacing para. 3 (vii). *One second before reaching the dropping zone.* Navigator switches on the green signal light. Paratroops leave the A/C, *those following moving aft in unison.* There is a pause of *3 secs.* between the dropping of paratroops Nos. 5 and 6 to allow the containers to fall clear.

(iv) Replacing para. 3 (x). Two of the crew go aft to *withdraw* the strops and close the aperture doors. *They must make sure static line carriage No. 5 is clear of the container release switch,* otherwise the distributor is liable to overheat.

Selector and distributor setting

25. Selector switches Nos. 1, 2, 4, 6, 7 and 9 are put "ON" by the navigator 20 minutes before dropping time. The auto-distributor is set to operate at an interval of 0·15 secs. The containers may not be salvoed.

Container dropping time

26. The interval between the jumping of Nos. 5 and 6 paratroops should be 3 seconds. The time is made up as follows:—

(i)   Between No. 5 paratroop and the release of the first container   ...   1   sec.

(ii) Travel of distributor arm   ...   .   1·2 sec.

(iii) For the last container to fall clear   ...   .   0·5 sec.

Flying speed over dropping zone

27. The aircraft is to be flown straight and level at 100–110 m.p.h. I.A.S. with flap applied at 15 deg.

C.G. conditions

28. The C.G. conditions of the Albemarle during a paratroop operation are described in Chap. 5. Provided the fuel is used in the manner described in Chap. 5, para. 51, the C.G. conditions are satisfactory with 6 items on the bomb carriers and 10 paratroops at take-off, flight to target, and action stations. After 5 paratroops have left the aircraft it is quite safe to release the containers. But if the paratroops do not leave the aircraft the containers must remain in place. If it is found necessary to land with paratroops aboard the aircraft their position should be as for take-off.

Length of stick of paratroops

29. The length of stick for ten paratroops and six items when dropped from 500 ft. at 100–110 m.p.h. I.A.S. is 500 yds.

Dakota I (C.47)

Special air drill

30. As the Dakota I is a transport aircraft with the exit door at the side, and the container release switches near the door, the typical air drill described in para. 3 does not apply.

31. Paratroops in the Dakota I will generally be from 15 to 20 in number. For training and operational purposes the paratroops will be divided into two sections of approximately equal numbers.

32. The Dakota I is not sensitive to minor movements of load within the fuselage, but it is advisable for the paratroops to be reasonably well spaced when making their exit during flight and not to crowd the door. The following notes are appended for the guidance of paratroops in the Dakota I:—

(i) All snap-hooks mounted on the static cable must face forward, otherwise there would be a danger of the tongues striking some obstacle and tending to open while the snap-hooks were sliding down the static cable. See that each snap-hook on the cable has a safety pin of the correct type and that there is only one set of holes for the safety pin.

(ii) There must be no obstacle preventing the folding down of the starboard seats.

(iii) The paratroops should be seated with odd numbers on the port side, and even numbers on the starboard side. For take-off they should be seated as far forward as practicable. During flight to target the weight of the men and equipment should be equally distributed laterally down the fuselage.

(iv) The pilot will give the command "Action Stations" to O.C. paratroops who will then order his troops to stand to. The paratroops will form into single (or slightly staggered) file facing aft.

(v) Fold down the starboard seats.

(vi) The paratroops attach their static lines to the static cable by means of the snap-hooks provided, or to the relevant 9 ft. 9 in. strop if these are fitted.

(vii) After the above operation has been checked, the O.C. paratroops should see that the aircraft door is removed and then report to the pilot "Ready to jump".

(viii) When the RED signal light shows the first paratroop prepares to jump.

(ix) When the GREEN signal light shows, all No. 1 Section should jump in rotation, including the O.C. paratroops who should be last of the Section.

Note.—It is essential that the member of the air crew who operates the container switches recognises the O.C. paratroops (preferably by some pre-arranged signal).

(x) Immediately O.C. paratroops has jumped the container release switches must be operated by the member of the air crew to whom that duty has been delegated. This operation takes approximately two seconds.

(xi) Immediately the last container has been dropped No. 2 Section leaves the aircraft.

(xii) Whilst moving down the fuselage each paratroop should guide his own snap-hook down the static cable until in the position of third from the door.

(xiii) With the Dakota I it is advisable to *step* outward, giving a slight turn to half left. If the paratroop *jumps* outward when making his exit it might involve his being blown much closer to the tail plane.

(xiv) Immediately all paratroops have left the aircraft the pilot operates the container jettison switch.

(xv) After the paratroops have jumped two members of the crew retrieve the static lines.

Note.—When dropping bicycles from the aircraft door it is essential that they are thrown *downwards* and not *outwards*.

Container dropping time

33. Containers are released by manually operated switches, one for each container, mounted on a panel forward of the exit door. If the operator—a member of the air crew—depresses each one in turn as quickly as possible the time taken to release all the containers is approximately two seconds. They are then spaced sufficiently to avoid interference consistent with the minimum stick length. *See* Sect. 2, Chap. 5, para. 63 of this manual.

Recommendations to Pilot (*see* fig. 2)

34.   Following are recommendations to pilots of Dakota I aircraft when taking part in a paratroop operation:—

(i)   Fly in formation up to approximately one mile from the dropping zone.   Then shake out into open formation with wide spacing between aircraft for dropping paratroops.

> *Note.*—The object of wide spacing is to enable each pilot to fly an individual steady course.   The use of throttle and rudder to maintain formation tends to cause yawing and creates a circular slip-stream which may result in paratroops fouling the tail wheel assembly.   Such a circumstance is extremely dangerous to the paratroop and to the aircraft, since an open parachute attached to an aircraft can result in complete loss of control.

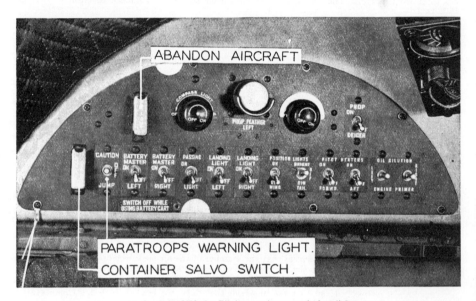

Fig. 2.   **DAKOTA I.   Pilot's paratroop control switches**

(ii)   During dropping operations the aircraft must be flown straight and level or in a shallow glide at a speed of not less than 100 m.p.h. I.A.S.

> *Note.*—A turn to the right or a climbing angle of the aircraft might result in the parachute or parachute bag fouling the tail plane or the tail wheel.   During training, paratroops will not be dropped from a height of less than 500 ft.   During operations it may be necessary for paratroops to be dropped from as low as 300 ft., according to the decision of the Force Commander.

(iii)   Maintain an Indicated Air Speed of 100 to 110 m.p.h. during the dropping of paratroops.

(iv)   Give the command "Action Stations" to O.C. paratroops approximately 15 minutes before the time for dropping.

(v)   Await message "Ready to jump" from O.C. paratroops.   When this message has been received, and 5 to 10 secs. before dropping is to commence, switch on the RED signal light.

(vi)   Determine the point where dropping is to commence and switch on the GREEN signal light.   Keep this light on until it is no longer safe to jump.   Then switch on the RED signal light.

(vii)   Immediately all paratroops have jumped operate the container jettison master switch.

(viii)   Should it be necessary to abandon the aircraft before reaching the dropping zone, give the order "Prepare to abandon aircraft". (A member of the crew will open the aircraft door, all paratroops will at once hook their static lines to the static cable, and the air crew will put on their parachutes), then give the command "Bale out". (The paratroops will jump in their operational order, followed by the air crew.)

> *Note.*—While containers (Mk. I or Mk. III) are carried on bomb racks three and four, the movement of the wing flaps is restricted to 50 per cent. In the event of a landing being made with the containers still attached, full flap cannot be used.

Length of stick of paratroops

35.   During tests the length of a stick of ten paratroops dropped at 100 m.p.h. was 260 yards. A stick of 20 men dropped at 100 m.p.h. measured 674 yards.

2

Transport of Troops and Equipment in Bombers and Transports, 1942

CHAPTER 2

CONVERSION OF BOMBER AIRCRAFT FOR TRANSPORT PURPOSES

General

1. For transporting troops by air, two classes of aircraft are employed, namely, bomber aircraft converted for troop carrying, and aircraft designed solely for transport purposes. This chapter deals with the conversion of bomber aircraft.

2. The conversion of a bomber aircraft for troop transport entails, in some instances, the removal of certain fittings, and, in most instances, the addition of troop transport seats. The number of seats fitted will not always coincide with the number of troops carried, since it is more economical of weight and space for certain troops to sit on packs or valises arranged on parts of the aircraft structure or equipment. It is of the utmost importance, for C.G. considerations, that the arrangement of seats described in the following paragraphs for each type of aircraft is adhered to closely.

3. The conversion of bomber aircraft for troop transport will be effected by the squadrons concerned.

Troop transport seat (see fig. 1)

4. The standard troop transport seat, Stores Ref. 27H/1977, comprises the following parts:—

Light-alloy tubular frame	Stores Ref. 27H/1978
Canvas seat and back	Stores Ref. 27H/1979
Safety strap, R.H.	Stores Ref. 27H/1980
Safety strap, L.H.	Stores Ref. 27H/1981
Rubber suction pads (4)	Stores Ref. 27H/1982
"Jubilee" clips (8)	Stores Ref. 27H/1983

5. The total weight of the seat is 6 lb.

Fixing the seat (see fig. 2)

6. The seat is intended to be secured to the floor of the aircraft by applying a coat of Bostik cement, Stores Ref. 33C/591, to the underside of the rubber pads, using the adhesive properties of the cement, combined with the suction effect obtained when the pads are pressed down on the floor and the air expelled from under them. Any grease that may be present on the floor of the aircraft must be removed before using the cement. To avoid contact between the rubber pads and any rivet heads or excrescences on the floor, the pads may be slid along the bottom members of the seat frame. The "Jubilee" clips should be loosened by a screwdriver before moving the pads, and subsequently tightened. It may be found preferable to cement the rubber pads to the floor before attaching them to the seat (see fig. 2).

7. Tests under flying conditions have shown that the troop transport seat is most stable when the pads are attached one at each extremity of the front and back lower frame members respectively (see fig. 1). If the seats are supplied with the pads in positions other than these, the pads should be removed and correctly positioned before attaching the seats to the aircraft floor.

Packs or valises used as seats

8. The following notes and diagrams, relevant to each type of aircraft used for troop transport, indicate which troops will be required to sit on packs or valises. It will generally be found that packs or valises which have been partially emptied afford greater comfort than full ones. The numbered arrows on the diagrams represent the positions of troops and the directions in which they face when travelling.

Special precautions

9. The accessibility of control wires and rods within the aircraft fuselage make special precautions imperative for the safe carriage of troops and stowage of their equipment. Sect. 3, Chap. 7 of this manual contains information on this subject.

Wellington Ic, II, III, IV, and X *(see* fig. 3)

Items removed for troop transport

10. The folding armour and pillar at the astrodome is removed from Wellington aircraft. The ammunition for the rear turret is limited to 2,000 rounds.

Troops and equipment carried

11. Eleven troops are carried, but fitted seats are not provided in Wellington aircraft. Each man has a rifle and pack, a valise, a gas cape and a steel helmet.

12. Additional equipment comprises one A/Tk rifle, two Bren guns, and four boxes of ammunition, all of which are stowed as far forward as possible.

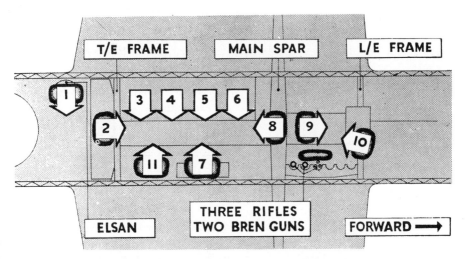

Fig. 3.—Wellington Ic, II. III, IV and X. Troops and equipment carried

13. The following table, read in conjunction with fig. 3, gives the travelling stations for eleven troops and equipment.

Troop	Position	Seating	Equipment carried	Equipment stowed
1	On Elsan	Use valise part empty	Carry rifle	
2	On T/E frame facing fwd.	Use valise	Carry rifle	
3	On rest bunk	—	Carry rifle	
4	On rest bunk	—	Carry rifle	Gas capes stowed on rest
5	On rest bunk	—	Carry rifle	bunk. Packs and steel
6	On rest bunk	—	Carry rifle	helmets stowed at station
7	On aux. oil tank	Use valise part empty	Rifle in flare rack	for No. 11
8	On main spar facing aft	Use valise part empty	Carry rifle	
9	On step facing fwd.	Use valise	Rifle in flare rack	
10	On L/E frame facing aft	Use valise	Rifle in flare rack	
11	Beside aux. oil tank	Use valise	Carry rifle	

Halifax I, II and V (*see* fig. 4)

Item removed for troop transport

14. The door aft of the rest compartment is removed from the aircraft. This will be a permanent modification.

Troops and equipment carried

15. Sixteen troops are carried, and six seats are fitted to the Halifax for this purpose. Each man has a rifle and pack, a valise, a gas cape and a steel helmet.

16. Additional equipment comprises one A/Tk rifle, two Bren guns, and six boxes of ammunition all of which are stowed as far forward as possible.

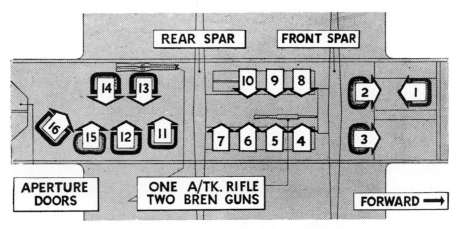

Fig. 4.—Halifax I, II and V. Troops and equipment carried

17. The following table, read in conjunction with fig. 4, gives the travelling stations for troops and equipment.

Troop	Position	Seating	Equipment carried	Equipment stowed
1	Port, aft of armoured blkh'd	Seat		
2	Port, 16 in. fwd. of front spar	Valise		A/Tk rifle at stbd. rest station.
3	Stbd., 16 in. fwd. of front spar	Valise	Rifles may be carried	Two Bren guns, port, aft of
4	Stbd. rest seat	—	by troops or stowed	rear spar.
5	Stbd. rest seat	—	against front and	Two boxes of ammunition
6	Stbd. rest seat	—	rear spars with butts	with Bren guns.
7	Stbd. rest seat	—	on rest station floor.	Two boxes of ammunition
8	Port rest seat	—		at port rest station.
9	Port rest seat	—		Two boxes of ammunition,
10	Port rest seat	—		port, aft of No. 14 troop
11	Stbd., 15 in. aft of rear spar	Seat		
12	Stbd., 35 in. aft of rear spar	Seat		
13	Port, 31 in. aft of rear spar	Seat		
14	Port, 55 in. aft of rear spar	Seat		
15	Stbd., aft of No. 12	Valise		
16	Stbd., forward of aperture	Seat		

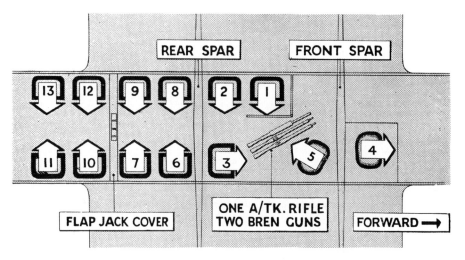

Fig. 5.—Manchester I. Troops and equipment carried

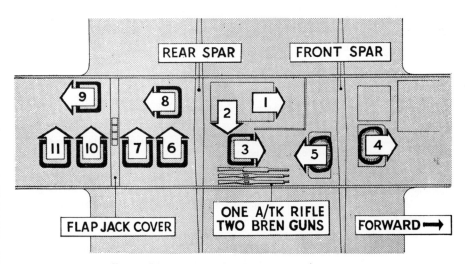

Fig. 6.—Lancaster I and II. Troops and equipment carried

Manchester I (*see* fig. 5)

Items removed for troop transport

18. The rest seat situated on the port side, immediately forward of the rear spar, is removed from its mounting.

Troops and equipment carried

19. Thirteen troops are carried and eleven seats are fitted to the Manchester I for this purpose. Each man has a rifle and pack, a valise, a gas cape and a steel helmet.

20. Additional equipment comprises one A/Tk rifle, two Bren guns, and four boxes of ammunition, all of which are stowed as far forward as possible.

21. The following table, read in conjunction with fig. 5, gives the travelling stations for troops and equipment.

Troop	Position	Seating	Equipment carried	Equipment stowed
1	Aft of armoured blkh'd facing inboard	Seat	Carry rifle	
2	Aft of No. 1	Seat	Carry rifle	
3	Opposite No. 2 facing forward	Seat	Carry rifle	
4	On step leading to cabin	Use valise	Carry rifle	Packs stowed between armour
5	On floor, back to front spar	Use valise	Carry rifle	bulkhead and front spar.
6	Stbd., aft of rear spar	Seat	Carry rifle	Helmets and valises stowed at
7	Stbd, forward of flap jack cover	Seat	Carry rifle	station for No. 11 troop.
8	Port, aft of rear spar	Seat	Carry rifle	A/Tk rifle and Bren guns stowed
9	Port, forward of flap jack cover	Seat	Carry rifle	between stations for Nos. 3 and
10	Stbd., aft of flap jack cover	Seat	Carry rifle	5 troops.
11	Stbd., aft of No. 10	Seat	Carry rifle	
12	Port, aft of flap jack cover	Seat	Carry rifle	
13	Port, aft of No. 12	Seat	Carry rifle	

Lancaster I and II (*see* fig. 6)

Troops and equipment carried

22. Eleven troops are carried and seven seats are fitted to the aircraft for this purpose. Each man has a rifle and pack, a valise, a gas cape and a steel helmet. The number of troops carried is limited by C.G. considerations.

23. Additional equipment comprises one A/Tk rifle, two Bren guns, and four boxes of ammunition, all of which are stowed as far forward as possible.

24. The following table, read in conjunction with fig. 6, gives the travelling stations for troops and equipment.

Troops	Position	Seating	Equipment carried	Equipment stowed
1	On port rest seat	—	Carry rifle	
2	On port rest seat	—	Carry rifle	
3	Stbd., beside rest seat	Seat	Carry rifle	
4	Stbd., step fwd. of front spar	Valise	Carry rifle	Packs stowed between armour
5	Stbd., step aft of front spar	Valise	Carry rifle	bulkhead and front spar.
6	Stbd., aft of rear spar	Seat	Carry rifle	Helmets and valises stowed by
7	Stbd., fwd. of flap jack	Seat	Carry rifle	No. 11 troop.
8	Port, aft of rear spar	Seat	Carry rifle	A/Tk rifle and Bren guns stowed
9	Port, aft of flap jack	Seat	Carry rifle	between troops Nos. 3 and 5.
10	Stbd., aft of flap jack	Seat	Carry rifle	
11	Stbd., aft of No. 10	Seat	Carry rifle	

This page issued with A.L. No. 3
December, 1942

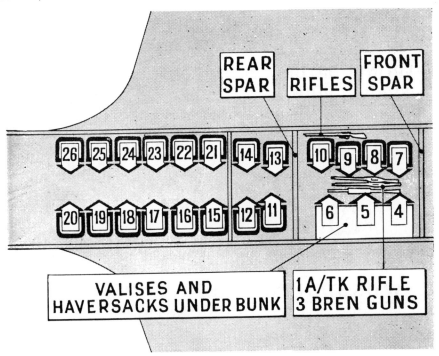

Fig. 7.—Stirling I. Troops and equipment carried aft of front spar

Stirling I, II and III (*see* figs. 7 and 8)

Items removed for troop transport

25.   The port side reserve ammunition boxes, the maintenance platform, maintenance ladder and trestle are removed from the aircraft.

Troops and equipment carried

26.   26 troops are carried, and 21 seats are fitted to the Stirling for this purpose.   Each man has a rifle, haversack, valise, gas cape and steel helmet.

27.   Additional equipment comprises 1 A/Tk rifle, three Bren guns and eight boxes of ammunition.

28.   The following table, read in conjunction with figs. 7 and 8 gives the travelling stations for troops and equipment.

85

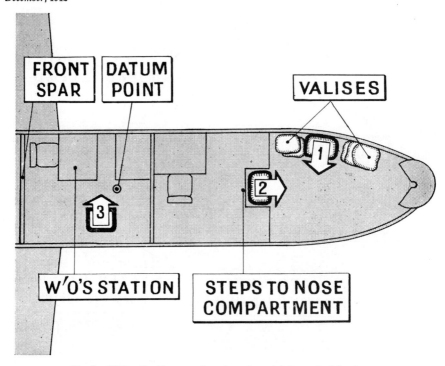

Fig. 8.—Stirling I. Troops and equipment carried forward of front spar

Troop	Position	Seating	Equipment stowed
1	Port, nose compartment	Valise	Four or five valises stowed in nose by
2	Step to nose compartment	Valise	No. 1 troop.
3	Stbd., W/O's compartment	Seat	
4	Stbd., rest bunk	—	
5	Stbd., rest bunk	—	Two boxes of A/Tk amm. stowed
6	Stbd., rest bunk (low headroom)	—	behind W/O.
7	Port, rest station	Seat	
8	Port, rest station	Seat	One A/Tk rifle and three Bren guns on
9	Port, rest station	Seat	rest station floor.
10	Port, rest station	Seat	
11	Stbd., aft of rear spar	Seat	
12	Stbd., aft of No. 11	Seat	Rifles stowed behind troops Nos. 7,
13	Port, aft of rear spar	Seat	8, 9 and 10.
14	Port, aft of No. 13	Seat	
15	Stbd., aft of Frame 26	Seat	Six boxes of Bren amm. on rest station
16	Stbd., aft of No. 15	Seat	floor.
17	Stbd., aft of No. 16	Seat	
18	Stbd., aft of No. 17	Seat	Rifles stowed behind troops Nos. 11,
19	Stbd., aft of No. 18	Seat	12, 13, and 14.
20	Stbd., aft of No. 19	Seat	
21	Port, aft of Frame 26	Seat	
22	Port, aft of No. 21	Seat	Haversacks, respirators and gas capes
23	Port, aft of No. 22	Seat	stowed under troop seats.
24	Port, aft of No. 23	Seat	
25	Port, aft of No. 24	Seat	
26	Port, aft of No. 25	Seat	

Albemarle I and II (*see* fig. 9)

Items removed for troop transport

29. The back of the rest seat on the step, the port and starboard flare racks, the stowage for spare ammunition and the maintenance ladder are removed from the aircraft.

Troops and equipment carried

30. Nine troops are carried, and three seats are fitted to the Albemarle for this purpose. Each man has a rifle, haversack, valise, gas cape, and steel helmet.

31. Additional equipment comprises one A/Tk rifle, two Bren guns and three boxes of ammunition, all of which are stowed as far forward as possible.

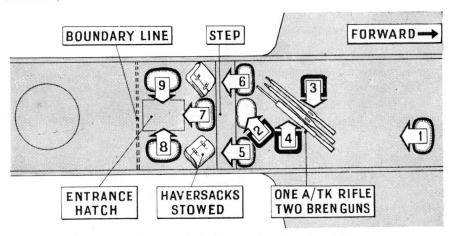

Fig. 9.—Albemarle I. Troops and equipment carried.

32. The following table, read in conjunction with fig. 9, gives the travelling stations for troops and equipment.

Troop	Position	Seating	Equipment stowed
1	Stbd., fwd. of upper turret	Valise	Three boxes of ammunition stowed on port step beside troop No. 1.
2	Stbd., aft of upper turret, at 45°	Seat	
3	Port, aft of upper turret	Seat	
4	Stbd., fwd. of No. 2	Seat	A/Tk rifle and two Bren guns on floor between troops Nos. 3 and 4.
5	Stbd., on step facing aft	Valise	
6	Port, on step facing aft	Valise	
7	Fwd. of rear entrance hatch	Valise	Rifles stowed behind troops Nos. 2, 3, and 4.
8	Stbd. of rear entrance hatch	Valise	
9	Port of rear entrance hatch	Valise	Valises and haversacks stowed by step and rear entrance hatch.

CHAPTER 5

AIRCRAFT CAPACITY AND LOADING

General

1. The object of the information contained in this chapter is to enable simple calculations to be made to ensure that the C.G. position for an aircraft loaded with troops and equipment is within the allowed limits.

2. General instructions for the use of Loading and C.G. Diagrams are contained in Vol. I, Sect. 4, of the aeroplane handbooks and will not be repeated here. There is, however, one departure from standard practice in the layout of the diagrams in this manual, the reason for this being as follows.

3. In the aeroplane handbooks it is usual to allocate identification numbers to the C.G. spots for reference against the weights and "X" arm dimensions tabulated. To prevent interference with the standard use of numerals for this purpose, troops and equipment have not been identified in this way. Instead each item is arranged in order along the horizontal datum line of the aircraft diagram, and is keyed by a "leader" to its C.G. spot on an enlarged section of the diagram.

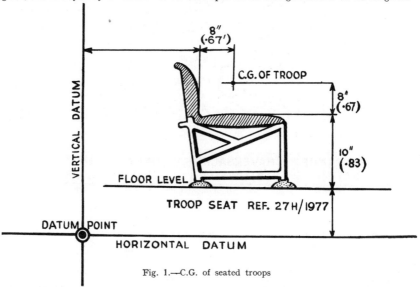

Fig. 1.—C.G. of seated troops

4. The weights and moments given in the following tables for Aeroplane Tare, Typical Service Load (excluding Airborne Forces Load), Fuel and Oil, must be regarded as representative only. These figures are constantly undergoing revision, and reference should be made to the relevant aeroplane handbook, Vol. I, Sect. 4, for the correct information in regard to the aircraft concerned.

5. The vertical displacement of the C.G., though indicated to scale on the diagrams, is not taken into account for the purpose of C.G. calculations.

C.G. of seated troops (see fig. 1)

6. Wherever a troop seat is positioned in line with the longitudinal axis of the aircraft, the C.G. of its occupant, relative to the frame of the seat, is determined as shown in fig. 1.

Range of operation

7. A practical range of 750 miles is at present envisaged for troop transport operations. This practical range is 75 per cent. of the "still-air" value, the safety margin being intended to allow for reasonable errors of pilotage, the effect of moderate wind and any other minor deviations from optimum flying conditions. **All figures for range which are quoted in subsequent loading statements are "practical" values.**

8. The fuel carried for the practical range of 750 miles has therefore to be determined on the following basis:—
   (i) 1,000 miles flight with troops and equipment, plus
   (ii) Fuel for taxying and take-off, plus
   (iii) Fuel used on climb in excess of that required for level flight.

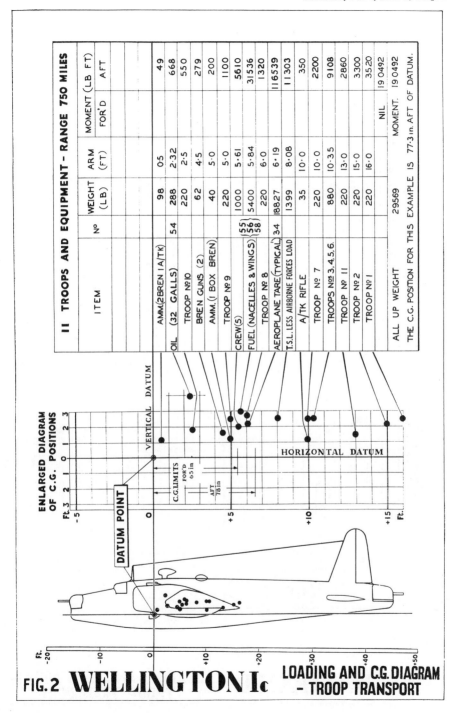

II TROOPS AND EQUIPMENT - RANGE 750 MILES

ITEM	Nº	WEIGHT (LB)	ARM (FT)	MOMENT (LB FT) FOR'D	MOMENT (LB FT) AFT
AMM.(2 BREN 1 A/TK)		98	0·5		49
OIL (32 GALLS)	54	288	2·32		668
TROOP Nº 10		220	2·5		550
BREN GUNS (2)		62	4·5		279
AMM.(1 BOX BREN)		40	5·0		200
TROOP Nº 9		220	5·0		1100
CREW(S)	(55)(56)(58)	1000	5·61		5610
FUEL (NACELLES & WINGS)		5400	5·84		31536
TROOP Nº 8		220	6·0		1320
AEROPLANE TARE (TYPICAL)	34	18827	6·19		116539
T.S.L. LESS AIRBORNE FORCES LOAD		1399	8·08		11303
A/TK RIFLE		35	10·0		350
TROOP Nº 7		220	10·0		2200
TROOPS Nºs 3,4,5,6.		880	10·35		9108
TROOP Nº 11		220	13·0		2860
TROOP Nº 2		220	15·0		3300
TROOP Nº 1		220	16·0		3520
ALL UP WEIGHT		29569		NIL	190492

MOMENT. 190492

THE C.G. POSITION FOR THIS EXAMPLE IS 77·3 in. AFT OF DATUM.

ENLARGED DIAGRAM OF C.G. POSITIONS

VERTICAL DATUM

HORIZONTAL DATUM

C.G.LIMITS FOR'D 65 in — AFT 78 in

DATUM POINT

FIG. 2 WELLINGTON Ic
LOADING AND C.G. DIAGRAM - TROOP TRANSPORT

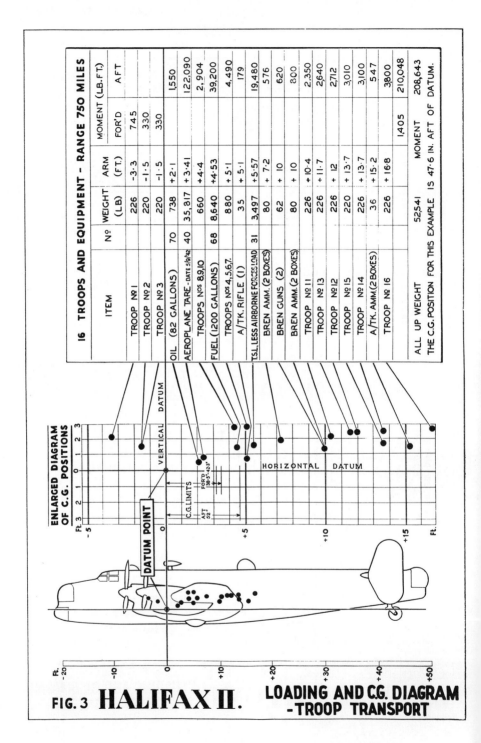

16 TROOPS AND EQUIPMENT – RANGE 750 MILES

ITEM	Nº	WEIGHT (LB)	ARM (FT.)	MOMENT (LB.FT.) FOR'D	MOMENT (LB.FT.) AFT
TROOP Nº 1		226	-3·3	745	
TROOP Nº 2		220	-1·5	330	
TROOP Nº 3		220	-1·5	330	
OIL (82 GALLONS)	70	738	+2·1		1,550
AEROPLANE TARE – DATE 5/9/42	40	35,817	+3·41		122,090
TROOPS Nºs 8,9,10		660	+4·4		2,904
FUEL (1200 GALLONS)	68	8,640	+4·53		39,200
TROOPS Nºs 4,5,6,7.		880	+5·1		4,490
A/TK. RIFLE (1)		35	+5·1		179
T.S.L.LESS AIRBORNE FORCES LOAD	31	3,497	+5·57		19,480
BREN AMM. (2 BOXES)		80	+7·2		576
BREN GUNS (2)		62	+10		620
BREN AMM. (2 BOXES)		80	+10		800
TROOP Nº 11		226	+10·4		2,350
TROOP Nº 13		226	+11·7		2,640
TROOP Nº 12		226	+12		2,712
TROOP Nº 15		220	+13·7		3,010
TROOP Nº 14		226	+13·7		3,100
A/TK. AMM.(2 BOXES)		36	+15·2		547
TROOP Nº 16		226	+16·8		3800
				1,405	210,048
ALL UP WEIGHT		52,541		MOMENT	208,643

THE C.G. POSITION FOR THIS EXAMPLE IS 47·6 IN. AFT OF DATUM.

ENLARGED DIAGRAM OF C.G. POSITIONS

VERTICAL DATUM

HORIZONTAL DATUM

C.G. LIMITS
FOR'D 38·5"–42·3"
AFT 52"

DATUM POINT

FIG. 3 HALIFAX II. LOADING AND C.G. DIAGRAM – TROOP TRANSPORT

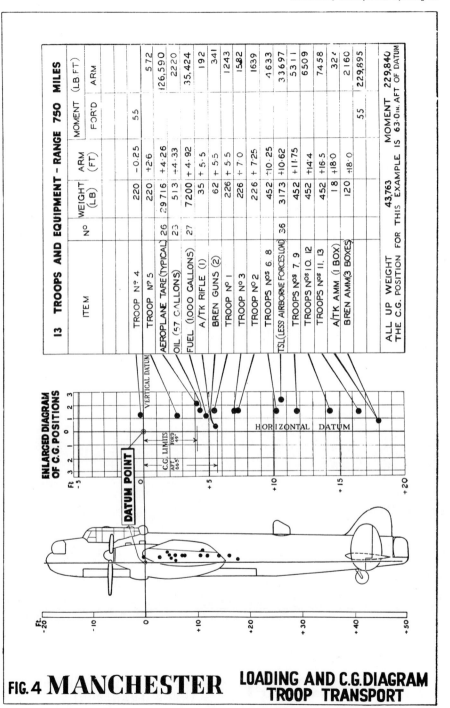

13 TROOPS AND EQUIPMENT – RANGE 750 MILES

ITEM	No	WEIGHT (LB)	ARM (FT)	MOMENT (LB.FT) FORD	ARM
TROOP No 4		220	-0.25	55	
TROOP No 5		220	+2.6		572
AEROPLANE TARE (TYPICAL)	26	29,716	+4.26		126,590
OIL (57 GALLONS)	23	513	+4.33		2220
FUEL (1,000 GALLONS)	27	7200	+4.92		35,424
A/TK RIFLE (1)		35	+5.5		192
BREN GUNS (2)		62	+5.5		341
TROOP No 1		226	+5.5		1243
TROOP No 3		226	+7.0		1582
TROOP No 2		226	+7.25		1639
TROOPS Nos 6, 8		452	+10.25		4633
TSL (LESS AIRBORNE FORCES LOAD)	36	3173	+10.62		33,697
TROOPS Nos 7, 9		452	+11.75		5311
TROOPS Nos 10, 12		452	+14.4		6509
TROOPS Nos 11, 13		452	+16.5		7458
A/TK AMM (1 BOX)		18	+18.0		324
BREN AMM (3 BOXES)		120	+18.0		2160
ALL UP WEIGHT		43,763		55	229,895

MOMENT 229,840
THE C.G. POSITION FOR THIS EXAMPLE IS 63·0 IN. AFT OF DATUM

ENLARGED DIAGRAM OF C.G. POSITIONS

VERTICAL DATUM

HORIZONTAL DATUM

C.G. LIMITS
FORD 49"
AFT 66·5"

DATUM POINT

FIG. 4 MANCHESTER **LOADING AND C.G.DIAGRAM TROOP TRANSPORT**

(A.L.6)

26 TROOPS AND EQUIPMENT – RANGE 750 MILES

ITEM	Nº	WEIGHT (LB)	ARM (FT.)	MOMENT (LB.FT.) FOR'D	MOMENT (LB.FT.) AFT
BALLAST WEIGHTS (25)		437·5	-13·3	5815	
TROOP Nº1		220	-13·0	2860	
TROOP Nº2		220	-10·0	2200	
TROOP Nº3		226	+ 1·0		226
OIL (60 GALLONS)	17	540	+ 4·1		2216
A/TK AMM. (2 BOXES)		36	+ 4·8		173
TROOP Nº7		226	+ 7·0		1582
TROOP Nº8		226	+ 8·5		1921
FUEL (662 GALLONS-TANK Nº2)	20	4766	+ 9·1		43550
" (508 GALLONS-TANK Nº4)		3658	+ 9·2		33520
A/TK. RIFLE (1)					
BREN GUNS (3)		368	+ 9·3		3422
BREN AMM. (6 BOXES)					
AEROPLANE TARE (TYPICAL) FEB.1943		43988	+ 9·5		419,760
TROOPS Nº4,5,6		660	+ 9·4		6204
TROOP Nº9		226	+ 10·0		2260
TROOP Nº10		226	+ 11·7		2644
TROOP Nº13		226	+ 14·5		3277
TROOP Nº11		226	+ 14·8		3345
T.S.L. (LESS AIRBORNE FORCES LOAD)		3477			44012
TROOPS Nº12,14		452	+ 16·2		7,322
TROOPS Nº15,21		452	+ 18·6		8407
TROOPS Nº16,22		452	+20·2		9,130
TROOPS Nº17,23		452	+22·0		9,944
TROOPS Nº18,24		452	+23·4		10,577
TROOPS Nº19,25		452	+25·3		11,436
TROOPS Nº20,26		452	+27·0		12,204
ALL-UP WEIGHT		63116·5		10875	637,132

TOTAL MOMENT 626,257

THE C.G. POSITION FOR THIS EXAMPLE IS 9·924 FT.(119·1 IN.) AFT OF DATUM

THE T.S.L. QUOTED COMPRISES ITEMS LISTED IN A.P.1660A & B VOL.1,SECT.4. THIS INCLUDES A NORMAL CREW OF SEVEN. ANY NECESSARY DEDUCTIONS FROM OR ADDITIONS TO THIS FIGURE SHOULD BE MADE TO DETERMINE THE C.G POSITION FOR A SPECIFIC OPERATION.

ENLARGED DIAGRAM OF C.G. POSITIONS
C.G LIMITS
FOR'D 9·25
AFT 10·083

DATUM POINT

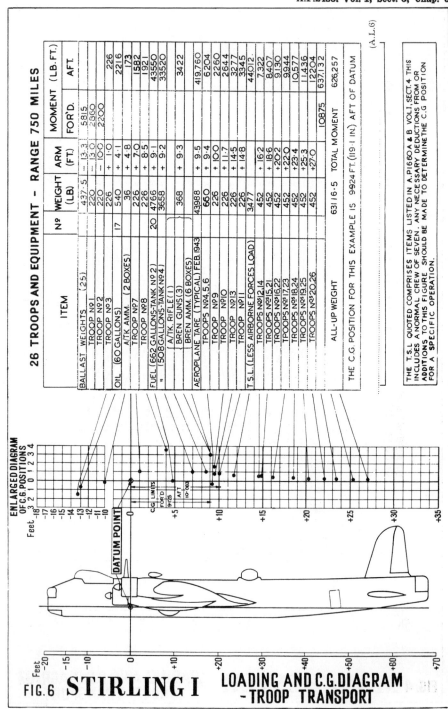

FIG.6 STIRLING I LOADING AND C.G.DIAGRAM - TROOP TRANSPORT

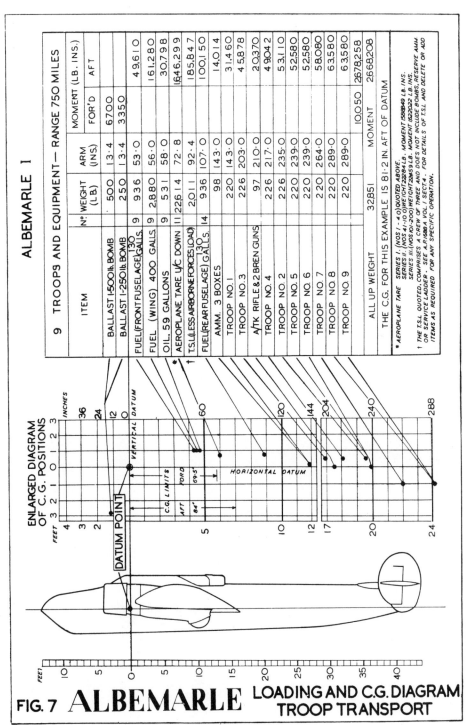

FIG. 7 ALBEMARLE
LOADING AND C.G. DIAGRAM TROOP TRANSPORT

3

Dakota CI, III and IV, July 1945

This leaf issued in reprint incorporating A.L's 1 to 15
July, 1945

DAKOTA CI, III, AND IV—PARACHUTE TROOP INSTALLATIONS

LIST OF CONTENTS

LIST OF ILLUSTRATIONS

General

1. The adaptation of the Dakota CI, III, and IV aircraft for the dropping of parachute troops involves the fitment of a static cable, the masking of protrusions inside and outside the fuselage, and the fitting of bomb carriers for supplies-dropping containers. Mats are required to prevent the parachute troops from slipping when making their way to the exit door.

2. Fig. 1 shows the interior of the fuselage modified for parachute operations.

Static line cable

3. The static line cable will be seen in fig. 1 on the starboard side of the cabin. It is of 60 cwt. steel cable, 24 ft. 6¾ in. long, and is spliced to a thimble at each end. It must not be taut when in position, as this puts an undue strain on the strong points, but should assume a slight curve, as shown in the illustration.

Forward strong point (fig. 2)

4. The strong point consists of an L-shaped bracket with a lug for attachment of the static line cable. It is bolted to a longitudinal stringer on the starboard side, just forward of fuselage transverse former No. 195½. In certain Dakota aircraft the bracket is bolted to both the longitudinal stringer and the fuselage former, whilst in others it is bolted to the longitudinal stringer only.

Aft strong point

5. There are three types of aft strong point for the static cable, as described below. The necessary fittings are in each case mounted on the starboard side of the cabin:—

(i) The static cable is attached to an idler pulley bracket between transverse fuselage frames No. 479 and 492. (In some aircraft the idler pulley bracket is located too far forward for this purpose, in which case one of the other methods of attachment is used). The bracket is used as the cable strong point by removing the pin holding the pulley bracket and replacing it by a bolt and Simmonds elastic stop nut carrying a shackle which is threaded through the thimble at the end of the static cable.

(ii) The cable anchorage is provided by a bracket clamped to a tube, the ends of which

DAKOTA CI, III, AND IV—PARACHUTE TROOP INSTALLATIONS

Fig. 1.—Interior of fuselage

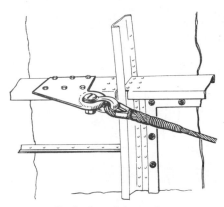

Fig. 2.—Forward strong point

are bolted to transverse fuselage frames No. 479 and 492. This strong point is illustrated in fig. 3.

(iii) The static cable is secured to a fitting bolted to two channels, which are secured to transverse fuselage frames No. 479 and 492. In some Dakota CI, III, and IV aircraft this type of strong point is located at a height of

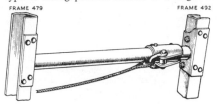

Fig. 3.—Aft strong point

DAKOTA CI, III, AND IV—PARACHUTE TROOP INSTALLATIONS

25 in. above the floor, whilst in others its height above the floor is 38 in.   See the important warning below.

WARNING

The use of an aft strong point located 38 in. above the floor surface creates a very definite hazard in parachuting. In such cases the strong point should be removed and re-installed as close to the floor as possible: the height above the floor surface should not exceed 25 in., as shown in fig. 4.

Attachment of static cable to the strong points (fig. 2, 3 and 4)

6. The forward end of the static cable is secured to the forward strong point by means of a shackle, a shackle pin and a split pin or cotter. The head of the shackle pin should be uppermost and the split pin well spread. (Alternatively the shackle may be attached by means of a bolt and locknut). The aft end of the static cable is secured to the aft strong point by means of a shackle and eye bolt. The eye bolt

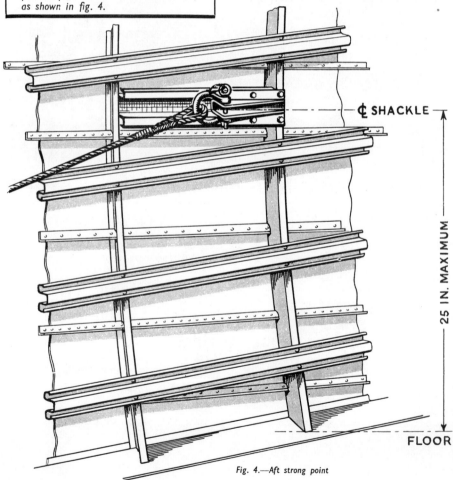

Fig. 4.—Aft strong point

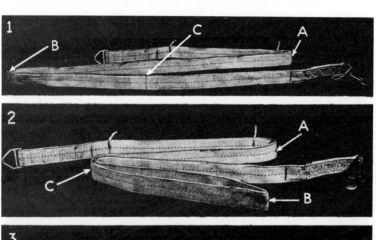

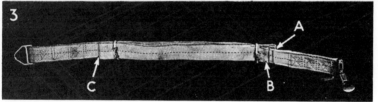

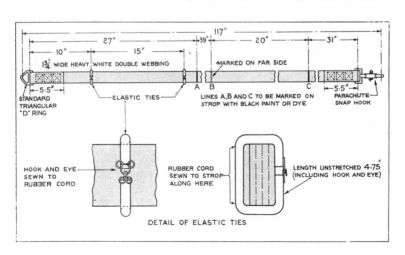

Fig. 5.—Folding of straps

DAKOTA CI, III, AND IV—PARACHUTE
TROOP INSTALLATIONS

is locked with wire which is threaded through the eye and the shackle, the ends being twisted together. When the idler pulley bracket is used as the aft strong point, a bolt and Simmonds elastic stop nut may be used to secure the shackle (as described in paragraph 5 (i)).

Strops

7. Strops of 9 ft. 9 in. length are used to connect the parachute static lines to the static cable. Each has a snap hook at one end and a D-ring at the other. Each strop must be folded as shown in fig. 5.

Fitment of strops

8. To attach the strops to the static cable, the latter is threaded through the strop D-rings before being secured. (Fig. 1 shows 25 strops attached and ready for use.)

Protection of strops and static lines

9. The object of masking is to cover all projections or sharp edges on the aircraft which might damage the static lines or interfere with their free movement. In addition to the

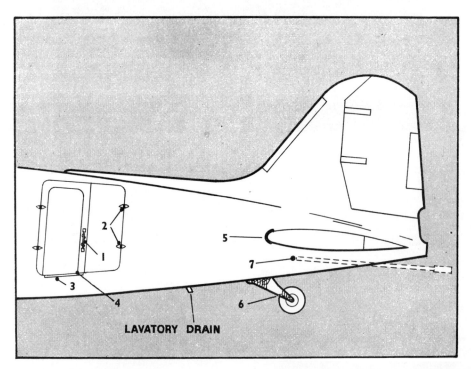

1. Door handle guard (positioned as shown in fig. 7)
2. Hinges at aft end of door
3. Lower outside edge of door frame; fire extinguisher bracket inside cabin, near the door
4. Corner formed by door frame and floor

5. Joint between the root fairing and the de-icing equipment on the leading edge of tailplane
6. Axle bobbins and front main "through bolt" of tail-wheel assembly
7. Forward end of glider towing attachment (if of the bridle type)

Fig. 6.—Masking

masking described in this Chapter the stretcher support guard (Dakota modification 1044) must be fitted.

10. For masking purposes 2 in. wide adhesive masking tape or doped fabric should be used. Projections such as the axle bobbins on the tail wheel assembly require padding with rag or paper before masking.

11. Fig. 6 indicates the main points that require masking, but a careful inspection should be made inside and outside the aircraft, and all sharp edges or obstructions likely to damage or interfere with the static lines must be masked. Particular care should be exercised if a glider-towing bridle is fitted.

12. If a venturi is fitted for the lavatory drain it must be removed. If a metal tube is used, this should be pushed up inside the aircraft or cut off short. A rubber tube may be safely left.

13. The rear mooring eye should be removed.

Door handle guard (fig. 6 and 7)

14. For the dropping of parachute troops the rear half of the door remains closed, and a guard over the external door handles is required to prevent fouling of the static lines. The guard should be positioned $\frac{1}{2}$ in. back from the forward edge of the dividing frame (as shown in fig. 6) to enable insertion of the key in the upper door handle.

WARNING

A canvas "wrapper" type door handle guard has been provided for use with the American parachute equipment. This must not be used for the guard when British parachute equipment is being employed, as it creates a definite hazard.

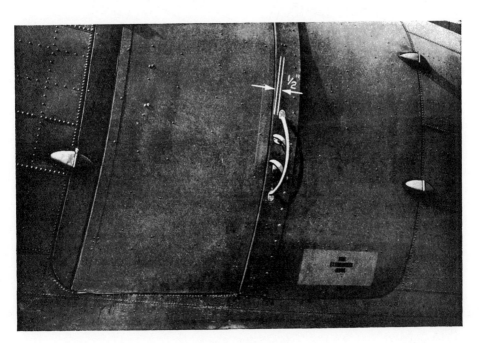

Fig. 7.—Door handle guard

This leaf issued in reprint incorporating A.L.'s I to 15
July, 1945

AIR   PUBLICATION   2453A
VOL. I PART 2 SECT. I CHAP. I

DAKOTA CI, III, AND IV—PARACHUTE TROOP INSTALLATIONS

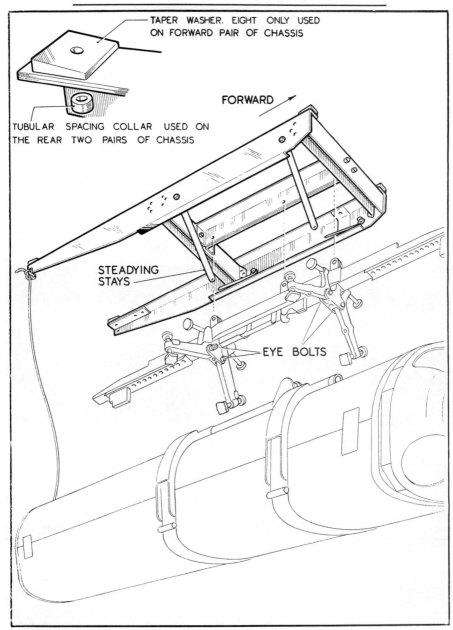

TAPER WASHER. EIGHT ONLY USED ON FORWARD PAIR OF CHASSIS

TUBULAR SPACING COLLAR USED ON THE REAR TWO PAIRS OF CHASSIS

FORWARD

STEADYING STAYS

EYE BOLTS

Fig. 8.—Chassis, bomb carrier and container

Container carrying equipment
(fig. 8 and 9)

15. Adaptation for the carriage of containers involves the fitting of six universal bomb carriers, attached to chassis which are bolted to existing strong points on the aircraft. These chassis are standard for all six positions.

Fitting the forward pair of universal bomb carriers

16. The procedure when fitting the forward pair of bomb carriers and chassis is as follows:—

(i) Fit the front pair of carrier chassis to the existing strong points on the aircraft, using the $\frac{3}{16}$ in. S.A.E. bolts from the existing attachment. Alternative holes are drilled in the rear end of the chassis to accommodate individual variations in different aircraft. Four wedge washers are supplied with each chassis. They are intended for use on the front pair only; they adjust the flat of the carrier chassis to the curvature of the underside of the aircraft.

(ii) Remove the nuts and bolts from the three suspension points on each of two No. 2 universal bomb carriers. The front and rear bolts screw out from the crutch brackets.

(iii) See that the release hook on the carrier is pointing forward and raise the carrier to the carrier chassis. Fit the bolt through the centre suspension point of the carrier and the centre strong point in the "T" member of the chassis. Fit the bolts to the front and the rear crutch brackets. Finally, tighten and lock all bolts and nuts.

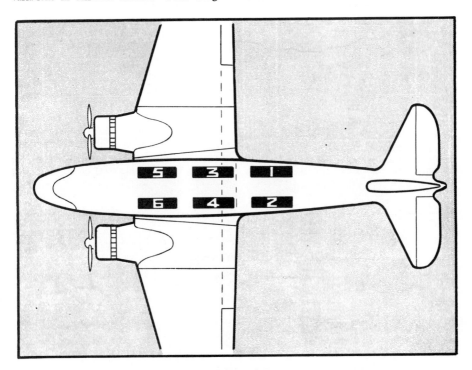

Fig. 9.—Location of containers

(iv) Adjust the four eye bolts which retain the crutches so that they face the correct way to take the bracing stays.

(v) Attach the bracing stays to the eye bolts and to the bomb carrier chassis and tighten up. The bomb carrier should be quite rigid.

(vi) The single electrical lead from the junction box is then inserted into No. 2 position in the appropriate socket in the aircraft fuselage. This is the positive lead from the electro-magnetic release unit to the release switchbox mounted beside the aircraft door. If a 3-pin cannon plug is available the lead is connected to the positive terminal of the plug which is then inserted in the 3-pin socket of the aircraft in the usual way. Any surplus cable should be secured to the carrier beam.

(vii) Ensure that all pins and nuts are locked with split pins or cotters.

(viii) Test the carriers as detailed in the daily inspection.

Note . . . When the universal bomb carriers are to be used exclusively for container dropping, the fuzing units, five-pin plug and wiring are to be removed from the bomb carriers.

Fitting the centre and rear universal bomb carriers
17. The method of fitting the centre and rear universal bomb carriers is similar to that described for the front carriers with the

exception of the attachment of the chassis to the aircraft. The wedge washers mentioned in para. 16 (i) are not used. The length of the bolts necessitates the use of four collars on the underside of each chassis.

Preparations for loading containers on to aircraft
18. Before commencing to load, ensure that all daily inspections have been completed, and that the static line of each container-dropping parachute has been prepared and stowed in the following manner:—

(1) The line marked at a point 3 ft from the free end.

(2) The line led from the rip-pin eye, doubled, and the loop tucked well into one of the stowage pockets provided for that purpose in the pack cover.

(3) The line led across the pack cover, doubled, and this second loop tucked into the other stowage pocket as far as the 3 ft. mark.

(4) The entry and exit of each of the loops to the pockets must be stitched, with single No. 18 thread (*Stores Ref. 32B/653*), *through* the static line, to the double edge of the stowage pocket and tied tightly with a double reef knot; there should be four ties in all.

After a container has been fitted to the aircraft, the static line must be led, as directly

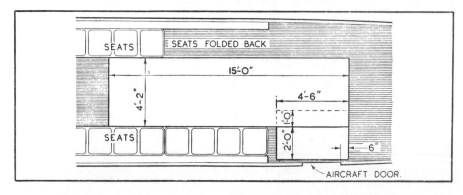

Fig. 10.—Arrangement of mats

as possible, to the strong point and secured so that the static line does not flap in the slipstream. The static line must not be subjected to any load which might strain the stitching.

Mattresses (fig. 10)

19. Two mattresses are placed as indicated in fig. 10. The main one is 15 ft. long and 4 ft. 2 in. wide, while the one at the aircraft door is 4 ft. 6 in. long and 3 ft. wide. It is important that there should be no wrinkles in the mats when they are in position.

Preparation for miscellaneous equipment dropping

20. When parachuting loose items of equipment from the floor of the aircraft, a 10 ft. long rope extension should be attached to the American static cable in the cabin roof: the

other end of the rope is then attached to the parachute static line.

21. A $\frac{3}{4}$ in. circumference rope (approximately $\frac{1}{4}$ in. diameter) is used for miscellaneous equipment dropping, and must be capable of bearing a snatch load of 400 lb. An eye is spliced in one end of the rope, and this end is connected to the parachute static line. A snap hook is spliced to the other end and is hooked on to the overhead static cable.

22. Because of the differences in the deployment of the British and American parachutes, it is dangerous to use the former in conjunction with the American overhead static cable.

Stores References

23. To convert the aircraft for the dropping of parachute troops and their equipment, the following items are required:—

	Item	Stores Ref.
STATIC CABLE AND ATTACH-MENTS	Static cable	126JQ/PC/31
	Shackle, A.G.S.**690**/F (for forward attachment of static cable) ...	28Y/2903
	Shackle, A.G.S.**914**/C (for aft attachment of static cable)	28Y/6431
	Strop (for attachment of parachute static lines)	126JQ/PC/120
	Pin, safety, locking, spring type (1·15 in.)	28P/5413
FLOOR MATS	Floor mat, **15** ft. × **4** ft. **2** in.	126JQ/PC/90
	Floor mat, **4** ft. **6** in. × **3** ft.	126JQ/PC/91
SPECIAL GUARD	Door handle guard	126JQ/PC/80
EQUIPMENT FOR CONTAINER DROPPING	Chassis for attachment of universal bomb carriers	126JQ/PC/100
	Bundles of six supply cables and six earthing cables for universal bomb carriers	126JQ/PC/70
	Pins for bracing stays (pins, shackle, steel, $\frac{3}{16}$ in. dia., **0·6** in. long) ...	28P/834
	Universal bomb carrier No. **1** (**2** off per aircraft)	11A/520 or 11A/598
	Universal bomb carrier No. **2** (**4** off per aircraft)	11A/533 or 11A/607
	Electro-magnetic release unit, Type C, Mk. 2	11A/466
	Note.—Electro-magnetic release units Type C, Mk. 2 or Mk. 3 are both suitable with **12** or **24**-volt supply.	
	Junction box, Type C	5D/579
	Crutch lever assembly, comprising:—	
	Buttons, adjusting screw	11A/1124
	Shoes	11A/1126
	Keep pins, adjusting screw	11A/1324
	Screw, adjusting, ball ended	11A/1325
	Rings, crutch pad retaining	11A/1871
	Nuts, for adjusting screws, M.S., $\frac{3}{8}$ in. B.S.F.	28M/760
	Release slip, Mk. 1	11A/487
	Cannon plug, 3-pin (RWK)	105X/857
	Linen thread	15A/108

This leaf issued in reprint incorporating A.L's I to 15
July, 1945

AIR PUBLICATION 2453A
VOLUME I PART 2 SECTION I

CHAPTER 2

DAKOTA CI, III, AND IV—LOADING AND C.G. DATA

LIST OF CONTENTS

Loading limitations

1. A Dakota C.I, III, or IV aircraft can be used to transport and drop a maximum of 25 parachute troops, together with the equipment carried by the men and in containers on the bomb racks.

2. For the approved loading cases the disposable loads are shown in the table at para. 3. In the table allowance is made for:—

(i) Type "J" dinghies on the basis of one for every ten, or portion of ten, parachute troops.
(ii) Ballast.
(iii) Full oil tanks.
(iv) All A.R.I. apparatus.

3. Table of disposable loads:—

4. The weight limitations of the aircraft are:—

(i) Maximum permissible take-off weight: 31,000 lb.

(ii) Maximum permissible landing weight: 26,500 lb.

5. The following are the forward and aft limits of the aircraft C.G. travel:—

(i) Forward: 239·6 in. from nose of aircraft (i.e. from fuselage station "0"). This corresponds to 11% M.A.C.

(ii) Aft: 263·1 in. from nose of aircraft (i.e. from fuselage station "0"). This corresponds to 28% M.A.C.

Loading case	Number of parachute troops Weight 237 lb. each	Number of kit bags Weight 60 lb. each	Number of containers Weight 400 lb. each	Fuel (Imperial gall.)	
				In normal tanks	In long range tanks
I	10	Nil	6	670	160
2	15	Nil	6	670	Nil
3	20	Nil	6	535	Nil
4	25	Nil	6	353	Nil
5	10	10	6	670	77
6	15	15	6	575	Nil
7	20	5	6	493	Nil
8	20	10	6	452	Nil
9	20	15	6	410	Nil

Note . . . The dispositions of men and equipment in the various loading cases are illustrated in chap. 3.

DAKOTA CI, III, AND IV—LOADING AND C.G. DATA

Note . . . These limitations are subject to amendment. If the limitations promulgated through normal official channels differ from those quoted above, the former should be considered as applicable.

Loading and C.G. requirements

6. Loading and C.G. tables for loads of 10 and 20 parachute troops (plus equipment) are given in para. 9. The calculations are for guidance only, however, and will be affected by the requirements of specific loading cases. Calculations of this nature must allow for:—

(i) The aircraft tare conditions.

(ii) Aircraft crew.

(iii) Typical service load of the aircraft.

(iv) Ballasting of the aircraft (if required).

(v) Aircraft parachuting equipment.

(vi) Parachute troops and their equipment.

(vii) Despatchers for the parachute troops (if required).

(viii) Petrol and oil.

7. For maintenance of the aircraft C.G. within the permissible limits it may be necessary to carry ballast in the lavatory compartment. The weight of ballast varies with the different loads, i.e. more ballast is made imperative if the dinghies and their packs are not carried. The table below is a guide to the ballasting of the aircraft.

Loading and C.G. tables

8. For the purpose of C.G. calculations similar to those at para. 9, it is not necessary to consider the weight and moment of each individual, but only of the group of men. The position of the "group C.G." for each approved loading case is given in the table on the opposite page. (The positions of the troops for each loading case are illustrated in fig. 1 to 9, Chapter 3.).

Number of parachute troops carried	Number of dinghies carried (if required)	Weight of ballast in lavatory compartment of aircraft in lb.		Remarks
		When dinghies are carried	When dinghies are not carried	
10	1	100	200	Aircraft fitted with long range fuel tanks
15 or 20	2	Nil	200	—
25	3	Nil	200	—

DAKOTA CI, III, AND IV—LOADING AND C.G. DATA

Description of load	Positioning of parachute troops	Position of group C.G.	
		Distance from nose of aircraft (i.e. from fuselage station "0"), in inches.	Cabin station number
Case I 10 men. Aircraft fitted with long range fuel tanks	Stations for take-off and flight to target Action stations	308 363	130 185
Case 2 15 men	Stations for take-off and flight to target Action stations	253 333	75 155
Case 3 20 men	Stations for take-off and flight to target Action stations	278 318	100 140
Case 4 25 men	Stations for take-off and flight to target Action stations	303 303	125 125
Case 5 10 men with kitbags. Aircraft fitted with long range fuel tanks	Stations for take-off and flight to target Action stations	308 (men) 258 (kitbags) 353	130 (men) 80 (kitbags) 175
Case 6 15 men with kitbags	Stations for take-off and flight to target Action stations	253 321	75 143
Case 7 20 men, 5 kitbags	Stations for take-off and flight to target Action stations	278 (men) 218 (kitbags) 420 (men with kitbags) 268 (men without kitbags)	100 (men) 40 (kitbags) 242 (men with kitbags) 90 (men without kitbags)
Case 8 20 men, 10 kitbags	Stations for take-off and flight to target Action stations	278 (men) 258 (kitbags) 368 (men with kitbags) 243 (men without kitbags)	100 (men) 80 (kitbags) 190 (men with kitbags) 65 (men without kitbags)
Case 9 20 men, 15 kitbags	Stations for take-off and flight to target Action stations	278 333 (men with kitbags) 218 (men without kitbags)	100 155 (men with kitbags) 40 (men without kitbags)

DAKOTA CI, III, AND IV—LOADING AND C.G. DATA

9. The following are loading and C.G. calculations for two typical cases—Loading cases 5 and 9:—

Items of Load	Weight (lb.)	Arm (in)	Moment (lb. in.)
Tare conditions (see note below)	**16,719**	**239·7**	**4,008,069**
(i)			
Signal pistol	3		316
Pistol holder	2	94	188
12 signal cartridges	4		474
Navigator's table	33	134	4,422
Navigator's stool	5	161	805
Fire extinguishers	7	85	595
Pilots' cushions	19	70	1,330
Lavatory equipment	15	550	8,250
First aid kit	1	582	582
Radio compass SCR.269, c/w accessories	74	169	12,453
Frequency meter SCR.211	37	171	6,327
R.3090	39·5	590	23,305
Cabin entrance step	9	535	4,815
Glider towing and release unit {	38	679	25,802
	8	745	5,960
Fittings for cargo anchorage, stowed	3	537	1,611
W/T Operator's tool kit	21	132	2,772
Black-out curtain	4	300	1,200
Locking pins for landing gear	1	580	580
Wing and tail jacking pads	2	450	900
Locks for control surfaces	9	580	5,220
A.R.I.5083 installation	83	105	8,715
British type static cable and 25 strops	40	327	13,080
Transmitter AN/APN–2	118	105	12,390
Folding ladder	13	89	1,157
Folding benches	86	309	26,574
18 sets of litter supports, stowed	239	312	74,568
Dinghy transmitter SCR.578	32	115	3,673
Dinghy Type H, stowed	50	520	26,000
Armour plate	130	70	9,100
Fireman's axe	4	180	720
Aldis lamp	3	130	390
Safety belts for folding seats	81	309	25,029
A.R.I.5183 installation	22	130	2,860
6 British type chassis for universal carriers	109		34,691
6 Universal carriers	89·5		27,489
2 V.G.O. guns and ammunition	95	450	42,750
2 V.G.O. guns and ammunition	95	180	17,100
Numnah mats	60	457	27,420
Non-skid floor piece, large	22	275	6,050
Non-skid floor piece, small	9	275	2,475
First aid kit	25	530	13,250
Sea landing safety belts	50	300	15,000
Total, removable items	**1,790**		**498,388**

CONTINUED—

DAKOTA CI, III, AND IV—LOADING AND C.G. DATA

CONTINUED—

Items of load	Weight (lb.)	Arm (in.)	Moment (lb. in.)
Tare conditions (see note below)			
(ii) Crew:—			
Pilot	180	70	12,600
Pilot's parachute	20	115	2,300
2nd pilot	180	70	12,600
2nd pilot's parachute	20	115	2,300
W/T operator	180	165	29,700
W/T operator's parachute	20	115	2,300
Navigator	180	165	29,700
Navigator's parachute	20	115	2,300
Total, crew	800		93,800

Note . . . The tare weight includes the weight of the following equipment:—Command Radio SCR. 274-N, including all associated parts. Liaison Radio SCR. 287-A, including all associated parts. Interphone R/C-36. Marker Beacon RC. 43-13 and Receiver BC. 357.

Items of Load	Weight (lb.)	Arm (in.)	Moment (lb. in.)
(iii) Basic weight (not including the parachute troops, containers, fuel or oil):—			
Tare	16,719		4,008,069
Removable	1,790		498,388
Crew	800		93,800
Total, basic	19,309		4,600,257
(iv) Loading Case 5			
(a) 10 parachute troops, each with 60 lb. kit bag			
(b) 6–400 lb. containers			
Take-off:—			
Basic (from (iii))	19,309		4,600,257
"J" type dinghy	70	520	36,400
No. 6 type pack	62	500	31,000
Long range fuel tanks	281	215	60,600
Parachute troops	2,370	308	729,960
Kitbags	600	258	154,800
Containers	2,400	307	736,800
Oil. 58 U.S. gall.	435	184	80,000
Fuel. Main wing tanks, rear: 400 U.S. gall.	2,400	276	662,400
Main wing tanks, front: 404 U.S. gall.	2,424	240·5	583,600
Long range tanks: 92 U.S. gall.	552	216	119,232
*Ballast in lavatory compartment	100	561	56,100
	31,003		7,850,549

C.G. position: **253·2** in. from nose of aircraft (i.e. from fuselage station "0")

DAKOTA CI, III, AND IV—LOADING AND C.G. DATA

Items of load	Weight (lb.)	Arm (in.)	Moment (lb. in.)
Action stations, at limit of radius:—			
Basic (from iii))	19,309		4,600,257
"J" type dinghy	70	520	36,400
No. 6 type pack	62	500	31,000
Long range fuel tanks	281	215	60,600
Parachute troops and kitbags	2,970	353	1,047,410
Containers	2,400	307	736,800
Oil. 58 U.S. gall.	435	184	80,000
Fuel. Main wing tanks, rear: 366 U.S. gall.	2,196	276	606,800
Moment for movement of W/T operator to despatcher's station			57,600
*Ballast in lavatory compartment	100	561	56,100
	27,823		7,312,967

C.G. position: **262·8** in. from nose of aircraft (i.e. from fuselage station "0")

	Weight (lb.)	Arm (in.)	Moment (lb. in.)
Landing. Fuel consumed: men and containers gone:—			
Basic	19,309		4,600,257
"J" type dinghy	70	520	36,400
No. 6 type pack	62	500	31,000
Long range fuel tanks	281	215	60,600
Oil. 58 U.S. gall.	435	184	80,000
*Ballast in lavatory compartment	100	561	56,100
	20,257		4,864,357

C.G. position: **240.1** in. from nose of aircraft (i.e. from fuselage station "0")

Items of load	Weight (lb.)	Arm (in.)	Moment (lb. in.)
(v) Loading Case 9			
(a) 20 parachute troops, 15 with 60 lb. kit bags			
(b) 6–400 lb. containers			
Take-off:—			
Basic (from (iii))	19,309		4,600,257
"J" type dinghies (2)	140	520	72,800
No. 6 type packs (2)	124	500	62,000
Parachute troops	4,740	278	1,317,720
Kitbags	900	278	250,000
Containers	2,400	307	736,800
Oil. 58 U.S. gall.	435	184	80,000
Fuel. Main wing tanks, rear: 400 U.S. gall.	2,400	276	662,400
Main wing tanks, front: 92 U.S. gall.	552	240·5	132,800
	31,000		7,914,977

C.G. position: **255·2** in. from nose of aircraft (i.e. from fuselage station "0") CONTINUED—

*Note . . . If the dinghy and pack are not carried, the ballast must be increased by 100 lb.

111

DAKOTA CI, III, AND IV—LOADING AND C.G. DATA

CONTINUED—

Items of Load	Weight (lb.)	Arm (in.)	Moment (lb. in.)
Action stations at limit of radius:—			
Basic (from (iii))	19,309		4,600,257
"J" type dinghies (2)	140	520	72,800
No. 6 type packs (2)	124	500	62,000
Parachute troops (5) without kitbags	1,185	218	258,330
Parachute troops (15) with kitbags	4,455	333	1,483,520
Containers	2,400	307	736,800
Oil. 58 U.S. gall.	435	184	80,000
Fuel. Main wing tanks, rear: 186 U.S. gall.	1,116	276	308,016
Moment for movement of W/T operator to dispatcher's station			57,600
	29,164		7,659,323

C.G. position: **263·0** in. from nose of aircraft (i.e. from fuselage station "0")

Items of Load	Weight (lb.)	Arm (in.)	Moment (lb. in.)
Landing. Fuel consumed: men and containers gone:—			
Basic	19,309		4,600,257
"J" type dinghies (2)	140	520	72,800
No. 6 type packs (2)	124	500	62,000
Oil. 58 U.S. gall.	435	184	80,000
	20,008		4,815,057

C.G. position: **240·8** in. from nose of aircraft (i.e. from fuselage station "0")

Note . . . If dinghies and packs are not carried, 200 lb. ballast is required in the lavatory compartment.

This leaf issued in reprint incorporating A.L's I to 15
July, 1945

CHAPTER 3

DAKOTA CI, III, AND IV —
TECHNICAL PROCEDURE IN FLYING

LIST OF CONTENTS

LIST OF ILLUSTRATIONS

General

1. The instructions contained in this chapter apply only to troops equipped with British X-type parachutes.

2. A Dakota C.I, III, or IV aircraft can be used to carry and drop a maximum of 25 fully-equipped parachute troops plus six supplies-dropping containers.

3. This chapter is concerned with loading cases consisting of 10, 15, 20, or 25 parachute troops, plus equipment carried in the aircraft with the men, and supplies dropping containers or other items which it is practicable to transport on the aircraft bomb carriers.

4. Door jumping technique is employed, the main door on the port side being utilised for this purpose.

5. Loading and C.G. data for the various authorised loading cases are given in Chapter 2.

Positioning of parachute troops

6. The take-off, flight to target, and action, stations are shown in fig. 1 to 9. The following table indicates the appropriate illustration for each loading case, together with a brief description of the troops' positions. The positioning of the men's kit bags, when these are carried, is also described.

DAKOTA CI, III, AND IV—
TECHNICAL PROCEDURE IN FLYING

Loading case No. and description	Fig. No.	Positioning of parachute troops (and kit bags, when carried)
No. 1 **10** men: aircraft fitted with long-range fuel tanks	1	(i) Take-off and flight to target:— 　Troops on side seats, port and starboard. (ii) Action stations:— 　No. 1 to **5**. Open single file, No. 1 at door. 　No. **6** to **10**. Close single file.
No. 2 **15** men	2	(i) Take-off and flight to target:— 　Troops on side seats, port and starboard. (ii) Action stations:— 　Troops in close single file along aircraft centre line, No. 1 at door
No. 3 **20** men	3	(i) Take-off and flight to target:— 　Troops on side seats, port and starboard. (ii) Action stations:— 　No. 1 to **9**. Close single file, No. 1 at door. 　No. **10** to **20**. Staggered in two lines in forward portion of cabin.
No. 4 **25** men	4	(i) Take-off and flight to target:— 　Troops on side seats, port and starboard. (ii) Action stations:— 　No. 1 to **9**. Close single file along aircraft centre line, No. 1 at door. 　No. **10** to **19**. Staggered in two lines between No. **9** and **20**. 　No. **20** to **25**. Staggered in three lines in forward portion of cabin.
No. 5 **10** men **10** kit bags: aircraft fitted with long-range fuel tanks	5	(i) Take-off and flight to target:— 　Troops on side seats, port and starboard. 　Kit bags. Along aircraft centre line, between the rows of men. (ii) Action stations:— 　No. 1 to **8**. Open single file, No. 1 at door. 　No. **9** and **10**. Side-by-side, behind No. **8**.

DAKOTA CI, III, AND IV—
TECHNICAL PROCEDURE IN FLYING

Leading case No. and description	Fig. No.	Positioning of parachute troops (and kit bags, when carried)
No. 6 15 men 15 kit bags	6	(i) Take-off and flight to target:— Troops. On side seats, port and starboard. Kit bags. In two lines, between the rows of men. (ii) Action stations:— No. I to 3. Open single file, No. I at door. No. 4 to 15. Staggered in two lines, behind No. 3 to bulkhead at cabin station "0".
No. 7 20 men 5 kit bags	7	(i) Take-off and flight to target:— Troops. On side seats, port and starboard. Kit bags. Along aircraft centre line in forward portion of cabin, between the rows of men. (ii) Action stations:— No. I to 5. Open single file, No. I at door. No. 6 to 20. Staggered in two lines behind No. 5.
No. 8 20 men 10 kit bags	8	(i) Take-off and flight to target:— Troops. On side seats, port and starboard. Kit bags. Along aircraft centre line, between the rows of men. (ii) Action stations:— No. I to 5. Open single file, No. I at door. No. 6 to 20. Staggered in two lines behind No. 5.
No. 9 20 men 15 kitbags	9	(i) Take-off and flight to target:— Troops. On side seats, port and starboard. Kit bags. Along aircraft centre line, between the rows of men. (ii) Action stations:— No. I to 5. Open single file, No. I at door. No. 6 to 20. Staggered in two lines behind No. 5.

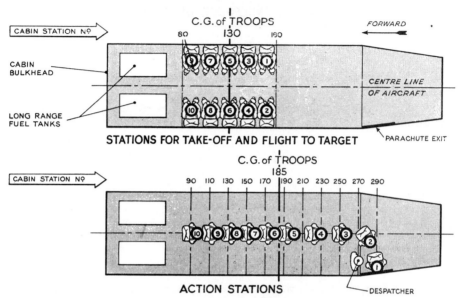

STATIONS FOR TAKE-OFF AND FLIGHT TO TARGET

ACTION STATIONS

Fig. I.—*Positioning of parachute troops: 10 men*

Drill in the air *(Fig. I to 9)*

7. The drill may be varied in detail according to circumstances, but it must be based on the following notes:—

(i) The take-off, flight to target, and action, stations should be substantially as laid down in para. 6 and fig. 1 to 9. If the men carry a considerable amount of equipment, they may not be able to stand comfortably at action stations, and in such instances each man can give himself more room by turning slightly to his right.

(ii) The duties of the despatcher are performed by the wireless operator, who is shown stationed forward of the parachute exit door in fig. 1 to 9. (This position is necessary in order that he can operate the container release switches, but he can place himself aft of the door if troops only are being dropped, or when he is required to despatch equipment from the door.)

(iii) For the best stick pattern the men should form one section, and the containers (fitted with canopy delayed opening devices), are then dropped simultaneously with them. If the containers are not fitted with canopy delayed opening devices, the men should be divided into two sections, composed of equal, or approximately equal, numbers; the stick is then arranged with the containers between the two sections. The men normally form one section if the stick is not to include containers. (For the container dropping procedure refer to para. 11 and 12.)

(iv) Each snap hook attaching a man's static line to the static cable, whether of the "self-locking" type or not, must be checked for secure locking. Safety pins, when required, must be of the correct type.

(v) There must be no obstruction to prevent the folding down of seats on the starboard side. (Refer to para. 7 (vi).)

DAKOTA CI, III, AND IV—
TECHNICAL PROCEDURE IN FLYING

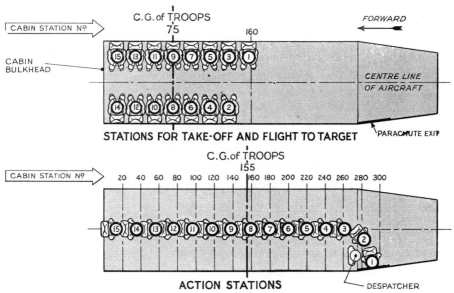

Fig. 2.—Positioning of parachute troops: 15 men

(vi) The pilot of the aircraft communicates with the O.C. parachute troops approximately 20 minutes before dropping is to commence. When the O.C. parachute troops considers it necessary, he orders his men to hook up their static lines to the strops and stand up. The four aft seats on the starboard side are then folded down out of the way. (These four seats at least must be folded down, but more may be folded to increase the floor space, if necessary.)

(vii) The panel in the forward half of the parachute exit door is removed.

Note . . . If a night descent is to take place, it is very important that the cabin lights should be extinguished before removal of the panel.

(viii) A check is carried out to make certain that each man is properly hooked up and that his equipment is in order. The O.C. parachute troops reports to the pilot when his men are ready to jump.

(ix) Five minutes before dropping time the men take up their appropriate action stations.

(x) 5–10 secs. before dropping is to start, the RED signal light is switched on, and the first man of the stick prepares to jump.

(xi) When the GREEN signal light is switched on, the troops begin jumping in rotation.

Note . . . It is essential that the despatcher should recognise the O.C. parachute troops.

(xii) Immediately the last man of Section No. 1 has jumped, the container release switches are operated by the despatcher. (Refer to para. 12 for the procedure to be followed when the containers are fitted with canopy delayed opening devices.)

(xiii) Immediately the last container has been dropped, Section No. 2 leaves the aircraft.

DAKOTA CI, III, AND IV—
TECHNICAL PROCEDURE IN FLYING

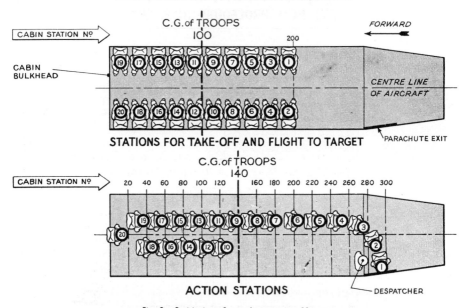

Fig. 3.—Positioning of parachute troops: 20 men

(xiv) Whilst moving down the fuselage, the static line and strop of each man is guided by the man immediately following him. The last man of the stick guides his own static line and strop until he is in the position of second from the door.

(xv) *When making his exit the parachutist should place his left foot on the door sill, with the toe almost over the edge,* and his hands should grip the door opening on each side. It is advisable to *step* outward. (If the parachutist *jumps* outward he is liable to be blown much closer to the tail plane.) For the procedure to be followed when a kit bag or rifle valise is being carried, see para. 8 and 9.

(xvi) Immediately all the parachute troops have jumped, the pilot should operate the container jettison switch.

(xvii) After all the parachute troops have jumped, two members of the crew retrieve the static lines and bags.

8. When kit bags are to be carried, the following points must be particularly noted. (Information regarding the kit bag and its method of use will be found in Part 4, Sect. 1):—

(i) The kit bag should be attached to the right leg.

(ii) When the parachute troop is making an exit, *the left foot should be placed on the edge of the door sill with the toe almost over the edge.* The left hand should hold on to the side of the door and the kit bag should be grasped with the right hand. The right leg should then be swung straight out of the door, and a downward push-off should be given. Immediately afterwards the legs should be brought together and the kit bag should be grasped by both hands; the body will then assume a semi-crouching position.

DAKOTA CI, III, AND IV—
TECHNICAL PROCEDURE IN FLYING

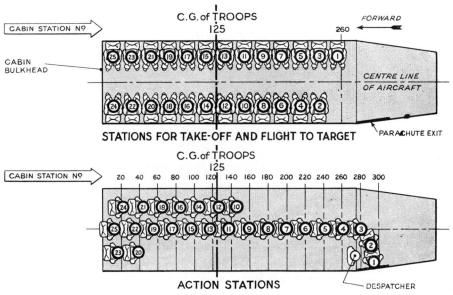

Fig. 4.—Positioning of parachute troops: 25 men

WARNING

> If the left foot is not placed on the edge of the door sill it is highly probable that twisting and somersaulting may develop owing to the left foot remaining in position until it is dragged out after the body has begun to fall.

9. When rifle valises are carried, the following points should be noted. (Information regarding the rifle valise and its method of use will be found in Part 4, Sect. 1):—

(i) The valise can only be used if the parachutist makes a standing exit from the aircraft.

(ii) No special precautions are required except that the valise should be released at the earliest moment after development of the parachute canopy, thus minimising the tendency towards the persistence of any twisting that may occur.

10. For emergency procedure refer to Chapter 4.

Container dropping

11. The containers are released by manually-operated switches (fig. 11), one for each container, mounted on a panel forward of the parachute exit door. If the operator—the man responsible for despatching—depresses each one in turn as quickly as possible, the time taken to release all the containers is approximately two secs. They are then spaced in such a way as to avoid interference, and a minimum stick length is ensured.

12. If the containers are fitted with canopy delayed opening devices, they can be dropped simultaneously with the troops in any desired "pattern". When 15 or more men are dropped, the switches for container stations No. 1 to 6 will normally be operated by the despatcher in sequence as No. 3, 5, 7, 9, 11, and 13 troops jump respectively. When less than 15 men are dropped the switches will normally be operated in sequence as the first six troops jump. The containers cannot be dropped in a single salvo without risk of interference.

DAKOTA CI, III, AND IV—
TECHNICAL PROCEDURE IN FLYING

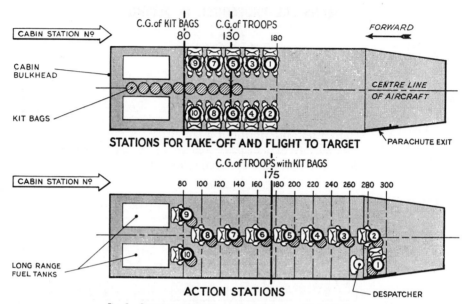

Fig. 5.—Positioning of parachute troops: 10 men with 10 kit bags

13. The maximum permissible landing weight of the aircraft is 26,500 lb. and if a landing has to be made with a considerable load of fuel, parachute troops, and containers on board, the weight should be reduced by jettisoning the containers. If the aircraft is to be landed when carrying 20 or 25 parachute troops, or 15 parachute troops with kit bags, container jettisoning is still essential, even though all the fuel may have been consumed. Container jettisoning is necessary to the following extent in order to comply with the landing weight limitation:—

Loading case No. and description	Container jettisoning details
No. 4: 25 men	Drop a total of five containers—from carriers 1, 2, 3, 4, 5 or 6.
No. 9: 20 men, 15 kit bags ⎫ No. 8: 20 men, 10 kit bags ⎬	Drop a total of four containers—from carriers 1, 2, 3 and 4.
No. 7: 20 men, 5 kit bags	Drop a total of three containers—from carriers 1, 2, 3 or 4.
No. 3: 20 men	Drop a total of two containers—from carriers 1 and 2.
No. 6: 15 men, 15 kit bags	Drop a total of one container—from carrier 1 or 2.

DAKOTA CI, III, AND IV—
TECHNICAL PROCEDURE IN FLYING

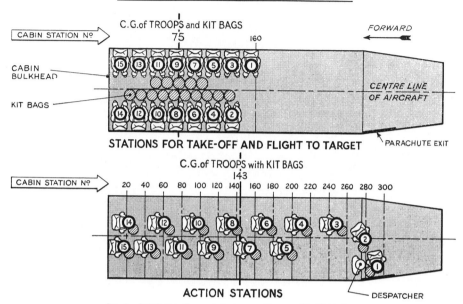

Fig. 6.—Positioning of parachute troops: 15 men with 15 kit bags

Dropping of miscellaneous equipment from parachute exit

14. Miscellaneous equipment such as bicycles can be dropped from the parachute exit door by the employment of a 10 ft. rope extension attached to the American static cable in the roof of the cabin. The rope extension is attached to the static line of the parachute with which the item is fitted.

Note . . . When bicycles are despatched from the parachute exit it is essential that they should be launched *downwards*, and not *outwards*.

15. If a camouflet set or similar heavy box is to be dropped, it should be placed on the floor of the aircraft opposite the parachute exit door with one end facing the exit and the pack uppermost. The loop on the end of the parachute static line is attached to the snap-hook on the end of the rearmost parachute troop strop, and the elastic stowage cord on the strop is removed.

16. A camouflet set or similar heavy box should be despatched by raising the inboard end about two feet from the floor and sliding the box through the doorway with a sharp push. This item should be dropped before the exit of the first parachute troop.

17. Owing to the differences in the deployment of British and American parachutes, it is considered dangerous to use the British X-type parachute in conjunction with the American overhead static cable.

18. The technique for dropping miscellaneous equipment (including light motor cycles) from the Dakota, is given in A.P.2453B, Vol. I, Part 4, Sect. 1.

Stick length

19. During tests a stick of 20 parachute troops, and 6 containers (fitted with canopy delayed opening devices), were dropped at an aircraft speed of 105 m.p.h. I.A.S. The stick length measured 430 yards.

DAKOTA CI, III, AND IV—
TECHNICAL PROCEDURE IN FLYING

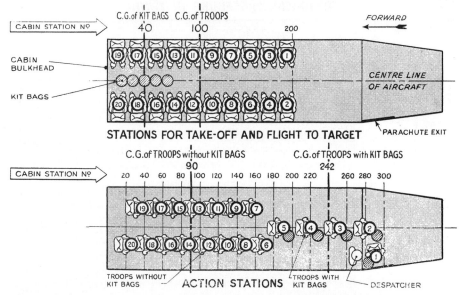

Fig. 7.—*Positioning of parachute troops: 20 men with 5 kit bags.*

Pilot's handling technique

20. The following are recommendations to pilots of Dakota CI, III, and IV aircraft when taking part in parachute operations:—

(i) Fly in formation up to approximately one mile from the dropping zone, then move into open formation with wide spacing between the aircraft for dropping purposes.

WARNING

> The object of the wide spacing is to enable pilots to fly an individual steady course. The use of throttle and rudder to maintain formation tends to cause yawing, and creates a circular slipstream which may result in parachute troops fouling the tail wheel assembly. Such a circumstance is extremely dangerous to the parachutist and to the aircraft; an open parachute attached to an aircraft can result in complete loss of control.

(ii) During dropping operations the aircraft must be flown straight and level or in a shallow glide, at a speed of not less than 100 m.p.h. I.A.S.

WARNING

> A turn to the right or a climbing attitude might result in the parachute or parachute bag fouling the tail plane or the tail wheel.

(iii) Maintain an indicated air speed of 100 to 115 m.p.h. during the dropping of parachute troops. The 125 c.c. motor cycle should not, however, be dropped at a speed in excess of 110 m.p.h. I.A.S.

(iv) Give the command "action stations" to the O.C. parachute troops approximately 15 minutes before the time for dropping.

(v) Await the message "ready to jump" from the O.C. parachute troops. When this message is received, and 5 to 10 seconds before

DAKOTA CI, III, AND IV—
TECHNICAL PROCEDURE IN FLYING

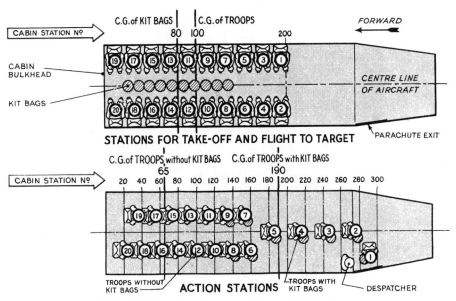

Fig 8.—Positioning of parachute troops : 20 men with 10 kit bags

dropping is to commence, switch on the RED signal light. (The signal light control panel for the pilot is illustrated in fig. 10).

(vi) At the moment when dropping is to commence, switch on the GREEN signal light. Keep this light on until it is no longer safe to jump, then switch on the RED signal light.

(vii) Immediately all the parachute troops have jumped, operate the container jettison switch.

(viii) Should it be necessary to abandon or ditch the aircraft, the drills detailed in Chapter 4—"Emergency Procedure"—should be carried out.

(ix) While Mk. I or Mk. III containers are carried on bomb carriers 3 and 4, the movement of the wing flaps is restricted to 50 per cent. In the event of a landing being made with these containers still attached, full flap cannot be used.

(x) The maximum permissible landing weight of the aircraft is 26,500 lb. If a landing with a considerable load of fuel, parachute troops and containers is unavoidable, the weight should be reduced by the jettisoning of containers in accordance with the instructions contained in para. 13.

Precautions for safety of aircraft

21. Serious accidents can occur if parachute troops interfere with aircraft fitments. For this reason precautions similar to those outlined in the following paragraphs should be taken to ensure that no interference occurs.

22. The Captain of the aircraft is in absolute control of all personnel on board. He will issue orders to the parachute troops through their commander. Prior to an operation the Captain of the aircraft should ensure that the commander of the parachute troops is familiar with the location of any aircraft fittings which

DAKOTA CI, III, AND IV—
TECHNICAL PROCEDURE IN FLYING

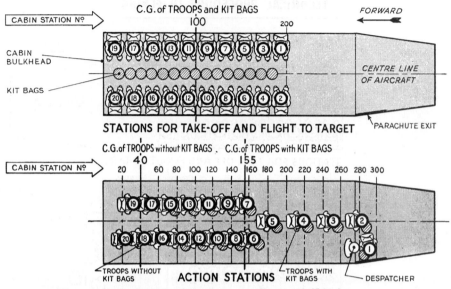

Fig. 9.—*Positioning of parachute troops: 20 men with 15 kit bags*

it may be necessary for him to use, such as intercommunication sockets, lighting switches, etc. No other controls should be touched.

23. The Captain of the aircraft might usefully address a few remarks to the parachute troops before take-off. The following is a suggestion for the substance of such remarks:—

(i) All troops will carry out the orders given by the Captain of the aircraft.

(ii) The parachute troops will stow equipment carefully in the cabin.

(iii) There will be no smoking in the aircraft.

(iv) The parachute troops will adhere to the specified take-off positions (*fig. 1* to *9*) until ordered to move by the Captain of the aircraft.

(v) There must be no undue movement of troops from their specified positions during flight.

(vi) No aircraft equipment must be touched by parachute troops, except under orders.

DAKOTA CI, III AND IV—
TECHNICAL PROCEDURE IN FLYING

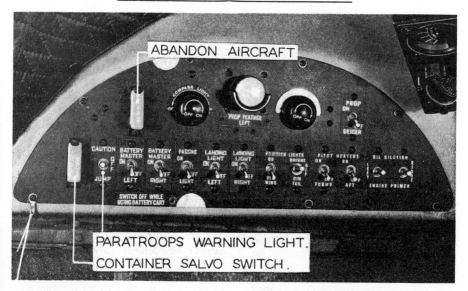

Fig. 10.—Pilot's control panel

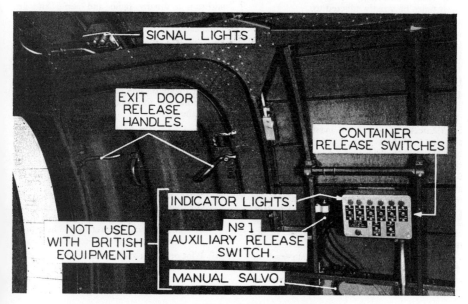

Fig. 11.—General view of parachute exit

DAKOTA C.I, III, and IV—EMERGENCY PROCEDURE

LIST OF CONTENTS

LIST OF ILLUSTRATIONS

General

1—It may be necessary for the parachute troops and crew to abandon the aircraft in an emergency, either by parachute if over the land, or by dinghy after the aircraft has ditched.

2—Special emergency drills for the parachute troops and crew have been evolved to meet both these conditions. These drills should at all times be strictly adhered to.

3—This chapter should be read in conjunction with Section 4 of A.P.2095, Pilot's Notes General and Section 4 of A.P.2445A, C, and D, Pilot's Notes for the Dakota C.I, III, and IV.

Emergency parachute drill

4—The pilot must not give the order to abandon the aircraft if below 300 ft. or if over the sea or some other large expanse of water.

5—Members of the crew must check their parachute harness and remove their flying helmets before abandoning the aircraft from the exits specified in the drill.

6—The parachute troops should abandon the aircraft in the same way as they leave it for a normal operation, the signal to abandon being given in the manner detailed in the drill. The method of giving the signal should be clearly understood by all personnel before take-off.

7—The drill to be carried out by the parachute troops and crew is given in the form of captions to fig. 1, insets 1 to 9, which depict the various stages of the drill.

8—If the aircraft has to crash-land from below 300 ft. with the troops and crew on board they should take up the same positions as for ditching.

Safety equipment carried

9—Two J and one H type dinghy, each packed in an H type valise, are carried. They are stowed on the floor against the starboard wall of the fuselage opposite the main door. In addition a dinghy radio and aerial kite are mounted on the starboard side of the rear bulkhead.

10—Six ditching belts are provided at intervals down the fuselage. They are fixed in position at either end as shown in fig. 2, inset (a). When not in use the top toggles on each side and the bottom toggle on one side of each belt should be undone and the belts rolled up and stowed under the seats.

Emergency ditching drill

11—The following drill must be observed in the event of the aircraft having to ditch.

(i) Pilot orders "Dinghy, dinghy, prepare for ditching". The crew will warn the troops.

(ii) The Stick Commander co-ordinates and supervises the parachute troops and sees that the ditching belts are securely fixed as shown in fig. 2, inset (a). The troops will then take up their ditching positions.

(iii) Pilot orders or signals "Brace for impact"; each man must then brace himself in the manner shown in fig. 2, inset (b) and prepare for severe deceleration.

(iv) After the aircraft has ditched, the ditching belts should be released if possible, so that the minimum obstruction is met. All personnel must then release their parachute harness. The parachute troops must dispose of any heavy equipment, retaining their life vests, water bottles and rations. The crew should put the dinghies into the water in the positions shown in fig. 3, while the parachute troops are discarding their heavy equipment.

(v) The parachute troops and crew should then leave the aircraft by the exit indicated in fig. 3, taking the dinghy radio and aerial kite with them. As they leave the aircraft the troops must inflate their life vests. The crew can assist and direct where possible. The Stick Commander will control the exit of the men, endeavouring to keep an even proportion of troops in each dinghy. Care should be exercised to prevent damage to the dinghies when boarding. The first man in each dinghy should help to control it while the rest of the men embark. Two or three parachute packs should be thrown into the water as a safety precaution to provide temporary support for any men who may fall overboard; in addition several parachutes should be taken into the dinghy for extra warmth.

(vi) The Stick Commander casts off each dinghy or cuts it adrift from the aircraft when full.

(vii) When clear of the aircraft every effort should be made to tie all the dinghies together; a safety line with quoit is attached to each dinghy and may be used for this purpose as well as for rescue purposes.

12—The glove paddles are for controlling the dinghies, and the weather aprons when fitted will save shipping much water under adverse weather conditions and provide a good protection against wind.

13—The crew follow their normal dinghy drill as far as they are able to do so, taking up the positions indicated in fig. 2 when ditching.

Release of parachutist entangled in strops

Use of special kit (Stores Ref. 15A/517)

14. The kit has been developed for the purpose of releasing a parachutist who has become entangled in the strops after jumping. The man is released by cutting the static cable and allowing him to descend by means of two standard observer-type parachutes. *The kit is for use only in parachuting operations in which the British method and installation are employed.*

15. *Whenever the British method and installation are to be used, the kit should be installed in the aircraft and available for immediate use in emergency.*

Details of the kit

16. Each kit is packed in a standard parachute travelling bag, and consists of the following items. The complete kit is identified under Stores Ref. 15A/517:—

(i) Two observer-type parachute packs (Stores Ref. 15A/141).

(ii) One flexible wire cable, 12 ft. long, complete with a shackle and pin (Stores Ref. 15A/515).

(iii) One hammer (Stores Ref. 1B/1329).

(iv) One cold chisel (Stores Ref. 1A/409).

(v) One duralumin "dolly bar", 1¼ in. diameter × 1 ft. long (Stores Ref. 20B/505).

(vi) One 10 ft. length of rope, 1½ in. circumference (Stores Ref. 32A/50).

(vii) One illustrated instruction sheet.

Inspection of kit before use

17. *It is extremely important that a check of the kit should be made before it is taken into the air, since the lack of any one item might make a release impossible if an emergency arose.* When the items comprising the kit have been checked, they should be packed into the bag in the following order:—

(i) One parachute pack, positioned so that the attachment D-rings are uppermost (i.e. towards the mouth of the bag).

(ii) Hammer, cold chisel, and dolly bar.

(iii) One parachute pack, positioned so that the attachment D-rings are downwards (i.e., towards the bottom of the bag).

(iv) Wire cable with shackle and pin.

(v) Length of rope.

(vi) Illustrated instruction sheet.

Method of using the kit

18. The method of use is described and illustrated in fig. 4, a reproduction of which is included with each kit.

1 Remove from the bag :—

   (i)   Two observer-type parachutes.
   (ii) Wire cable, shackle and pin.
   (iii) Hammer.
   (iv) Cold chisel.
   (v) Dolly bar.
   (vi) Rope, 10 ft.

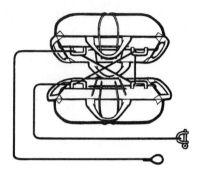

CABLE

2 Thread one end of the wire cable through both D-rings of each of the two parachute packs as illustrated.

3 Thread one end of the wire cable through all the trailing strop D-rings. Join the ends of the cable by means of the pin and shackle.

ROPE

4 Pass one end of the rope through the rip cord handle of each parachute pack and tie a bowline. Tie the free end to the cargo lashing point just forward of the door, leaving an effective length of about 7 feet between the parachutes and the lashing point. Place the parachutes on the floor as close to the door as possible.

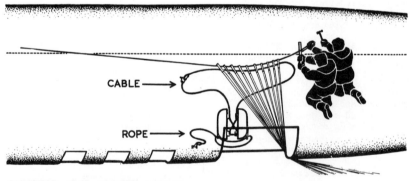

CABLE ⟶

ROPE ⟶

CUTTING THE STATIC CABLE

5 WARNING : For this operation all personnel should take steps to keep clear of the static cable in case it whips when it is cut.

6 One of the safety belts on the starboard side should be fastened round the static cable forward of the D-rings to minimize the whipping effect of the cable when it is released.

7 Cut the static cable aft of the strops near the aft attachment bracket to release all the trailing strops. This is done by one man holding the dolly bar, suitably supported on the side of the aircraft as an anvil underneath the static cable, and another man cutting the cable with a hammer and chisel.

FIG. 4

Vol. I Part 2 Sect. I Chap. 4

128

This leaf issued in reprint incorporating A.L's 1 to 15
July, 1945

AIR PUBLICATION 2453A
Vol. I   Part 2   Sect. I   Chap. 4

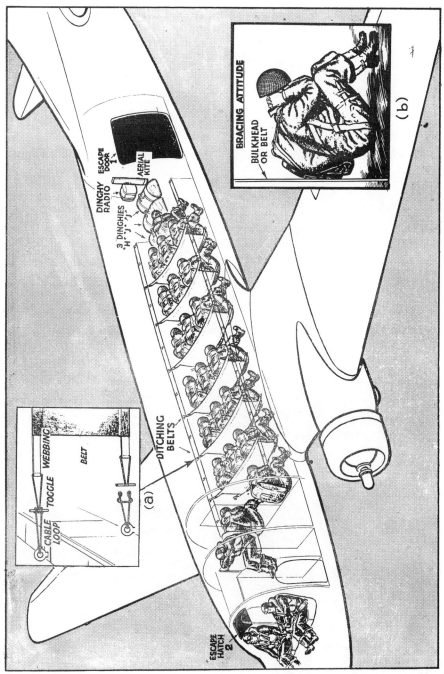

FIG. 2

Troops and crew in ditching or crash positions

1. All crew at action stations. Pilot switches alternative red and green lights, gives order "Section, section, prepare to abandon aircraft." Crew and Stick Cmdr. acknowledge.

2. Pilot destroys I.F.F., 2nd Pilot leaves seat and fits parachute, Nav. gives position of aircraft to Stick Cmdr., W/Op. jettisons trailing aerial.

3. Pilot maintains control. 2nd Pilot moves aft and confirms order to parachute troops, giving position of aircraft ; removes or jettisons parachuting door, if in position. Nav. fits parachutes. W/Op., if time, sends emergency signal. Stick Cmdr. gives order "Hook up."

4. 2nd Pilot stands by to leave after parachute troops. Nav. moves aft. W/Op. fits parachute. Stick Cmdr. (when stick is ready) reports to Pilot (who acknowledges) and removes flying helmet.

DAKOTA

5 — Pilot puts on green light. 2nd Pilot informs Pilot "Leaving aircraft." W/Op. moves aft. Stick jumps.

6 — Pilot orders crew to jump. 2nd Pilot leaves aircraft from main exit, diving out head first.

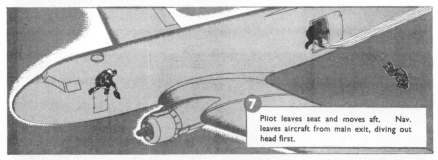

7 — Pilot leaves seat and moves aft. Nav. leaves aircraft from main exit, diving out head first.

8 — Pilot fits parachute. W/Op. leaves aircraft from main exit, diving ou head first.

9 — Pilot leaves aircraft from main exit, diving out head first.

COMBINED EMERGENCY PARACHUTE DRILL FOR PARACHUTE TROOPS AND CREV
FIG. I

This leaf issued with A.L. No. 4
JUNE 1944

AIR PUBLICATION 2453A
Vol. I   Part 2   Sect. I   Chap. 4

Troops and crew boarding dinghies

FIG 3.

4
Stirling IV, July 1945

STIRLING IV PARACHUTE TROOP INSTALLATIONS

FIG. 1   *Parachuting installation—top door open*

General

1. The Stirling IV has been cleared to carry a maximum of twenty-two parachute troops and twelve containers. Alternative loadings of parachute troops and containers are given in Chapter 2.

2. Information on how to load the containers will be found in A.P.2453B, Part 2, Section 2.

Floor aperture (fig. 1 and 2)

3. The floor aperture is situated just forward of the fuselage door. It is rectangular in shape and tapers slightly from the top to the bottom. It measures 85 in. long and 54 in. wide at the top, 72 in. long and 36 in. wide at the bottom and is 30 in. deep.

4. The floor aperture is covered during the

STIRLING IV PARACHUTE TROOP INSTALLATIONS

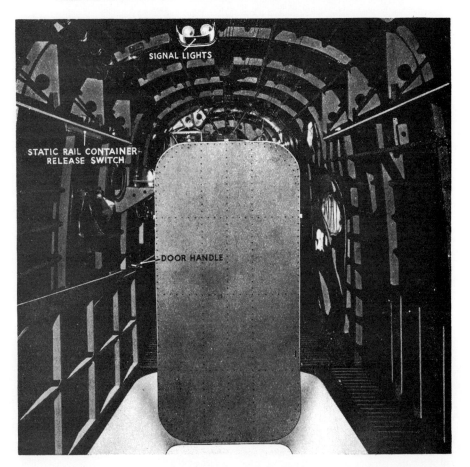

FIG. 2 *Parachute troops' aperture—bottom door open*

flight to the target by two doors, one at the top and the other at the bottom of the aperture.

5. The top door, when closed, forms part of the floor. It is secured by two turn fasteners on the floor which fit over lugs on the port edge of the door. The door hinges about its centre and is also hinged to the floor at the starboard side. When open, it is folded in

half and secured to the starboard side of the fuselage by two straps and fasteners.

6. The bottom door, which forms part of the aircraft skin, is hinged to the fuselage at the back edge. It is strengthened by cross-members and has a tread-way down the centre so that personnel may walk across it. Five latches secure it when closed, one at the

This leaf issued in reprint incorporating A.L's 1 to 15
July, 1945

AIR PUBLICATION 2453A
Vol. I   Part 2   Sect. 2   Chap. I

STIRLING   IV   PARACHUTE   TROOP   INSTALLATIONS

FIG. 3   *Tail guard retracted*

forward end and two at each side. The door is opened by means of a long handle attached to the forward end by a universal joint. The handle should be stowed in the spring clip at the rear end of the door when not in use. When the door is open, the handle is secured to the starboard side of the fuselage by a strap.

Tail guard (fig. 3, 4 and 5)

7. A retractable tail guard, which fits against the underside of the fuselage when retracted and is fixed vertically when lowered, is fitted just aft of the aperture and prevents the parachute static lines and bags from fouling the tail after the parachute troops have left the aircraft.

8. The tail guard is raised by means of a strut welded to a sleeve on the bottom member of the guard. The strut projects through a hole just aft of the fuselage door, and is secured with the guard in both the retracted and lowered positions by a pin passing through the strut and through angle plate fittings bolted to the floor as shown in fig. 5.

9. The guard should be lowered after the Captain has given the order "Prepare for

action" and must be raised directly after the strops have been retrieved.

Static line rail (fig. 6)

10. A static line rail of inverted "T" section to carry the strop carriages is fitted to each wall of the fuselage. The strop carriages are prevented from riding off the forward end of the rails by spring catches, while permanent stops are provided at the rear ends to prevent the carriages from running off after the exit of the parachute troops.

Strops (fig. 7)

11. The strops are made of $1\frac{3}{4}$ inch wide heavy white double webbing, and are all 16 ft. long; the method of folding them is detailed in fig. 7. When moving down the fuselage towards the aperture the parachute troops should grasp their strops just below the carriage and guide the carriage down the rail, letting go just before making their exit. The position of the carriage carrying the plunger depends on whether or not the container parachutes are fitted with the parachute delay opening device.

STIRLING IV PARACHUTE TROOP INSTALLATIONS

FIG. 4 *Tail guard lowered*

12. The permissible tolerance allowed on the length of the strops is ± 2 in. The dead length of the strops is to be measured from the inside face of the snap hook to the end of the webbing at the carriage end.

13. The strop carriages are threaded onto the static rails in ascending order, even numbers on the starboard rail and odd numbers on the port rail.

14. If the containers are to be dropped without the parachute delay opening device, No. 8 of a stick of 15 operates the static rail container release switch and No. 10 of a stick of 20 or 22. No. 2 of any size stick always operates the switch if the containers are to be dropped with the parachute delay opening device fitted.

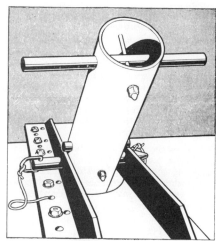

FIG. 5 *Locking of tail guard*

This leaf issued in reprint incorporating A.L's I to I5
July, 1945

AIR PUBLICATION 2453A
Vol. I   Part 2   Sect. 2   Chap. I

STIRLING IV PARACHUTE TROOP INSTALLATIONS

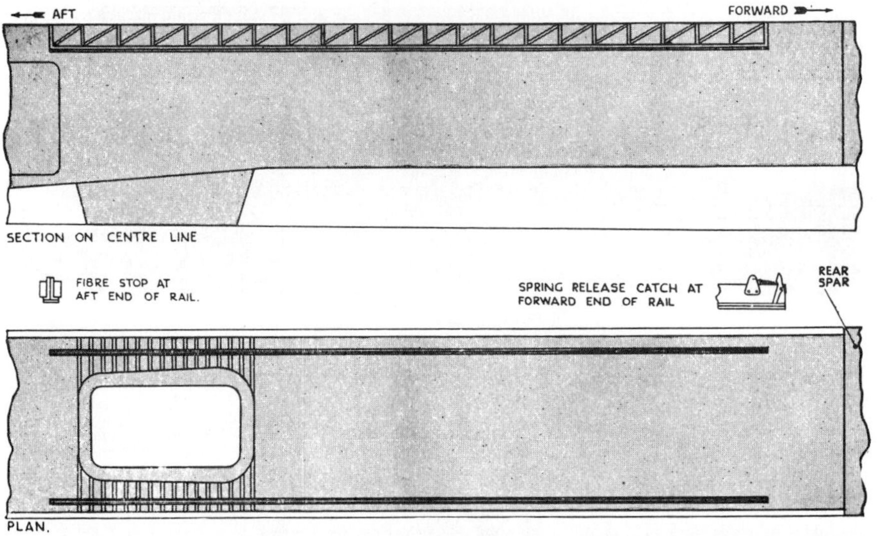

AFT

FORWARD

SECTION ON CENTRE LINE

FIBRE STOP AT
AFT END OF RAIL.

SPRING RELEASE CATCH AT
FORWARD END OF RAIL

REAR
SPAR

PLAN.

FIG. 6   Static line rails

15. Any strops that are not in use must be tied back at the forward ends of the static line rails; this must be done whether or not the aircraft is being used on a parachuting operation.

Plunger for operation of static rail container release switch (fig. 8)

16. A plunger sliding in a tube mounted on the outboard side of one of the strop carriages is held against a spring by a pin passing through the tube. A lanyard is spliced to a ring on the lower end of the pin, the other end being attached to a becket on the strop. The lanyard is slack while the strop to which it is attached remains folded.

17. When the parachutist to whose static line is attached the strop operating the plunger, leaves the aircraft, the lanyard becomes taut, withdrawing the pin and releasing the plunger, thus operating the static rail container release switch as described in para. 19.

18. A breaking tie of No. 8 linen thread, Stores Ref. 15A/108, looped through the ring on the pin and over the tube containing the

plunger, prevents the premature withdrawal of the pin.

Static rail container release switch
(fig. 8)

19. The static rail container release switch is mounted on the outboard side of the starboard static line rail, above the aperture. It consists of a spring loaded bar behind which are mounted two micro-switches wired in parallel. The switch is operated by the spring loaded plunger, described in para. 16, which depresses the bar onto one or both the micro-switches, thereby starting the distributors.

Signal lights (fig. 2)

20. Two signal lights are mounted on a bracket in the roof of the fuselage over the rear end of the aperture. A shroud over the lights prevents their being seen from the ground when the aperture doors are open. The lamps, one red and one green, are of the cockpit type Mk. I (Stores Ref. 5C/446) and are wired to switches under the control of the pilot, second pilot, navigator and air bomber. Masks prevent inadvertent operation of the switches.

STIRLING IV PARACHUTE TROOP INSTALLATIONS

21. The red light is a warning to the troops to be ready to jump, the green light is for giving the troops the signal to jump.

Bomb distributors and selectors

22. Stirling IV aircraft are fitted with either two sixteen point bomb distributors and two sixteen point bomb selectors, or one thirty-two point bomb distributor and one thirty-two point bomb selector.

23. The time interval settings of the distributors for four representative cases are detailed in Chap. 3.

Pre-selector

24. A thirty-two point pre-selector is fitted on the Stirling IV. The order in which the containers are dropped is pre-selected after setting the bomb selector or selectors. The setting of the pre-selector for the various representative cases is detailed in Chap. 3.

Mattresses (fig. 9)

25. Eight standard Numna mattresses, each measuring 5 ft. by 3 ft. are laid lengthwise in pairs down the fuselage floor and are tied at the edges to the fuselage frames and each other.

26. When the parachute troops have left the aircraft the two forward mattresses are untied from the fuselage frames and laid back to permit the fitting of the strop retrieving winches.

Strop retrieving winches (fig. 10)

27. Two Mk. VI winches are provided for retrieval of the strops. They are secured in position between angle iron fittings which are bolted to the floor on each side of the aircraft just aft of the rear spar, by bolts and wing nuts.

Accessories

28. The following accessories may be required in aircraft used for parachute troop operations:—

  (i) Three sanitary containers.

  (ii) Two Elsans.

  (iii) 22 paper "sick" bags.

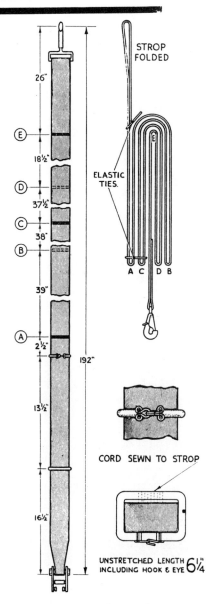

FIG. 7 *Folding of strops*

STIRLING IV PARACHUTE TROOP INSTALLATIONS

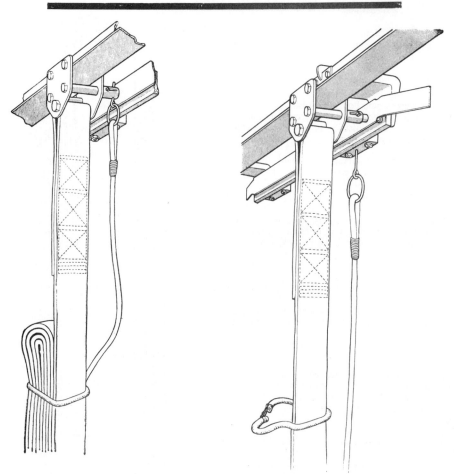

FIG. 8 *Special carriage for operation of static rail container release switch*

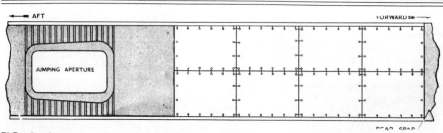

FIG. 9 *Position of parachute troop mattresses*

STIRLING IV PARACHUTE TROOP INSTALLATIONS

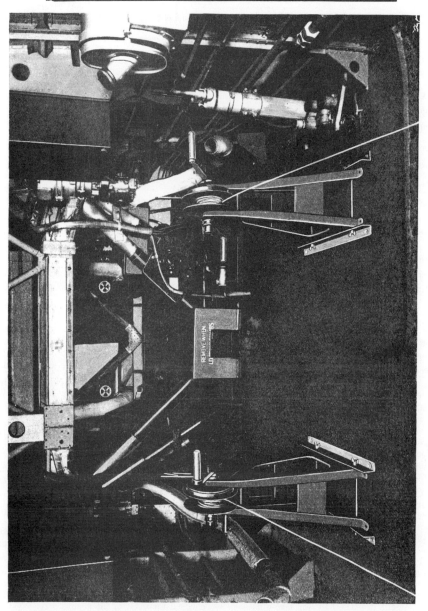

FIG. 10 Mk. VI strop retrieving winches (cables extended)

$\equiv\equiv\equiv$ **STIRLING IV - LOADING AND C.G. DATA** $\equiv\equiv\equiv$

General

1. This chapter deals with the C.G. and loading of the aircraft when used for the carriage and dropping of parachute troops and containers.

Weight limitations

2. The all-up weight of the aircraft must not exceed 70,000 lb. for take-off.

3. The maximum permissible landing weight is 60,000 lb. If the aircraft has to land without dropping its parachute troops or containers the weight may have to be reduced by consuming or jettisoning fuel. With 1,400 gallons consumed the weight will, in each loading case, be sufficiently reduced.

4. Containers must not be dropped to reduce the maximum permissible all-up weight of the aircraft for landing.

Loading

5. In all loading cases, and in the typical loading and C.G. schedule given in this chapter, it has been assumed that the aircraft has been loaded to the maximum permissible all-up weight of 70,000 lb. for take-off.

Aircrew

6. The number of aircrew carried is given below together with their weights:—

Pilot
Co-pilot
Wireless operator
Navigator
Rear gunner
Flight engineer

Each man with his parachute weighs 200 lb. making a total load of 1,200 lb.

Parachuting service load

7. The removable equipment comprising the parachuting service load is as scheduled in Appendix "A" No. 1484, and in weight data in A.P.1660D, Vol. I, Sect. 4.

8. The following items of alternative service loads have been included in the C.G. and weight calculations:—
  (i) 6,000 rounds of rear turret ammunition
  (ii) Two J type dinghies for parachute troops

Tactical load including fuel and oil

9. The aircraft has been cleared to carry a tactical load of a maximum weight of 23,264 lb. It is assumed to be loaded to this maximum in the sixteen cases tabulated below.

10. Any tactical loading case departing from those quoted, either at the maximum permissible weight or a lesser weight, should be checked for C.G. in the normal way.

(i) Containers at 350 lb. each, no kit bags

CASE	NO. OF PARACHUTE TROOPS	NO. OF CONTAINERS (MK. I (T) OR MK. III)	NO. OF KIT BAGS	GALL. OF FUEL				TOTAL FUEL	GALL. OF OIL
				TANK NOS.					
				1	2–5	6	7		
1	15	9	—	41	FULL	FULL	FULL	2,135	
2	20	8	—	—	FULL	FULL	233	2,019	FULL
3	20	12	—	—	FULL	FULL	38	1,824	(132)
4	22	12	—	—	FULL	135	—	1,759	

(ii) Containers at 400 lb. each, no kit bags

CASE	NO. OF PARACHUTE TROOPS	NO. OF CONTAINERS (MK. I (T) OR MK. III)	NO. OF KIT BAGS	GALL. OF FUEL				TOTAL FUEL	GALL. OF OIL
				TANK NOS.					
				1	2–5	6	7		
5	15	9	—	—	FULL	FULL	287	2,073	
6	20	8	—	—	FULL	FULL	177	1,963	FULL
7	20	12	—	—	FULL	117	—	1,741	(132)
8	22	12	—	—	FULL	51	—	1,675	

(iii) Containers at 400 lb. each, kit bags at 40 lb. each

CASE	NO. OF PARACHUTE TROOPS	NO. OF CONTAINERS (MK. I (T) OR MK. III)	NO. OF KIT BAGS	GALL. OF FUEL				TOTAL FUEL	GALL. OF OIL
				TANK NOS.					
				1	2–5	6	7		
9	15	9	15	—	FULL	FULL	183	1,969	
10	20	9	5	—	FULL	FULL	74	1,860	FULL
11	20	9	8	—	FULL	FULL	57	1,843	(132)
12	20	6	10	—	FULL	FULL	213	1,999	

(iv) Containers at 400 lb. each, kit bags at 60 lb. each

CASE	NO. OF PARACHUTE TROOPS	NO. OF CONTAINERS (MK. I (T) OR MK. III)	NO. OF KIT BAGS	GALL. OF FUEL				TOTAL FUEL	GALL. OF OIL
				TANK NOS.					
				1	2–5	6	7		
13	15	9	15	—	FULL	FULL	141	1,927	
14	20	9	5	—	FULL	FULL	60	1,846	FULL
15	20	9	8	—	FULL	FULL	35	1,821	(132)
16	20	6	10	—	FULL	131	188	1,943	

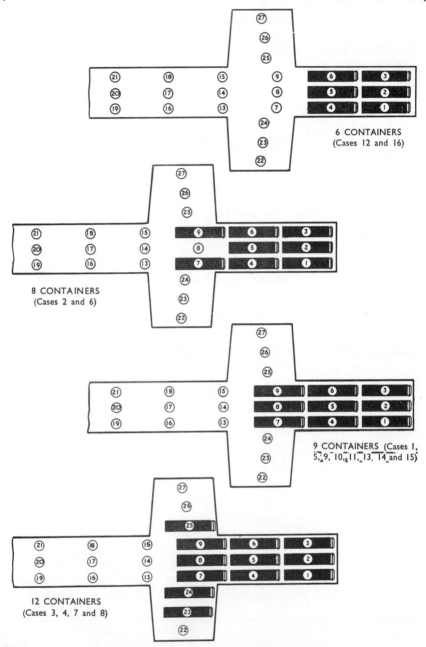

6 CONTAINERS
(Cases 12 and 16)

8 CONTAINERS
(Cases 2 and 6)

9 CONTAINERS (Cases 1,
5, 9, 10, 11, 13, 14 and 15)

12 CONTAINERS
(Cases 3, 4, 7 and 8)

FIG. 1   Position of containers on bomb carriers

STIRLING IV - LOADING AND C.G. DATA

Ballast

11. In the tactical loading cases 9 to 15, 140 lb. of ballast must be carried in the nose ballast stowage. In case 16, the ballast weight must be increased to 340 lb.

Parachute troop positions

12. The table below gives the mean C.G. of the parachute troops in feet aft of datum for the three conditions, take-off, flight to target, and action stations.

Mk. I (T) or Mk. III containers carried and the bomb racks on to which they are loaded for each of the sixteen tactical loads for which the aircraft has been cleared. The various loadings are illustrated in fig. 1.

16. The maximum weight of the containers is given in the sub-para. headings in para. 10

CASE	NUMBER OF PARACHUTE TROOPS	NUMBER OF KITBAGS	POSITION OF MEAN C.G. OF PARACHUTE TROOPS (FT. AFT OF DATUM)			
			TAKE-OFF AND LANDING	FLIGHT TO TARGET	ACTION STATIONS	
					PARACHUTE TROOPS WITHOUT KITBAGS	PARACHUTE TROOPS WITH KITBAGS
			(KITBAGS AT REST STATION)			
1 & 5	15	—	23·0	23·0	23·5	—
2 & 6	20	—	21·0	23·0	22·75	—
3 & 7	20	—	21·0	23·0	22·75	—
4 & 8	22	—	18·0	21·0	21·5	—
9 & 13	15	15	23·0	23·0	—	23·5
10 & 14	20	5	21·0	23·0	18·25	31·5
11 & 15	20	8	21·0	23·0	16·0	28·3
12 & 16	20	10	21·0	23·0	17·0	27·5

13. Kit bags, when carried, should be stowed at the rest station so that their C.G. is 8·8 ft. aft of datum during take-off and flight to target. The kit bags must be collected when the troops move to action stations. One C.G. position is quoted for the troops with kit bags and another for those without kit bags when they are at action stations.

Weight of parachute troops

14. The weight of each parachutist with rifle valise and without kit bag must not exceed 237 lb.

Container loading

15. The following table gives the number of

Centre of gravity

17. When the aircraft is loaded according to the above instructions and with the crew at their normal stations, except in the circumstances detailed in the table in para. 18, the C.G. will at all times remain within the permissible ranges of C.G. movement as follows:—

Take-off: 9·125 to 10·083 ft. aft of datum

Flight to target: 9·15 to 10·333 ft. aft of datum

Landing: 8·55 to 10·208 ft. aft of datum

CASE	NUMBER OF MK. I (T) OR MK. III CONTAINERS	BOMB STATIONS			
		ROW 1	ROW 2	ROW 3	WING CELLS
1, 5, 9, 10, 11, 13, 14, and 15	9	1, 2, 3	4, 5, 6	7, 8, 9	—
2 and 6	8	1, 2, 3	4, 5, 6	7, 9	—
3, 4, 7, and 8	12	1, 2, 3	4, 5, 6	7, 8, 9	23, 24, 25
12 and 16	6	1, 2, 3	4, 5, 6	—	—

STIRLING IV - LOADING AND C.G. DATA

18. The table below gives the movements of the crew that are necessary under certain conditions to keep the C.G. within the permissible range of C.G. movement.

CONDITION	POSITION OF CREW
Parachute troops at action stations	In each loading case the BOMB AIMER should be at his station
Limitation of range (extreme range)	In each loading case the REAR GUNNER should move to nose before troops take up action stations
Landing with parachute troops and containers aboard	In each loading case the REAR GUNNER should move to nose

Loading and C.G. schedule

19. When the load to be carried in the aircraft has been decided upon, a loading and C.G. schedule must be compiled to check that the C.G. positions and all-up weights for the various conditions are within the prescribed limits.

20. Care should be taken when compiling the schedule to establish accurate figures for the aircraft tare and military load as well as for the airborne forces load. It is recommended that a separate schedule be compiled for each aircraft.

21. If any further information on the compilation of the schedules is required, reference should be made to Sect. 4, Chap. 1 of A.P.1660 C and D, Vol. I.

22. The schedule given below is for a typical case only, 20 parachute troops and 12 containers at 400 lb., and should only be used as a guide.

ITEM OF LOAD	WEIGHT lb.	MOMENT ARM (ft.) −	MOMENT ARM (ft.) +	MOMENTS (lb. ft.) −	MOMENTS (lb. ft.) +
TAKE-OFF					
Basic weight (tare plus removable military load) ...	46,736				464,862
Fuel tank. No. 2 662 gallons (full)	4,766		9·14		43,550
3 126 gallons (full)	907		13·35		12,070
4 508 gallons (full)	3,658		9·16		33,520
5 328 gallons (full)	2,362		9·18		21,676
6 117 gallons (full)	842		9·19		7,738
Oil: 132 gallons (full) ...	1,188				4,882
Containers: 3 at row 1	1,200	5·6		6,720	
3 at row 2	1,200		0·9		1,080
3 at row 3	1,200		7·4		8,880
3 in wing cells	1,200		8·2		9,840
20 parachute troops at take-off positions	4,740		21·0		99,540
	69,999			6,720	707,638
					6,720
C.G.: 10·01 aft of datum					700,918
FLIGHT TO TARGET					
Basic weight (tare plus removable military load) ...	46,736				464,862
Fuel tank: No. 2 522 gallons	3,758		9·14		34,348
3 126 gallons (full)	907		13·31		12,070
4 508 gallons (full)	3,658		9·16		33,520
5 328 gallons (full)	2,362		9·18		21,676
6 117 gallons (full)	842		9·19		7,738
Oil: 132 gallons (full)	1,188				4,882
Containers: 3 at row 1	1,200	5·6		6,720	
3 at row 2	1,200		0·9		1,080
3 at row 3	1,200		7·4		8,880
3 in wing cells	1,200		8·2		9,840
20 parachute troops at flight to target positions ...	4,740		23·0		109,020
	68,991			6,720	707,916
					6,720
C.G.: 10·16 ft. aft of datum					701,196

STIRLING IV - LOADING AND C.G. DATA

ITEM OF LOAD	WEIGHT lb.	MOMENT ARM (ft.) −	MOMENT ARM (ft.) +	MOMENTS (lb. ft.) −	MOMENTS (lb. ft.) +
FLIGHT TO TARGET (AT LIMIT OF RADIUS)					
Basic weight (tare plus removable military load) ...	46,736				464,862
Fuel tank: No. 3 126 gallons (full)	907		13·31		12,070
4 138 gallons	994		9·16		9,105
5 328 gallons (full)	2,362		9·18		21,676
6 117 gallons	842		9·19		7,738
Oil: 132 gallons (full)	1,188				4,882
Containers: 3 at row 1	1,200	5·6		6,720	
3 at row 2	1,200		0·9		1,080
3 at row 3	1,200		7·4		8,880
3 in wing cells	1,200		8·2		9,840
20 parachute troops at flight to target positions ...	4,740		23·0		109,020
	62,569			6,720	649,153
					6,720
C.G.: 10·27 ft. aft of datum					642,433
FLIGHT TO TARGET (AT LIMIT OF RANGE)					
Basic weight (tare plus removable military load) ...	46,736				464,862
Oil: 132 gallons	1,188				4,882
Containers: 3 at row 1	1,200	5·6		6,720	
3 at row 2	1,200				1,080
3 at row 3	1,200				8,880
3 in wing cells	1,200				9,840
20 parachute troops at flight to target positions ...	4,740				109,020
	57,464			6,720	598,564
					6,720
C.G.: 10·29 ft. aft of datum					591,844
ACTION STATIONS (AT LIMIT OF RADIUS)					
Basic weight (tare plus removable military load) ...	46,736				464,862
Fuel tank: No. 3 126 gallons (full)	907		13·31		12,070
4 138 gallons	994		9·16		9,105
5 328 gallons (full)	2,362		9·18		21,676
6 117 gallons	842		9·19		7,738
Oil: 132 gallons (full)	1,188				4,882
Containers: 3 at row 1	1,200	5·6		6,720	
3 at row 2	1,200		0·9		1,080
3 at row 3	1,200		7·4		8,880
3 in wing cells	1,200		8·2		9,840
20 parachute troops at action stations	4,740		22·75		107,835
Moment for bomb aimer moving to station				1,685	
Moment for wireless operator moving aft of aperture					8,678
	62,569			8,405	656,646
					8,405
C.G.: 10·36 ft. aft of datum					648,241
ACTION STATIONS (AT LIMIT OF RADIUS) *(Men and containers dropped)*					
Basic weight (tare plus removable military load) ...	46,736				464,862
Fuel tank: No. 3 126 gallons (full)	907		13·31		12,070
4 138 gallons	994		9·16		9,105
5 328 gallons (full)	2,362		9·18		21,676
6 117 gallons	842		9·19		7,738
Oil: 132 gallons (full)	1,188				4,882
Moment for bomb aimer moving to station				1,685	
Moment for wireless operator moving aft of aperture					8,678
	53,029			1,685	529,011
					1,685
C.G.: 9·94 ft. aft of datum					527,326

STIRLING IV - LOADING AND C.G. DATA

ITEM OF LOAD	WEIGHT lb.	MOMENT ARM (ft.)		MOMENT (lb. ft.)	
		−	+	−	+
ACTION STATIONS (*AT LIMIT OF RANGE*)					
Basic weight (tare plus removable military load) ...	46,736				464,862
Oil: 132 gallons (full)	1,188				4,882
Containers: 3 at row 1	1,200	5·6		6,720	
3 at row 2	1,200		0·9		1,080
3 at row 3	1,200		7·4		8,880
3 in wing cells	1,200		8·2		9,840
20 parachute troops at action stations ...	4,740		22·75		107,835
Moment for bomb aimer moving to station				1,685	
Moment for rear gunner moving to nose				14,060	
Moment for wireless operator moving aft of aperture					8,678
	57,464			22,465	606,057
					22,465
C.G.: 10·15 ft. aft of datum					583,592
ACTION STATIONS (*AT LIMIT OF RANGE*)					
(*Men and containers dropped*)					
Basic weight (tare plus removable military load) ...	46,736				464,862
Oil: 132 gallons (full)	1,188				4,882
Moment for bomb aimer moving to station				1,685	
Moment for rear gunner moving to nose				14,060	
	47,924			15,745	469,744
					15,745
C.G.: 9·47 ft. aft of datum					453,999
LANDING (*ALL FUEL USED*)					
Basic weight (tare plus removable military load) ...	46,736				464,862
Oil: 132 gallons (full)	1,188				4,882
C.G.: 9·80 ft. aft of datum	47,924				469,744
LANDING (*ALL FUEL USED*)					
(*Men and containers aboard*)					
Basic weight (tare plus removable military load) ...	46,736				464,862
Oil: 132 gallons (full)	1,188				4,882
Containers: 3 at row 1	1,200	5·6		6,720	
3 at row 2	1,200		0·9		1,080
3 at row 3	1,200		7·4		8,880
3 in wing cells	1,200		8·2		9,840
20 parachute troops at take-off positions	4,740		21·0		99,540
Moment for rear gunner moving to nose				14,060	
	57,464			20,780	589,084
					20,780
C.G.: 9·87 ft. aft of datum					568,304

This leaf issued in reprint incorporating A.L's 1 to 15
July, 1945

AIR PUBLICATION 2453A
Vol. I   Part 2   Sect. 2

≡STIRLING IV-TECHNICAL PROCEDURE IN FLYING≡

LIST OF CONTENTS

LIST OF ILLUSTRATIONS

General

1. This chapter deals with the technical procedure in flight when the aircraft is used for the carriage and dropping of parachute troops and equipment.

Air drill

2. The special duties of the aircrew during a parachuting operation are as follows:—

(i) *Before taxying out for take-off:* The captain of the aircraft ensures that the parachute troops know their ditching drill, if flying over the sea, and their crash positions in case of an emergency landing. He tests the intercomm. with the stick commander. The bomb aimer checks the signal lights, strops and snap hook pins and ensures that his bomb panel is working satisfactorily. The parachute troops normally bring with them certain items of equipment and it is the responsibility of the captain to see that these items of equipment are arranged in a position where they will not foul any controls or interfere with the opening of the parachute troop doors. Such equipment will normally be stacked as far forward in the aircraft as possible for the take-off.

(ii) *Before take-off:* The captain orders "Take-off positions" and, after the troops have taken up their positions as indicated in fig. 1 to 7, the stick commander replies: "O.K. take-off positions".

(iii) *Normal flying after take-off:* The captain orders: "Travelling positions" and the troops take up positions as indicated in fig. 1 to 7.

(iv) *20 minutes before dropping time:* The captain orders "Prepare for action". The wireless operator moves aft and checks that the static rail container release switch is not depressed, and that the retaining pin on the special roller carriage is correctly positioned. He reports to the bomb aimer, who selects the containers and the order in which they are to be dropped. The engineer moves aft and assists the wireless operator to lower and lock the tail guard down. The engineer returns to his panel. If any parachute troops are dropping with kit bags, they collect them from the rest station stowage and put them on in the manner described in para. 4. All the troops then arrange themselves in their correct order for dropping and attach their static line D-rings to the appropriate strops. The wireless operator opens the top door of the aperture and reports to the captain: "Tail guard down, top door open". He remains aft of the aperture facing the parachute troops.

Note.—If the troops are to be dropped at the extreme range of action the rear gunner should move forward to the nose before any members of the crew, or any of the parachute troops, move.

(v) 5 minutes before dropping time: Captain orders: "Action stations" and then reduces speed to 130/135 m.p.h. I.A.S., increases the engine revs. to 2,400 and opens the bomb doors. The parachute troops stand up facing the aperture ready to jump. The stick commander removes his intercomm. helmet and replaces it with his steel helmet. He holds his intercomm. helmet to his ear until the red signal light goes on in order to maintain intercomm. with the captain. The wireless operator opens the bottom aperture door and reports to the captain, "Bottom door open". The air bomber calls out the minutes to go, on the intercomm. before the parachutists leave the aircraft, and the wireless operator holds up the relative number of fingers representing the minutes to go, to the parachute troops.

(vi) 15 seconds before dropping time: The air bomber or navigator switches on the red signal light and calls out the seconds to go to the dropping time. He switches on the green signal light one second before the dropping time and the parachute troops leave the aircraft.

WARNING

The parachute troops should stand as near the centre of the forward edge of the aperture as possible to avoid a twisting effect as they enter the slipstream.

(vii) Container dropping: If the containers are dropped with the delay action device, the men may leave the aircraft in an unbroken stick. If the delay action device is not fitted, a pause must be made at some point in the stick to allow the containers to fall clear. The duration of this pause and the point at which it occurs in the stick is given in para. 11 and 13.

(viii) Immediately after dropping: The wireless operator reports: "All gone". The air bomber pulls the bomb jettison toggle. The captain keeps his air speed under 140 m.p.h. I.A.S. and closes his bomb doors. The engineer moves aft and prepares the strops for winding in. When he is ready he reports to the captain who orders the navigator aft. The navigator and engineer then wind in the strops. If the strops have to be jettisoned the engineer must cut the webbing inside the fuselage.

Note.—Particular attention should be paid to para. 14, 15, and 16 which fully describe the procedure for retrieving or jettisoning the strops.

When the strops have been retrieved or jettisoned the wireless operator closes the aperture doors and reports to the captain, "Doors closed". The captain then returns to normal cruising speed and engine settings. The engineer moves right aft and assists the wireless operator to raise and lock the tail guard. The wireless operator reports to the captain: "Tail guard up". He and the engineer then return to their normal duties.

Note.—The composition of the tactical loading cases referred to in fig. 1 to 7 is given in Chap. 2, para. 10 (i) to (iv).

Method of jumping

3. Each parachutist must jump from the centre of the forward edge of the aperture. He should drop through the aperture in the normal alert position. If a kitbag is carried it should be steadied by holding the top of it with both hands.

This leaf issued in reprint incorporating A.L's I to 15
July, 1945

AIR PUBLICATION 2453A
Vol. I   Part 2   Sect. 2   Chap. 3

STIRLING IV-TECHNICAL PROCEDURE IN FLYING

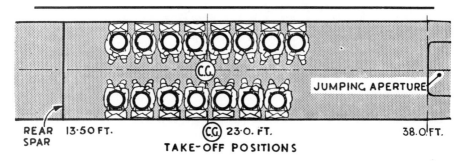

REAR SPAR   13·50 FT.   (C.G) 23·0. FT.   38.0 FT.

TAKE-OFF POSITIONS

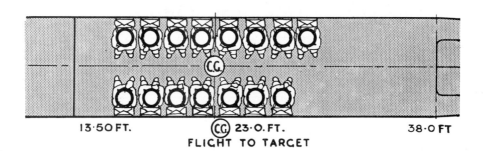

13·50 FT.   (C.G) 23·0. FT.   38·0 FT

FLIGHT TO TARGET

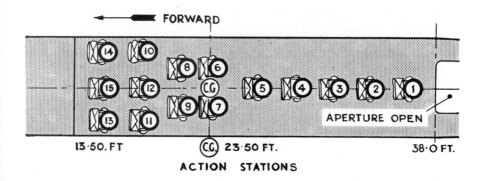

13·50. FT   (C.G) 23·50 FT.   38·0 FT.

ACTION STATIONS

(C.G) MEAN C.G. OF TROOPS WITHOUT KIT BAGS IN FT AFT OF DATUM

FIG. I   *Troop positions (cases I and 5)*

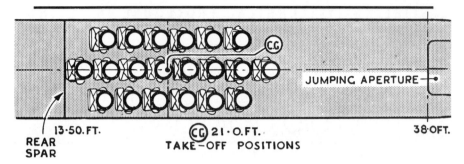

13·50.FT.   C.G 21·0.FT.   38·0FT.

REAR SPAR   **TAKE-OFF POSITIONS**

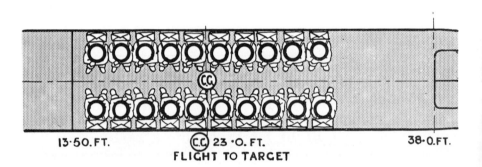

13·50.FT.   C.G 23·0.FT.   38·0.FT.

FLIGHT TO TARGET

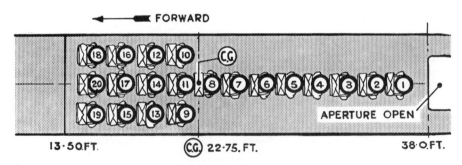

13·50.FT.   C.G 22·75.FT.   38·0.FT.

ACTION STATIONS

(C.G.) MEAN C.G OF TROOPS WITHOUT KIT BAGS IN FT. AFT OF DATUM

FIG. 2   *Troop positions (cases 2, 3, 6 and 7)*

This leaf issued in reprint incorporating A.L's 1 to 15
July, 1945

AIR   PUBLICATION   2453A
Vol. 1   Part 2   Sect. 2   Chap. 3

≡STIRLING IV-TECHNICAL PROCEDURE IN FLYING≡

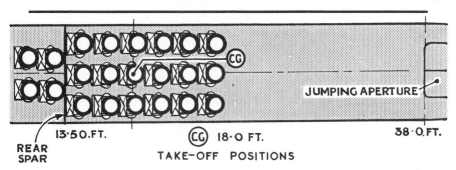

13·50.FT.   (CG) 18·0 FT.   38·0.FT.

REAR
SPAR   TAKE–OFF POSITIONS

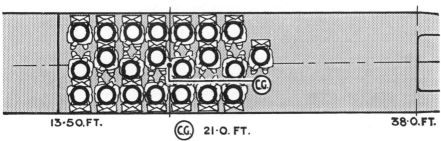

13·50.FT.   (CG) 21·0. FT.   38·0.FT.

FLIGHT TO TARGET

← FORWARD

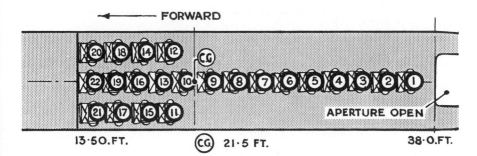

13·50.FT.   (CG) 21·5 FT.   38·0.FT.

ACTION STATIONS

(CG) MEAN   C.G. OF TROOPS WITHOUT KIT BAGS IN FT. AFT OF DATUM

FIG. 3   *Troop positions (cases 4 and 8)*

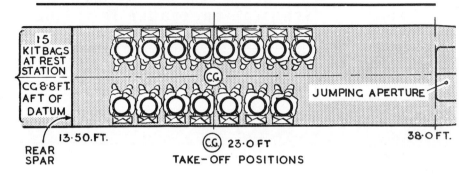

15 KITBAGS AT REST STATION

CG 8·8FT. AFT OF DATUM

JUMPING APERTURE

13·50.FT.

REAR SPAR

(CG) 23·0 FT

38·0 FT.

TAKE-OFF POSITIONS

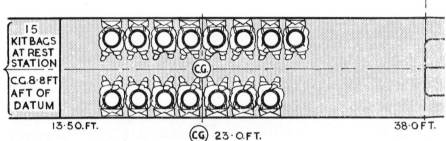

15 KITBAGS AT REST STATION

C.G. 8·8 FT AFT OF DATUM

13·50.FT.

38·0 FT.

(CG) 23·0.FT.

FLIGHT TO TARGET

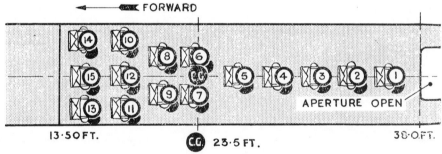

FORWARD

APERTURE OPEN

13·50FT.

38·0.FT.

(CG) 23·5 FT.

ACTION STATIONS

(CG) MEAN   CG OF TROOPS WITHOUT KIT BAGS IN FT AFT OF DATUM

(CG) MEAN   CG OF TROOPS WITH KIT BAGS IN FT AFT OF DATUM

FIG. 4

Troop positions (cases 9 and 13)

STIRLING IV-TECHNICAL PROCEDURE IN FLYING

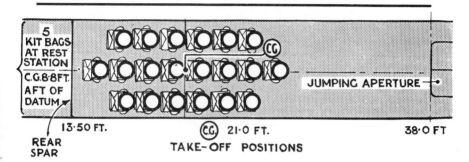

TAKE-OFF POSITIONS

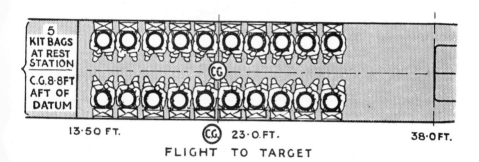

FLIGHT TO TARGET

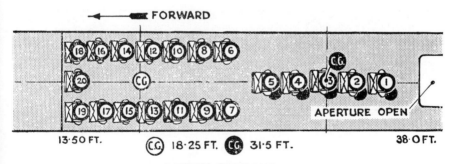

ACTION STATIONS

(CG) MEAN C.G. OF TROOPS WITHOUT KIT BAGS IN FT. AFT OF DATUM

(CG) MEAN C.G. OF TROOPS WITH KIT BAGS IN FT. AFT OF DATUM

FIG. 5   *Troop positions (cases 10 and 14)*

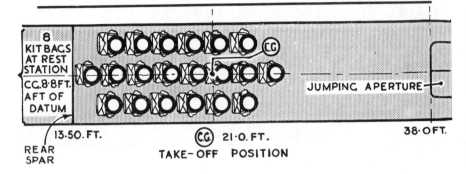

8 KIT BAGS AT REST STATION

C.C.8·8FT. AFT OF DATUM

JUMPING APERTURE

13·50. FT.

REAR SPAR

(C.G) 21·0. FT.

38·0 FT.

TAKE–OFF POSITION

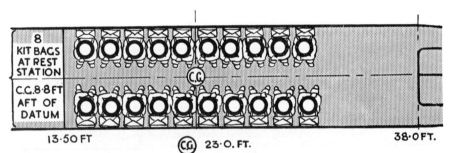

8 KIT BAGS AT REST STATION

C.C.8·8FT AFT OF DATUM

13·50 FT

(C.G) 23·0. FT.

38·0 FT.

FLIGHT TO TARGET

FORWARD

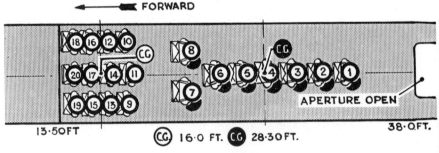

APERTURE OPEN

13·50 FT

(C.G) 16·0 FT. (C.G) 28·30 FT.

38·0 FT.

ACTION STATIONS

(C.G) MEAN   C.G. OF TROOPS WITHOUT KIT BAGS IN FT AFT OF DATUM

(C.G) MEAN   C.G OF TROOPS WITH KIT BAGS IN FT AFT OF DATUM

FIG. 6

Troop positions (cases 11 and 15)

≡STIRLING IV-TECHNICAL PROCEDURE IN FLYING≡

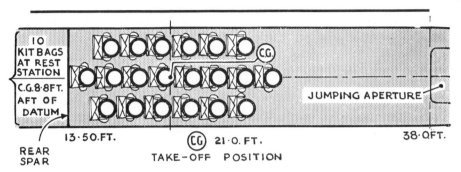

TAKE-OFF POSITION

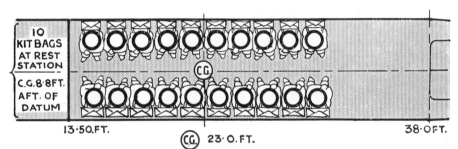

FLIGHT TO TARGET

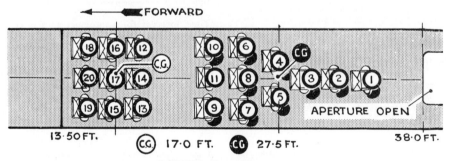

ACTION STATIONS

(CG) MEAN C.G. OF TROOPS WITHOUT KIT BAGS IN FT. AFT OF DATUM

(CG) MEAN C.G. OF TROOPS WITH KIT BAGS IN FT. AFT OF DATUM

FIG. 7

Troop positions (cases 12 and 16)

Wearing of kitbags

4. When the parachute troops who are to jump with kitbags have collected them from the rest station stowage they should strap them to their right legs and take up their action station positions.

Setting of pre-selector

5. If the containers are to be dropped with the delay action device, any pre-selector setting may be used, but a dead station must be selected between successive containers. To avoid sudden change of trim, however, it is recommended that the same settings as given in the table in para. 6 be used, with the addition of the dead stations between the containers.

6. The settings when the containers are to be dropped without the delay action device are tabulated below, together with the number of containers in the stick and the cases to which they refer.

No. OF CON- TAINERS	CASE	SETTING OF PRE-SELECTOR
6	12 and 16	4, 3, 6, 1, 5, 2
8	2 and 6	7, 3, 9, 1, 5, 2, 4, 6
9	1, 5, 9, 10, 11, 13, 14 and 15	7, 3, 9, 1, 5, 2, 4, 6, 8
12	3, 4, 7 and 8	23, 1, 25, 3, 24, 2, 7, 6, 8, 4, 9, 5

Setting of bomb selectors

7. The switches on the bomb selectors which correspond with the numbers on the pre-selector must be switched on. The drum switch must be set to distributor.

Setting of bomb distributor

8. The contact arm of the distributor must be set to 1. The time intervals setting between containers is as follows:—
  (i) *Containers dropped with delay action device.* The time interval setting on the distributor must be 0·35 secs.
  (ii) *Containers dropped without delay action device.* The time interval setting on the distributor must be 0·25 secs.
Some aircraft are fitted with two 16 point distributors and two settings are necessary in these cases.

Setting of delay action device

9. If the parachutes of the containers to be dropped are fitted with the delay opening device, it should be set to a time delay of 1·5 secs. This is most easily done before the parachutes are attached to the containers.

Position of special strop and carriage

10. The position the special strop and carriage occupies on the starboard static rail depends on whether or not the delay action device is fitted to the container parachutes and on how many parachute troops are in the stick to be dropped.

11. The positions the special strop and carriage occupy for the various conditions are tabulated below:—

CONDITION	POSITION OF SPECIAL STROP AND CARRIAGE
Containers dropped with delay action device	Snap hook attached to the static line D-ring of No. 2 parachutist
15 men in stick	Snap hook attached to the static line D-ring of No. 8 parachutist
20 or 22 men in stick	Snap hook attached to the static line D-ring of No. 10 parachutist

Time interval for containers to fall clear of parachutists

12. If the containers are dropped with the delay action device fitted, they are dropped throughout the stick, therefore no pause in the stick is necessary.

13. To allow the containers, when they are not fitted with the parachute delay opening device, to fall clear of the parachutists, one man must pause before jumping. This pause must occur between the jumping of the parachutist operating the container release switch and the next man's jump. The position in the stick of the parachutist attached to the special strop and carriage is given in para. 11.

≡STIRLING IV-TECHNICAL PROCEDURE IN FLYING≡

The pause is made up as follows:—

No. of containers ...	6	8	9	12
Between jumping of parachutist operating static rail container release switch and release of first container (secs.) ...	1·2	1·2	1·2	1·2
Travel of distributor arm (secs.) ...	1·25	1·75	2·0	2·75
For last container to fall clear (secs.) ...	0·9	0·9	0·9	0·9
Total time interval (secs.)	3·35	3·85	4·1	4·85

Retrieval of strops

14. The strops must be retrieved by the engineer and navigator. The engineer pulls out the cables from each winch drum in turn while the navigator holds the pawl out of engagement with the toothed wheel on the side of the drum. The engineer then loops the cables round all the strops on their own sides, pushing the loops as far down the strops as he can. He and the navigator then operate both winches simultaneously to bring in both sets of strops together. If the strops become entangled, the cable on the side affected should be slackened off slightly and the other wound up. This has the effect of pulling the strops away from the side on which the tangle occurs.

15. If necessary the strops may be retrieved manually by three men. All the strops should be encircled by a rope and then hauled in.

WARNING

Care must be taken not to allow the strops and bags to slip back after they have been pulled forward of the tail guard, as they may pass over the guard rail and foul the tail.

Jettisoning of strops

16. If necessary the strops may be jettisoned in an emergency by first raising the tail guard, to avoid any risk of the free ends passing over the guard rail and becoming entangled with it, and then cutting the webbing inside the fuselage as quickly as possible. The aircraft must be flown straight and level during the jettisoning.

WARNING

Great care must be exercised when raising the tail guard as it is likely to slam back violently under the load of the trailing strops, static lines and bags.

Handling

17. For the dropping operation the aircraft should be flown straight and level at 130/135 m.p.h. I.A.S. under the following conditions and settings:—

    (i) Bomb doors open

    (ii) Tail guard lowered

    (iii) Elevator trim + 8½

18. The use of ⅓ flap may be found to assist, particularly if the aircraft weight at the time of dropping the parachute troops and containers is still high and if the weather conditions are bumpy.

19. At the speed recommended above, turns up to rate 1 can be accomplished. When a stick of 20 men and 12 containers are dropped the trim settings change from +8½ to +5 approximately.

20. For all other handling information reference should be made to A.P.1660A, C and D—P.N. Pilot's Notes for the Stirling I, III, and IV.

This leaf issued in reprint incorporating A.L's I to 15
July, 1945

CHAPTER 4

STIRLING IV - EMERGENCY PROCEDURE

General

1—It may be necessary for the parachute troops and crew to abandon the aircraft in an emergency, either by parachute if over the land, or by dinghy after the aircraft has ditched.

2—Special emergency drills for the parachute troops and crew have been evolved to meet both these conditions. These drills should at all times be strictly adhered to.

3—This chapter should be read in conjunction with Section 4 of A.P.2095, Pilot's Notes General and Section 4 of A.P.1660A, and A.P.1660C, & D, Pilot's and Flight Engineer's Notes for the Stirling I, III, and IV.

Emergency parachute drill

4—The pilot must not give the order to abandon the aircraft if below 300 ft. or if over the sea or some other large expanse of water.

5—Members of the crew must check their parachute harness and remove their flying helmets before abandoning the aircraft from the exits specified in the drill.

6—The parachute troops should abandon the aircraft in the same way as they leave it for a normal operation. The method of giving the signal to abandon should be decided upon and clearly understood by all personnel before take-off.

7—The drill to be carried out by the parachute troops and crew is given in the form of captions to fig. 1, insets 1 to 9, which depict the various stages of the drill.

8—If the aircraft has to crash-land from below 300 ft. with the troops and crew on board they should take up the same positions as for ditching.

Safety equipment which may be carried

9—The normal port wing built-in stowage for the J type dinghy with complete provision for a crew of seven is retained in the Stirling IV.

10—In addition a maximum of three extra J type dinghies packed in H type valises may be carried for the use of the parachute troops. They are secured by means of quick-release straps in a stowage on the floor against the starboard wall of the fuselage between the wing spars.

11—The number of extra dinghies to be carried is left to the discretion of the Command concerned.

Ditching belts

12—Six ditching belts are provided at intervals down the fuselage. They are fixed in position at either end as shown in fig. 2, inset (a). When not in use the port toggles should be undone and the belts rolled up and stowed against the starboard wall of the fuselage and strapped to stiffener N, the third up from the floor.

Emergency ditching drill

13—The following drill must be observed in the event of the aircraft having to ditch:—

(i) Pilot orders "Dinghy, dinghy, prepare for ditching". The crew will warn the troops.

(ii) The Stick Commander co-ordinates and supervises the parachute troops and sees that the ditching belts are securely fixed as shown in fig. 2, inset (a). The troops will then take up their ditching positions.

(iii) Pilot orders or signals "Brace for impact"; each man must then brace himself in the manner shown in fig. 2, inset (b) and prepare for severe deceleration.

(iv) After the aircraft has ditched, the ditching belts should be released if possible, so that the minimum obstruction is presented. All personnel must then release their parachute harness. The parachute troops must dispose of any heavy equipment, retaining their life vests, water bottles and rations. The crew should put the dinghies into the water in the positions shown in fig. 3, while the parachute troops are discarding their heavy equipment.

(v) The parachute troops and crew should then leave the aircraft by the exits indicated in fig. 3, the troops inflating their life vests as they leave the aircraft. The crew can assist and direct where possible. The Stick Commander will control the exit of the men, endeavouring to keep an even proportion of troops in each dinghy. Care should be exercised to prevent damage to the dinghies when boarding. The first man in each dinghy should help to control it while the rest of the men embark. Two or three parachute packs should be thrown into the water as a safety precaution to provide temporary support for any men who may fall overboard; in addition several parachutes should be taken into the dinghies for extra warmth.

(vi) The Stick Commander casts off each dinghy or cuts it adrift from the aircraft, when full.

(vii) When clear of the aircraft every effort should be made to tie all the dinghies together; a safety line with quoit is attached to each dinghy and may be used for this purpose as well as for rescue purposes.

14—The glove paddles are for controlling the dinghies, and the weather aprons when fitted will save shipping much water under adverse weather conditions and provide a good protection against wind.

15—The crew should follow their normal dinghy drill as far as they are able to so do, taking up the positions indicated in fig. 2 when ditching.

PILOT NAV W/Op A/B ENG R/G TROOPS

① All crew at action stations. Pilot gives order, " Section, section, prepare to abandon aircraft." Crew and Stick Cmdr. acknowledge.

② Pilot destroys I.F.F. Nav. gives position of aircraft to Stick Cmdr., who acknowledges. W/Op., jettisons trailing aerial. A.B. fits parachute. Engineer fits parachute. R.G. leaves turret.

③ Pilot maintains control. Nav. leaves seat and fits parachute. W/Op., if time, sends emergency signal. A.B. opens front hatch. Engineer moves to aft of rear spar and plugs in i/c. R.G. collects and fits parachute and moves forward to parachute troops' aperture. Stick Cmdr. gives order " Hook up."

④ Nav. moves forward. W/Op. fits parachute. R.G. assists No. I to open and secure top door, opens lower hatch and secures handle. Stick Cmdr. (when stick is ready) reports to Pilot (who acknowledges).

STIRLING

5 Pilot orders Stick Cmdr. "Jump." Stick Cmdr. removes flying helmet. W/Op. moves forward. Stick jumps. Eng. informs Pilot when last parachute troop has gone.

6 Pilot orders crew to jump. A.B. leaves aircraft from front exit feet first, facing aft. Engineer moves aft to parachute troops' aperture. R.G. moves aft and leaves aircraft through OWN escape hatch.

7 Pilot leaves seat. Nav. leaves aircraft from front exit feet first, facing aft. Engineer leaves aircraft feet first, facing aft.

8 Pilot fits parachute, moves forward. W/Op. leaves aircraft from front exit, feet first facing aft.

9 Pilot leaves aircraft from front exit, feet first facing aft.

COMBINED EMERGENCY PARACHUTE DRILL FOR PARACHUTE TROOPS AND CREW FIG. I

This leaf issued in reprint incorporating A.L's 1 to 15
July, 1945

AIR PUBLICATION 2453A
Vol. I Part 2 Sect. 2 Chap. 4

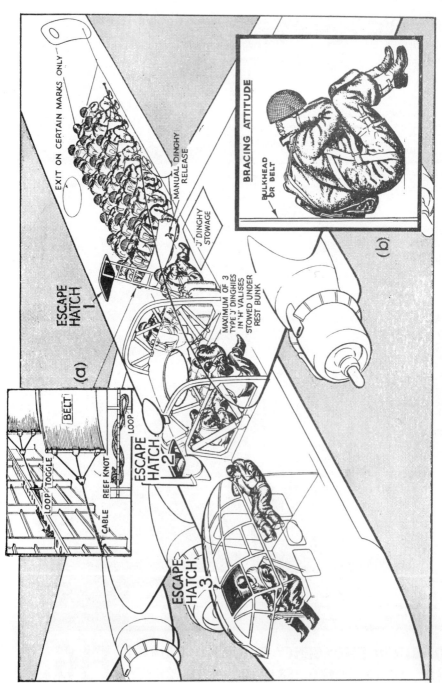

Troops and crew in ditching or crash positions

FIG. 2

Troops and crew boarding dinghies

FIG. 3

5

Albemarle I, II, V and VI, July 1945

ALBEMARLE I, II, V, AND VI—PARACHUTE TROOP INSTALLATIONS

LIST OF CONTENTS

LIST OF ILLUSTRATIONS

General

1. The Albemarles I, II, V, and VI have been cleared for the carriage and dropping of a maximum of 10 parachute troops and their equipment.

2. This chapter describes the parachute troop installations. Details of the C.G. and loading for all the tactical loads which the aircraft have been cleared to carry are given in Chapter 2. Chapter 3 describes the technical procedure in flying, while the emergency procedure for ditching, crash landing and abandoning in the air is given in Chapter 4.

3. The methods of loading the containers and other equipment carried on the bomb carriers will be found in A.P.2453B, Part 2, Section 3.

Modifications

4. Before the aircraft may be flown on a parachuting operation the following modifications must have been embodied:—

Mod. No.	Description
A.542	Airframe structure
A.543	Fixed electrics
A.544	Removable parts
A.689	Re-positioning of A.R.I.5506 and addition of A.R.I.5083
A.786	Non-slip covering on floor adjacent to aperture

Note . . . Embodiment of Mod. A.786 is only essential if parachute troops carrying rifle valises are to be dropped.

5. The following modifications may be incorporated:

Mod. No.	Description
A.688	Stowage for "J" type dinghy
A.743 A.744 }	Cooling aids, fans and spinners

ALBEMARLE I, II, V, AND VI—PARACHUTE TROOP INSTALLATIONS

Fig. 1.—Parachute troop installations—Looking aft

ALBEMARLE I, II, V, AND VI—PARACHUTE TROOP INSTALLATIONS

Fig. 2.—Parachute troop installations—Looking forward

Floor aperture (fig. I and 2)

6. An extension of the ventral turret hole gives an elongated aperture situated approximately six feet aft of the step. It is covered during the flight to the target by two doors; each door is hinged at its outboard edge. The starboard door has a flange along the top of its inboard edge which holds down the port door when both are closed and is itself fastened to the floor by a bolt at each end.

7. Each door, when open, is secured to the wall of the fuselage by a strap carrying a metal plate in which a slot is cut. The slot passes over the head of a turnbutton attached to the underside of each door.

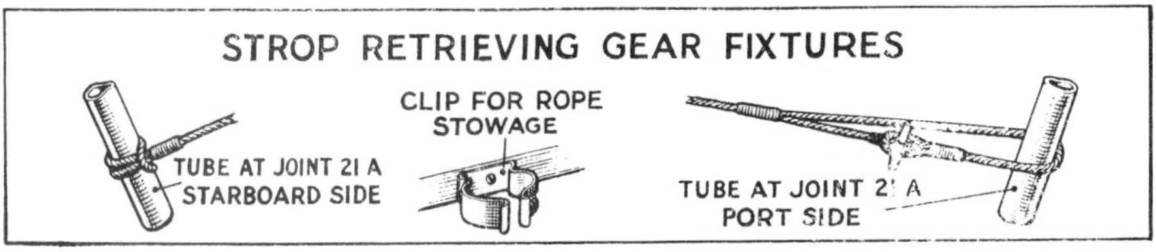

STROP RETRIEVING GEAR FIXTURES

CLIP FOR ROPE
STOWAGE

TUBE AT JOINT 21 A
STARBOARD SIDE

TUBE AT JOINT 2' A
PORT SIDE

Fig. 3.—Attachment of strop retrieving gear

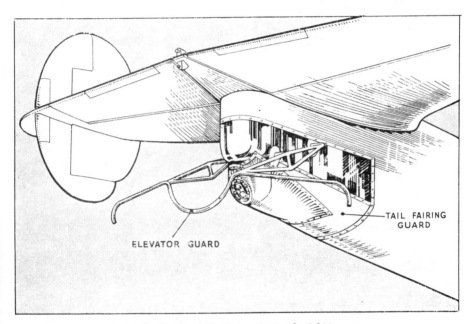

TAIL FAIRING
GUARD

ELEVATOR GUARD

Fig. 4.—Elevator guard and strengthening of tail fairing

WARNING

Great care should be taken to see that the doors are held securely open as the troops may hold the open edges for support as they jump.

Guard for tail fairing (fig. 4)

8. A shield of 20 s.w.g. metal is fitted over the lower part of the transparent tail fairing as shown in fig. 4 to prevent damage caused by the impact of the parachute bags during retrieval.

Elevator guard (fig. 4)

9. A tubular guard of curved construction

ALBEMARLE I, II, V, AND VI—PARACHUTE TROOP INSTALLATIONS

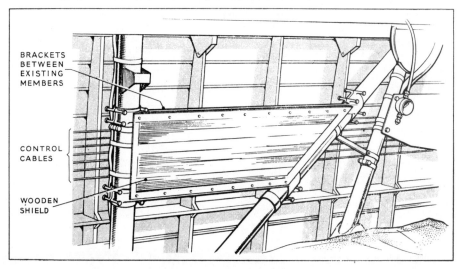

Fig. 5.—Guard for control wires

is mounted in a transverse position below the tail plane as shown in fig. 4 to prevent the parachute bags or static lines from fouling the elevators.

Control cable guard (fig. 5)

10. A wooden panel fitted over the control wires on the port side, just aft of the turret, as shown in fig. 5, prevents interference from parachute troops or their kit.

Static line rail (fig. 1, 2, and 6)

11. A static line rail of inverted "T" section to carry the strop carriages of the odd numbered strops is attached to the fuselage members near the roof on the starboard side, by means of tubular struts.

12. The strop carriages are prevented from riding off the forward end of the rail by a spring catch, while a permanent stop is provided at the aft end to prevent the carriages from running off the rail after the exit of the parachute troops

Static line cable (fig. 1, 2, and 6)

13. A static line cable of 60 cwt. steel, attached at each end to the port wall of the fuselage near the roof, as shown in fig. 1, 2, and 6, carries the triangular D rings of the strops on the port side.

Strops (fig. 7)

14. The strops are made of 1¾ in. wide heavy white double webbing and are all 6 ft. long. The method of folding them is illustrated in fig. 7.

15. The permissible tolerance on the dead length of the strops is ±1 inch   The dead length of the strops is to be measured from the inside face of the snap hook to the end of the webbing at the carriage or D ring end.

16. The position of the special strop and carriage, mentioned in para. 18, on the static line rail is given in Chapter 3.

Caution.—Due to cases of accidental release of containers by strop carriages running down the

172

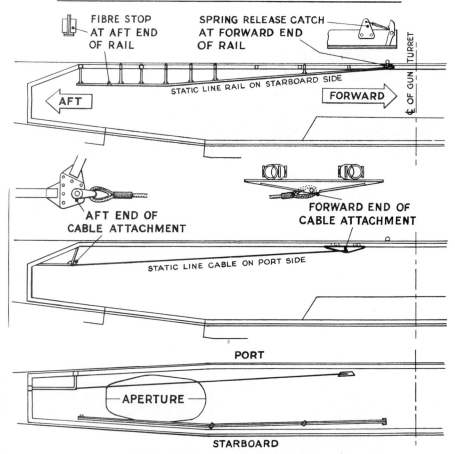

FIBRE STOP AT AFT END OF RAIL

SPRING RELEASE CATCH AT FORWARD END OF RAIL

STATIC LINE RAIL ON STARBOARD SIDE

AFT

FORWARD

℄ OF GUN TURRET

AFT END OF CABLE ATTACHMENT

FORWARD END OF CABLE ATTACHMENT

STATIC LINE CABLE ON PORT SIDE

PORT

APERTURE

STARBOARD

Fig. 6.—Static line rail and cable attachments

static line rail, the strops must be tied back at the forward end of the rail when the aircraft is not being used for parachuting.

Strop retrieving gear (fig. 1, 2, and 3)

17. To enable the strops, static lines, and parachute bags to be retrieved after the troops have jumped, a strop retrieving gear has been devised. A rope secured at floor level to the tube at joint 21a on the starboard side is passed underneath the door hinges, across to the port side wall aft of the aperture and back along the port side, under the door hinges, and fastened to the tube at joint 21a on the port side. The rope is held in position by ten spring clips, distributed along its length, screwed to wooden longerons at floor level.

173

ALBEMARLE I, II, V, AND VI—PARACHUTE TROOP INSTALLATIONS

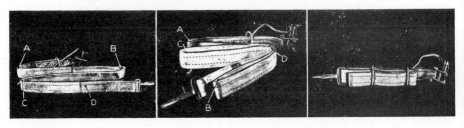

FOLDING OF STROPS
(I) FACING THE CLOSED SIDE OF SNAP HOOK, FOLD AT POINTS 'A','B' AND 'C'
(II) TAKE FOLD 'B' AND SNAP HOOK, BRING TO POINT 'C', FOLDING AT 'D'
(III) FASTEN WITH THE TWO RUBBER BANDS

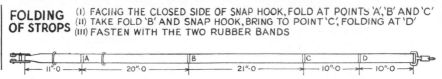

Fig. 7.—Folding the strops

Static rail container release switch (fig. 8)

18. The static rail container release switch is mounted on the outboard side of the static line rail above the centre of the aperture. It consists of a fixed plate carrying two micro-switches, wired in parallel, one at each end, and a second movable plate mounted in front of, and parallel to it, on two pins. The plates are held apart by springs passed over the pins and confined between the plates.

19. When the spring-loaded plunger on the special strop carriages is released by the withdrawal of the retaining pin, it presses the

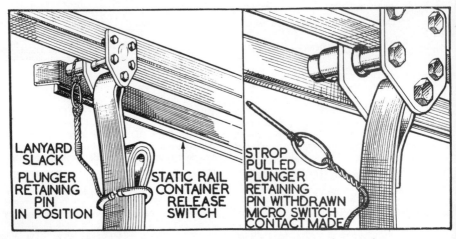

Fig. 8.—Special carriage for operation of static rail container release switch

ALBEMARLE I, II, V, AND VI—PARACHUTE TROOP INSTALLATIONS

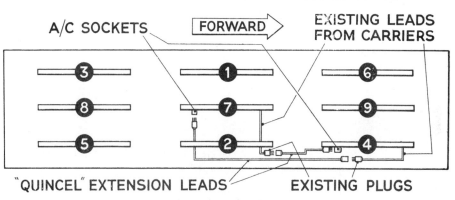

Fig. 9.—Re-wiring of bomb carriers

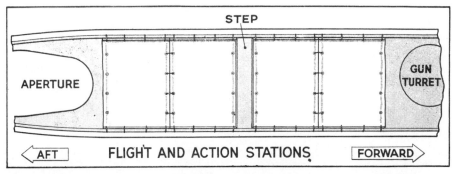

Fig. 10.—Positions of troop mattresses

plate outwards towards the fixed plate and actuates one or both of the micro-switches thereby starting the distributor.

20. The aft stop on the static line rail is placed so that there is sufficient length of rail beyond the switch to enable the plunger to ride out of engagement with it thus avoiding the possibility of overheating the distributor.

21. When micro-switches, Stores Ref. 5C/2126, are used, the rubber dust covers must be removed or the switches will remain permanently inoperative.

Plunger for operation of static rail container release switch (fig. 8)

22. A plunger sliding in a tube mounted on the outboard side of one of the strop carriages is held against a spring by a pin passing through the tube. A lanyard is spliced to a ring on the lower end of the pin, its other end being attached to a becket on the strop; the lanyard is slack whilst the strop to which it is attached remains folded.

23. When the parachutist, whose static line is attached to the strop operating the plunger,

ALBEMARLE I, II, V, AND VI—PARACHUTE TROOP INSTALLATIONS

leaves the aircraft, the lanyard becomes taut, withdrawing the pin and releasing the plunger which operates the static rail container release switch described in para. 18.

24. A breaking tie of No. 8 linen thread, Stores Ref. 15A/108, looped through the ring on the pin and over the tube containing the plunger, prevents the premature withdrawal of the pin.

Signal lights (fig. 1)

25. Two signal lights are mounted on a bracket in the roof of the fuselage over the middle of the aperture. The bottom of the bracket is parallel to the floor and prevents the lights being seen from the ground when the aperture doors are open.

26. The lamps, one red and one green, are of the cockpit type, Mk. I (Stores Ref. 5C/446).

27. The red light is a warning to the troops to be ready to jump, the green light is for giving the troops the signal to jump.

Abandon aircraft light (fig. 1)

28. An abandon aircraft light is mounted on a bracket in the roof of the fuselage on the port side of the signal lights.

Bomb distributor and selector

29. A 16-point bomb distributor and 16-point bomb selector are fitted in this aircraft. The distributor is operated by the static rail container release switch.

Bomb distributor circuit (fig. 9)

30. The bomb distributor circuit comprises the bomb distributor, the bomb selector and a series of numbered sockets in the bomb cells into which the cables from the bomb carrier electro-magnetic release units are plugged. The circuit is arranged so that stud No. 1 of the distributor corresponds to switch No. 1 of the selector and socket No. 1 of the bomb cell and so on. For the safe release of the containers dropped with parachute troops, how-ever, it is necessary to release container No. 7 before container No. 4. This is effected by using extension leads to connect bomb carriers 4 and 7 to sockets 7 and 4 respectively. This changes the firing order of the bomb stations from 1, 2, 3, 4, 6, 7, 9 to 1, 2, 3, 7, 6, 4, 9.

Mattresses (fig. 10)

31. To ensure a good foothold for the troops when moving down the fuselage towards the aperture, four mattresses, each measuring 5 ft. by 3 ft., are laid lengthwise in pairs across the floor of the aircraft, two forward and two aft of the step. The pairs are tied at the edges to the fuselage members and to each other by lengths of 16 oz. cord and are not moved during a parachuting operation.

Dim lighting installation

32. A standard dim lighting installation (Stores Ref. 50/2299) is provided to accustom the eyes of the parachute troops to a gradual reduction in illumination prior to leaving the aircraft during the hours of darkness. It comprises two six watt lamps attached to the fuselage roof by bulldog clips, a dimmer switch and plug for insertion in the existing ceiling socket. The forward light is positioned adjacent to the turret, the aft light on the former adjacent to the dinghy stowage. The dimmer is clipped to the gusset plates on joint 20.

Special cradles and straps for carrying containers

33. Mk. I(T) and Mk. III containers, when carried on the Albemarle, must be fitted with Mk. II cradles (Stores Ref. 15C/205) and straps (Stores Ref. 15C/2020).

Positioning of container location device on containers

34. The fitting of the container location device to the containers carried on the Albemarle may be found in A.P.2453B, Vol. I, Part 4.

ALBEMARLE I, II, V, AND VI—PARACHUTE TROOP INSTALLATIONS

Method of loading trolleys when containers fitted with the delay action device are carried

35. Mk. II trolleys must be packed in Mk. I(T) containers when carried with containers fitted with the parachute delay opening device.

Accessories

36. The following accessories are required in aircraft used for parachute troop operations:—

    (i) One thermos flask.

    (ii) Two rubber urine bottles.

    (iii) A supply of paper "sick" bags.

ALBEMARLE I, II, V, AND VI—LOADING AND C.G. DATA

LIST OF CONTENTS

General

1. This Chapter deals with the effect on the C.G. of the specified tactical loads which may be carried in the Albemarle I, II, V, and VI for parachuting operations. The Aircraft Handbook, A.P.1688A, B, F, & G, Vol. I, Section 4, Chapter 1, gives a Loading and C.G. Diagram and Loading and C.G. Data Sheet for the aircraft. It also gives the effect of modifications on the tare weights and C.G. position.

2. A Loading and C.G. Schedule should be compiled for each aircraft. The weight and moment arms of the items which make up the tactical loads are listed in para. 23.

3. The Mk. VI aircraft referred to in this chapter are Albemarle Mk. VI Series I aircraft and are fitted with side loading doors.

WARNING

The tare C.G. of Mk. VI Series II aircraft may differ from that of Mk. VI Series I aircraft. This must be determined for each aircraft and the C.G. positions experienced under various load conditions must be very carefully checked.

Weight limitations

4. The all-up take-off weight of the Albemarle I, II, V, and VI must not exceed 36,500 lb.

5. The maximum permissible landing weight of the various marks of aircraft are as follows:—

Albemarle I ... ... 32,500 lb.

Albemarle II, V, and VI 34,500 lb.

Parachute troop loads

6. The aircraft has been cleared to carry the parachute troop loads listed below:—

(i) Ten men.

(ii) Ten men with ten 40 lb. kitbags.

(iii) Ten men with ten 60 lb. kitbags.

(iv) Ten men, three with rifle valises. The number of kitbags which may be carried are tabulated in para. 8.

Note.—When carrying the load mentioned in sub-para. (iii) a minimum of three containers must be carried which must be positioned on bomb carriers 4, 6, and 9.

7. Any tactical load differing from those quoted above either at the maximum permissible weight or a lesser weight should be checked for C.G. in the normal way.

ALBEMARLE I, II, V, AND VI—LOADING AND C.G. DATA

8. The maximum number of 40 lb. or 60 lb. kitbags which may be carried when the first three men in the stick carry rifle valises are tabulated below:—

WEIGHT OF KITBAG	NUMBER OF KITBAGS		
	ALBEMARLE I, II, and V	ALBEMARLE VI	
40 lb. 60 lb.	4 2	1 1	} Cooling aids not fitted
40 lb. 60 lb.	6 4	4 2	} Cooling aids fitted

Fuel

9. The full normal fuel capacity is 769 gall. To keep the C.G. within the specified limits the fuel must be consumed as detailed in para. 19 (i).

10. The maximum permissible fuel load for the Albemarle VI when ten parachute troops with ten 60 lb. kitbags and six 400 lb. Mk. I (T) or Mk. III containers are carried, is 753 gall. if the aircraft is not fitted with cooling aids. When cooling aids are fitted this must be reduced to 743 gall. For all other cases the full tankage may be utilised.

Oil

11. The full normal quantity of 59·25 gall. of oil is always carried.

Ballast—Albemarle VI

12. If cooling aids are not fitted, 55 lb. of ballast must be carried at the second pilot's position when ten parachute troops with 60 lb. kitbags are carried.

Parachute troop positions

13. The distance of the mean C.G. of the parachute troops in inches aft of the datum point, for the parachute troop load of ten men only, is given in Chapter 3, fig. 1. The C.G. positions for the other parachute troop loads must be determined for each loading and C.G. schedule compiled.

Weight of parachute troops

14. The weight of each parachutist with rifle valise and without kitbag must not exceed 237 lb.

Bomb carrier loadings

15. The following maximum loadings are possible:—

(i) Six Mk. I (T) or Mk. III containers each of a maximum weight of 400 lb., on bomb carriers 1, 2, 4, 6, 7, and 9.

(ii) Five Mk. I (T) or Mk. III containers, each of a maximum weight of 400 lb., on bomb carriers 2, 4, 6, 7, and 9, and two folding trolleys at stations 1 and 3.

(iii) A combination in which Type E or F containers may replace Mk. I (T) or Mk. III containers on bomb carriers 7 and 9.

16. If the container parachutes are fitted with the delay action device, the folding trolleys, if carried, must be packed in Mk. I (T) containers.

17. When ten men each with a 40 lb. or 60 lb. kitbag, or ten men with three rifle valises, are carried, a minimum of three containers must also be carried on bomb carriers 4, 6, and 9.

Centre of gravity

18. The permissible range of travel of the C.G. for all forms of flying is 69·5 in. to 84·0 in. aft of the datum point. For gentle manoeuvres only, however, movement of the C.G. to an extended aft limit of 85·4 ins. aft of the datum point is permissible.

19. In order to maintain the C.G. within the authorised limits it is essential that the following instructions be observed.

(i) *Consumption of fuel.*—Fuel from the wing tanks must be consumed first. If

This leaf issued in reprint incorporating A.L's 1 to 15
July, 1945

AIR   PUBLICATION   2453A
Vol. 1   Part 2   Sect. 3   Chap. 2

ALBEMARLE I, II, V, AND VI—LOADING
AND C.G. DATA

the full quantity of fuel is not required for a particular range, the fuselage tanks must be filled first and the remainder put in the wing tanks.

(ii) *Container loading.*—When ten men, each with a 40 lb. or 60 lb. kitbag, or ten men with three rifle valises and the maximum number of kitbags, as given in the table in para. 8, are carried, a minimum of three containers must also be carried, positioned on bomb carriers 4, 6, and 9.

(iii) *Troops and containers dropped.*—In all marks of aircraft fitted with cooling aids, except the Mk. VI, if more than 680 gall. of fuel remain in the tanks after the troops and containers have been dropped, the air gunner or some other member of the crew must move to a position aft of the turret.

(iv) *Landing with troops and containers dropped.*—In all marks of aircraft fitted with cooling aids, except the Mk. VI, the movement of a member of the crew is necessary as in (iii) above. This must be done irrespective of the quantity of fuel remaining in the tanks.

(v) *Landing with troops and containers on board.*—Movement forward of the aft parachutist, or an equivalent move forward by one or more of the other parachutists, to a position forward of the turret, is necessary if the aircraft has to land with parachute troops carrying 60 lb. kitbags on board at any time after the fuel from the wing tanks has been consumed. Alternatively the five kitbags carried by the men nearest the aperture may be moved forward to the crawlway or jettisoned. The foregoing instructions also apply if ten men, each with a 40 lb. kitbag, are carried in an Albemarle VI which is not fitted with cooling aids.

Practical ranges and radii of action

20. The practical ranges and radii of action for the tactical loads are 75 per cent. of the "still air" values, the safety margin being intended to allow for reasonable errors of

pilotage, a reasonable time over the target, the effect of moderate winds and other minor deviations from optimum flying conditions.

PARACHUTE TROOP LOAD	PRACTICAL RANGE IN MILES	PRACTICAL RADIUS OF ACTION IN MILES
Ten men	1,050	550

21. When ten men with 60 lb. kitbags, and six 400 lb. Mk. I (T) or Mk. III containers are carried in the Albemarle VI, the practical ranges and radii are limited because of the reduced maximum fuel load which may be carried, as detailed in para. 10.

22. The reduced ranges and radii are tabulated below:—

PARACHUTE TROOP LOAD	PRACTICAL RANGE IN MILES	PRACTICAL RADIUS OF ACTION IN MILES
Ten men with ten 60 lb. kitbags and six Mk. I(T) or Mk. III containers of 400 lb. weight— cooling aids not fitted	1,025	535
Ten men with ten 60 lb. kitbags and six Mk. I (T) or Mk. III containers of 400 lb. weight— cooling aids fitted	1,000	525

Note.—The practical range figures are calculated on the assumption that the troops are either dropped or landed with the aircraft at the end of its outward flight. The practical radius of action figures are calculated on the assumption that the troops and containers are dropped at the end of the outward flight and the aircraft returns to base.—

Weight and moment arm of main items of tactical loads

23. The following list gives the weight, moment arm, and moment of the main items included in the tactical loads:-

ITEM OF LOAD	WEIGHT lb.	MOMENT ARM (in.) −	+	MOMENT (lb. in.) −	÷
Mk. I(T) or Mk. III container on bomb carriers 4, 6, or 9 ...	350	13·4		4,690	
Mk. I(T) or Mk. III container on bomb carriers 4, 6, or 9 ...	400	13·4		5,360	
Mk. I(T) or Mk. III container on bomb carriers 1, 2, or 7 ...	350		87·2		30,500
Mk. I(T) or Mk. III container on bomb carriers 1, 2, or 7 ...	400		87·2		34,900
Type E container on bomb carrier 9	160	13·4		2,145	
Type E container on bomb carrier 7	160		87·2		14,000
Type F container on bomb carrier 9	200	13·4		2,680	
Type F container on bomb carrier 7	200		87·2		17,440
Mk. I folding trolley on bomb carrier 1	98		87·2		8,550
Mk. I folding trolley on bomb carrier 3	98		191·3		18,790
Mk. I folding trolley packed in a Mk. I(T) container on bomb carrier 1	180		87·2		15,700
Mk. I folding trolley packed in Mk. I(T) container on bomb carrier 3	180		191·3		34,500
Oil 59·25 gall.	533		58		30,900
Fuel centre section tank 204 gall.	1,469		53		77,860
Fuel rear fuselage tank 165 gall.	1,188		107		127,000
Fuel wing tanks (200 gall. each) 400 gall.	2,880		56		161,280
Ten parachute troops (take-off and flight to target positions) ...	2,370		251		595,000
Ten parachute troops (action stations positions)	2,370		261		619,000
Ten parachute troops with ten 40 lb. kitbags (take-off and flight to target positions)	2,770		251		695,000
Ten parachute troops with ten 40 lb. kitbags (action stations positions)	2,770		261		723,000
Ten parachute troops with ten 60 lb. kitbags (take-off and flight to target positions)	2,970		251		745,000
Ten parachute troops with ten 60 lb. kitbags (action stations positions)	2,970		261		775,000

This leaf issued in reprint incorporating A.L's 1 to 15
July, 1945

AIR PUBLICATION 2453 A
Vol. I   Part 2   Sect. 3

CHAPTER 3

≡ ALBEMARLE I, II, V, and VI—TECHNICAL PROCEDURE IN FLYING ≡

General

1. This chapter deals with the technical procedure in flying when the aircraft is used for the carriage and dropping of parachute troops and equipment.

Drill in the air

2. The drill given below only describes the procedure to be followed when ten men without kitbags or rifle valises are carried. The necessary additions to the drill when kitbags or rifle valises are carried are given in para. 3 and 4. The drill is intended as a guide only, and may be varied to suit local conditions and circumstances, except where reference is made to other parts of the book which definitely lay down the procedure to be adopted.

(i) *Before taxying out for take-off:* The captain of the aircraft ensures that the parachute troops know their emergency drills as laid down in Chapter 4 of this section. He tests the intercomm. with the stick commander. The bomb aimer checks the signal lights, strops, snap hook pins (if old type snap hooks are used), the position of the special strop and carriage, and ensures that his bomb panel is working satisfactorily. The parachute troops normally bring with them certain items of equipment and it is the responsibility of the captain to see that these are arranged in a position where they will not foul any controls or interfere with the opening of the

parachute troop aperture doors. Such equipment will normally be stowed as far forward in the aircraft as possible for the take-off.

(ii) *Take-off and normal flying:* The captain orders: "Take-off positions" and after the troops have taken up their positions as indicated in fig. 1, the stick commander replies: "O.K. take-off positions".

(iii) *20 minutes before dropping time:* The captain orders: "Prepare for action". The stick commander ensures that the static rail container release switch is free and reports to the air bomber who makes his bomb selector and bomb distributor settings. No. 1 will pass back the strops on the starboard side retaining the end strop for himself, and each succeeding man passes the remainder of the strops along in turn retaining the last one, and so on until each man has one. The same proceedure takes place on the port side, starting with No. 2. Each man, as he takes his strop will call out his number. Each man will hook-up. The stick commander orders: "Check equipment" and each man will check:—

(a) The position of his own static line.

(b) The fitting of his own snap hook and snap hook safety pin, if the old type of snap hook is used.

(c) The security of his own release box.

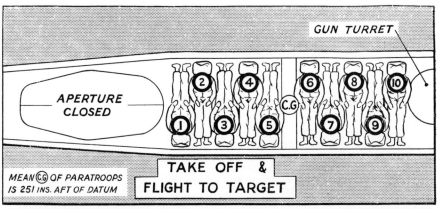

TAKE OFF &
FLIGHT TO TARGET

MEAN C.G OF PARATROOPS
IS 251 INS. AFT OF DATUM

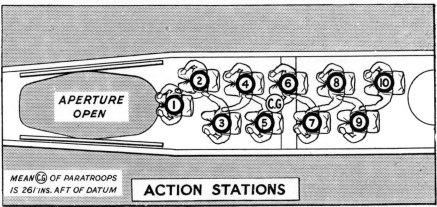

MEAN C.G OF PARATROOPS
IS 261 INS. AFT OF DATUM

ACTION STATIONS

FIG. I

Parachute troop positions—10 men

(d) The shoulder ties and static line of the man in front of him.
The shoulder ties and static lines of No. 9 and 10 will be checked by No. 7 and 8 respectively. The stick commander orders: "Tell off for equipment check". The men will call out: "No. 1 O.K.", "No. 2 O.K." . . . "No. 10 O.K.". The stick commander reports to the captain: "Ready for action".

(iv) *Five minutes before dropping time:* The captain orders: "Action stations"; the stick commander orders: "Action stations". If a night descent is being made the stick commander will switch off the fuselage interior lights. He then removes his intercomm. helmet, replacing it with his steel helmet, and holds the earpiece of the intercomm. helmet to his ear to maintain communication with the captain. No. 1

≡ ALBEMARLE I, II, V, and VI—TECHNICAL PROCEDURE IN FLYING ≡

and 2 will open the aperture doois and fasten them back securely. The wireless operator takes up a position from which he can watch the parachute troops make their exit. The captain will inform the stick commander at each minute interval thus: "Four minutes to go", "Thiee minutes to go", "Two minutes to go". Immediately after the captain has announced "Two minutes to go" the stick commander orders "Stand up". The men then take up the "knees bend" rosition facing the tail. Each man on the port side places his left hand, and each man on the starboard side places his right hand, on the shoulder of the man who precedes him. The men arrange themselves as illustrated in fig. 1.

(v) *Fifteen seconds before dropping:* The navigator switches on the red signal light. The stick prepares for immediate exit.

(vi) *Over the dropping zone:* The navigator puts on the green signal light one second before the dropping time and the parachute troops make their exit from the aircraft. As they move down the fuselage each man must guide his strop carriage or D-ring along with his thumb, taking care to keep the strop behind his hand.

(vii) *Container dropping:* If the containers are dropped with delay action devices, the men may leave the aircraft in an unbroken stick. If the delay action devices are not fitted a pause must be made between parachutists No. 5 and 6 to allow the containers to fall clear of the men. The duration of this pause is given in para. 20.

(viii) *Immediately after dropping:* The wireless operator reports to the captain: "All gone". The air bomber pulls the bomb jettison toggle. One or two of the crew go aft and retrieve the strops. The captain closes the bomb doors.

(ix) When the strops have been retrieved the air gunner closes the aperture doors

and reports to the captain: "Doors closed". The captain returns the aircraft to normal cruising speed and the engines to their normal settings.

3. If kitbags are carried the following should be added to the standard drill:

(i) When the order "Prepare for action" has been given the men carrying kitbags must attach them to their right legs.

(ii) When the order: "Check equipment" is given those men carrying kitbags will also inspect the kitbag, quick release, and jettison devices.

4. If rifle valises are carried the following should be added to the standard drill.

(i) When the order: "Prepare for action" is given those men carrying rifle valises must attach them to their right legs and their waists.

(ii) When the order: "Check equipment" is given those men carrying rifle valises will also inspect the rifle valise, quick release, and jettison devices.

(iii) When the order "Stand up" is given those men carrying rifle valises take up their action stations positions astride the forward half of the aperture.

WARNING

The stick commander must make certain that the men jumping with rifle valises understand the special precautions given in para. 12. Serious injury or death may result if these precautions are not fully understood and observed.

Method of jumping without kitbag or rifle valise

5. Each man in turn takes up a "knees bend" attitude on the centre line of the forward edge of the aperture. The head is held erect, the hands *rest* upon the tops of the aperture doors, the toe of the left foot projects slightly over the edge of the aperture, and the right foot is placed some distance behind the left. Fig. 2 illustrates the correct position.

FIG. 2

Attitude of parachutist when preparing to jump

6. Each man steps off into the aperture with his right foot and brings his left foot forward, assuming the normal alert position.

Method of jumping with kitbag

7. The attitude of the man when preparing to jump with a kitbag attached to his right leg differs slightly from that illustrated in fig. 2. He should grasp the top of the kitbag with his right hand.

8. When jumping he must bring his right leg forward, supporting the kitbag with his right hand as he does so, and step into the aperture. He must not swing his right leg forward too violently or the weight of the kitbag will cause

it to swing across the body and the man will start spinning.

9. As he steps off into the aperture, the man should bring his left hand across his body and assist his right hand to steady the kitbag during his exit. He should assume a position as near the normal alert position as possible.

Method of jumping with rifle valise

10. The men who are to jump with rifle valises stand astride the aperture.

11. When jumping, each man in turn brings his legs together and his arms to his sides, dropping through the aperture in the normal alert position.

≡ ALBEMARLE I, II, V, and VI—TECHNICAL PROCEDURE IN FLYING ≡

Special precautions necessary when rifle valises are carried

12. If the first three men in the stick have to jump with rifle valises the stick commander must make certain that they know the special precautions, listed below, which must be observed:—

(i) An alternative form of signal to the men to jump will have to be adopted, as the head of the first man will be aft of the signal lights and his parachute pack will obscure the lights from the men behind him.

(ii) The first man to jump must be careful to avoid touching the static rail container release switch as this might cause the premature release of the containers. The most suitable hand hold for this man is on the static line rail adjacent to the switch.

(iii) The men astride the aperture must take care to avoid catching the right arm in the static line cable when jumping.

(iv) To avoid the possibility of being thrown out of the aircraft should the pilot for any reason bank steeply, the three men astride the aperture should secure a good foothold and hand grip.

(v) If the containers to be dropped are fitted with parachute delay action devices, the strop carriage of No. 1 parachutist must be kept forward of the static rail container release switch until jumping commences.

Setting of bomb selector

13. The bomb selector switches 1, 2, 3, 4, 6, 7, and 9 must be switched on.

Setting of bomb distributor

14. The contact arm of the distributor must be set to 1.

15. The time interval setting between containers is as follows:—

(i) *Containers dropped with the delay action device:* The time interval setting on the distributor must be 0·5 sec.

(ii) *Containers dropped without the delay action device:* The time interval setting on the distributor must be 0·25 sec.

Setting of delay action device

16. If the containers are to be dropped with the delay action device it should be set to a time delay of 1·5 sec. This is most easily done before the parachutes are attached to the containers.

Position of special strop and carriage

17. If the containers are to be dropped with the delay action device, the special strop and carriage is attached to the static line of No. 1 parachutist.

18. When the containers are dropped without the delay action device the special strop and carriage is attached to the static line of No. 5 parachutist.

Time interval for containers to fall clear of parachutists

19. If the containers are dropped with the delay action device, they may be dropped throughout the stick length and therefore no pause is necessary.

20. If the delay action device is not used, a pause must be made between the jumping of No. 5 and 6 parachutists to allow the containers to fall clear of the men. This pause is determined as follows:—

		Sec.
(i) Between the jumping of No. 5 parachutist and release of first container		1·0
(ii) Travel of distributor arm ...		1·5
(iii) For last container to fall clear of parachutists		1·0
(iv) Total time interval		3·5

Retrieval of strops

21. The strops are retrieved by one, or preferably two, members of the aircrew.

22. The strop retrieving rope loop is removed from its spring retaining clips by pulling on one end, and the strops are hauled in. Once the kit bags have passed the elevator guard they must not be allowed to slip back, as they may pass over the guard rail and foul the elevators.

Handling

23. For the dropping operation the aircraft should be flown straight and level at 100/110 m.p.h. I.A.S. with flaps applied 15° and bomb doors open.

24. For all other handling information reference should be made to A.P.1688A, B, F, & G—Pilot's Notes for the Albemarle I, II, V, and VI.

ALBEMARLE I, II, V AND VI — EMERGENCY PROCEDURE

LIST OF CONTENTS

LIST OF ILLUSTRATIONS

General

1—It may be necessary for the parachute troops and crew to abandon the aircraft in an emergency, either by parachute if over the land, or by dinghy after the aircraft has ditched.

2—Special emergency drills for the parachute troops and crew have been evolved to meet both these conditions. These drills should at all times be strictly adhered to.

3—This chapter should be read in conjunction with Section 4 of AP.2095 Pilot's Notes General and Section 4 of A.P. 1688 A, B, F & G, Pilot's Notes for the Albemarle I, II, V and VI.

Emergency parachute drill

4—The pilot must not give the order to abandon the aircraft if below 300 ft. or if over the sea or some other large expanse of water.

5—Members of the crew must check their parachute harness and remove their flying helmets before abandoning the aircraft from the exits specified in the drill.

6—The parachute troops should abandon the aircraft in the same way as they leave it for a normal operation. The method of giving the signal to abandon being detailed in the drill. The method of giving the signal should be clearly understood by all personnel before take-off.

7—The drill to be carried out by the parachute troops and crew is given in the form of captions to fig. 1, insets 1 to 9, which depict the various stages of the drill.

8—If the aircraft has to crash-land from below 300 ft. with troops and crew on board they should take up the same positions as for ditching.

Safety equipment carried

9—The standard built-in stowage in the roof between Nos. 1 and 2 escape hatches, for the H type dinghy normally used by the crew, is retained; in this drill, however, for convenience this dinghy is used by the troops. A manual release is provided in the roof over the floor covering the aft end of the bomb bay. The J type dinghy packed in an H type valise, which is stowed on the starboard side of the aft end of the crawlway, is operated by the crew and used by the crew and some of the troops.

10—A ditching belt is provided aft of the mid-upper turret; it should be kept permanently in position in the manner shown in fig. 2 inset (a), the amount of slack being sufficient to allow ready access forward at all times.

Emergency ditching drill

11—The following drill must be observed in the event of an aircraft having to ditch.

(i) Pilot orders "Dinghy, dinghy, prepare for ditching". The crew will warn the troops.

(ii) The Stick Commander co-ordinates and supervises the parachute troops and sees that the ditching belt is securely fixed as shown in fig. 2, inset (a). The troops will then take up their ditching positions.

(iii) Pilot orders or signals "Brace for impact"; each man must then brace himself in the manner shown in fig. 2 inset (b) and prepare for severe deceleration.

(iv) After the aircraft has ditched, the ditching belts should be released if possible, so that the minimum obstruction is presented. All personnel must then release their parachute harness. The parachute troops must dispose of any heavy equipment, retaining their life vests, water bottles and rations. The dinghies should be put into the water in the positions shown in fig. 3, while the parachute troops are discarding their heavy equipment.

(v) The parachute troops and crew should then leave the aircraft by the exits indicated in fig. 3. After they have left the aircraft the troops must inflate their life vests. The crew can assist and direct where possible. The Stick Commander will control the exit of the men. Care should be exercised to prevent damage to the dinghy when boarding. The first man in the dinghy should help to control it while the rest of the men embark. Two or three parachute packs should be thrown into the water as a safety precaution to provide temporary support for any men who may fall overboard. In addition several parachutes should be taken into the dinghy for extra warmth.

(vi) When the dinghy is full the Stick Commander casts off or cuts it adrift from the aircraft.

(vii) When clear of the aircraft every effort should be made to tie the dinghies together; a safety line with quoit is attached to each dinghy and may be used for this purpose as well as for rescue purposes.

12—The glove paddles are for controlling the dinghies, and the weather aprons when fitted will save shipping much water under adverse weather conditions and provide a good protection against wind.

13—The crew should follow their normal dinghy drill as far as they are able to do so, taking up the positions indicated in fig. 2 when ditching.

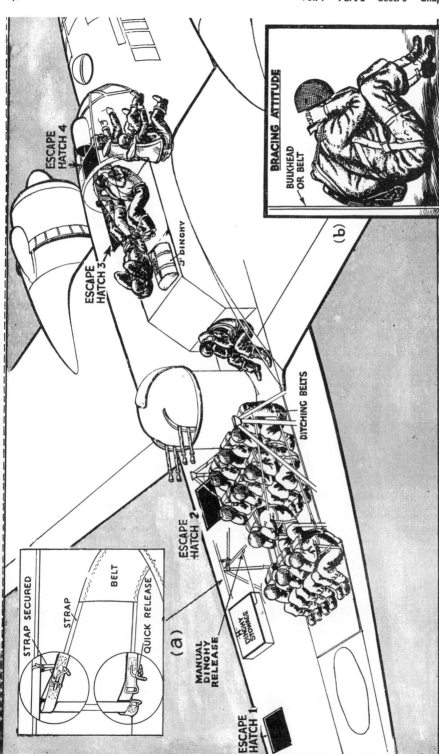

FIG. 2

Troops and crew in ditching or crash positions

PILOT   **NAV.**   **A.B.**   **W/Op**   **A.G.**   **PARACHUTE TROOPS**

① All crew at action stations. Pilot flashes abandon aircraft light and gives order "Section, section, prepare to abandon aircraft." Crew and Stick Cmdr. acknowledge.

② Pilot destroys I.F.F. Nav. gives position of aircraft to Stick Cmdr., who acknowledges. A.B. fits parachute. W/Op. jettisons trailing aerial. R.G. leaves turret.

③ Pilot maintains control. Nav. fits parachute. W/Op. if time, sends emergency signal. R.G. fits parachute. Stick Cmdr. gives order "Hook up."

④ Nav. moves aft, A.B. follows him. W/Op. fits parachute. When stick is ready, Stick Cmdr. reports to Pilot (who acknowledges), and removes flying helmet.

ALBEMARLE

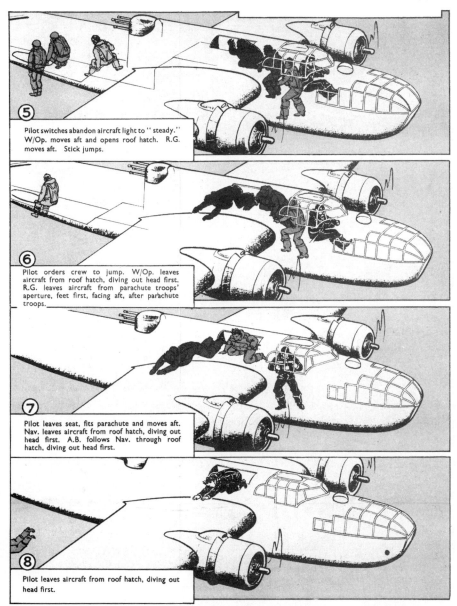

⑤ Pilot switches abandon aircraft light to " steady." W/Op. moves aft and opens roof hatch. R.G. moves aft. Stick jumps.

⑥ Pilot orders crew to jump. W/Op. leaves aircraft from roof hatch, diving out head first. R.G. leaves aircraft from parachute troops' aperture, feet first, facing aft, after parachute troops.

⑦ Pilot leaves seat, fits parachute and moves aft. Nav. leaves aircraft from roof hatch, diving out head first. A.B. follows Nav. through roof hatch, diving out head first.

⑧ Pilot leaves aircraft from roof hatch, diving out head first.

COMBINED EMERGENCY PARACHUTE DRILL FOR PARACHUTE TROOPS AND CREW FIG.I

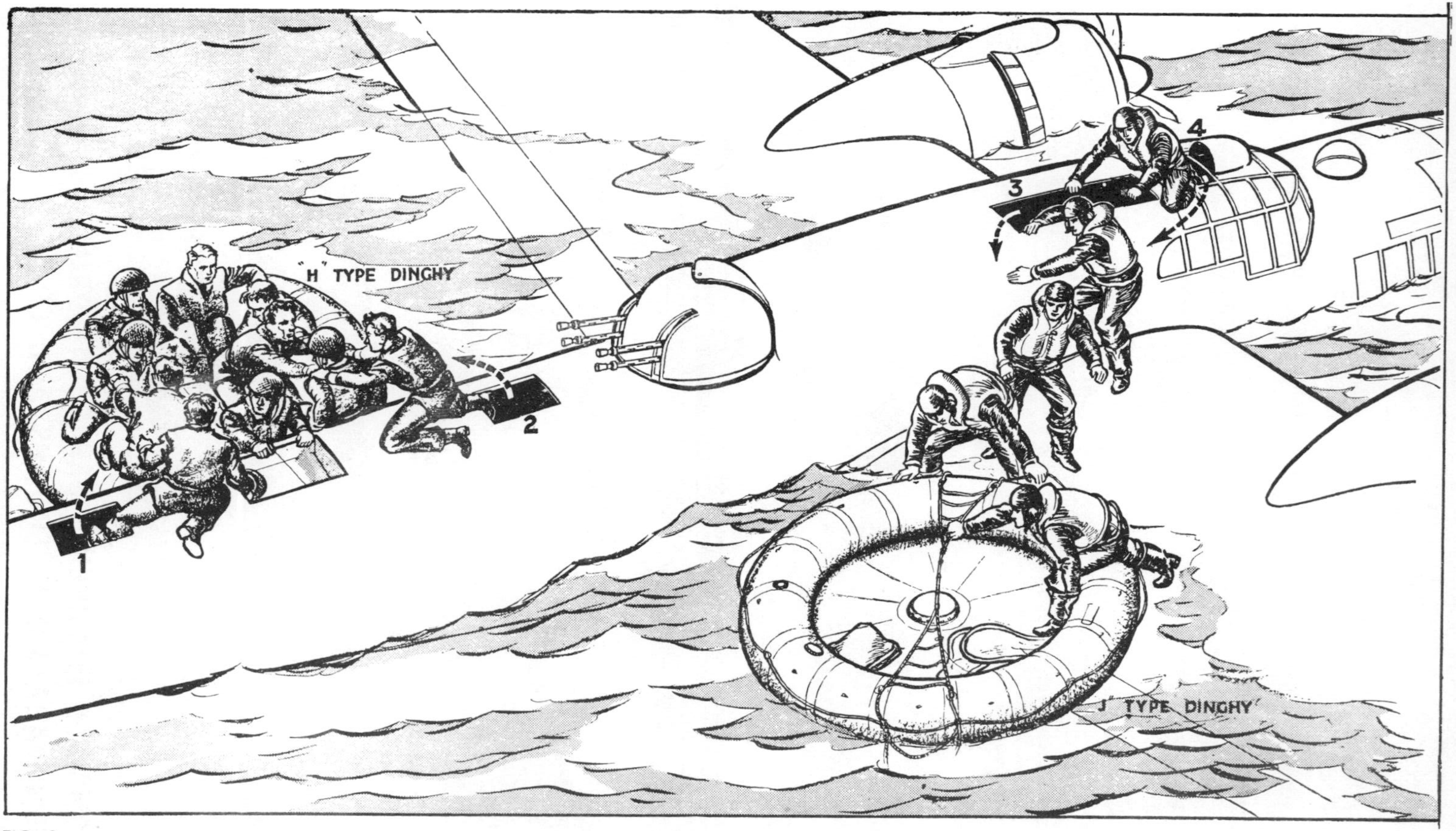
"H" TYPE DINGHY
1
2
3
4
"J" TYPE DINGHY

FIG. 3

Troops and crew boarding dinghies

6
Halifax III, July 1945

This leaf issued with A.L. No. 16
July, 1945

AIR PUBLICATION 2453A
VOL. I   PART 2   SECT. 4

HALIFAX III - PARACHUTE TROOP INSTALLATIONS

LIST OF CONTENTS

LIST OF ILLUSTRATIONS

General

1. A Halifax III aircraft can be used to carry and drop a maximum of ten parachute troops with their supplies-dropping containers. The fifteen bomb carriers on the aircraft can all be employed, but the actual number of containers in a given parachute troop load will depend upon the nature of the stores to be dropped.

2. A general view of the fuselage interior is given in fig. 1.

3. The following are the principal modifications necessary for the parachute installation:—

Modification No.	Description
—	Removal of the mid-upper turret complete.
22	Paratroop installation, fixed parts.
286A	To provide static bar.
286B	To provide windshield, strops, and panels.
287	To separate S.O.O. items from Modification No. 22.
356	Additional items for paratroop installation.
555	To provide a cover for the mid-upper turret aperture.
746	Repositioning of Type 90 aerial.
775	Non-metallic windshield for paratroop aperture.
892	Paratroop warning-light switch guard.
950	Paratroop strops, panels, and mattresses.
1045A	Alterations to paratroop warning lights, fixed parts.
1045B	Alterations to paratroop warning lights, removable parts.
1256	Re-designed shackle for paratroop lines.

4. Where the aircraft modification leaflets make reference to A.P.2453, Vol. I, it should be noted that the Air Publication in question is being superseded by a new series of publications, of which this chapter forms a portion. Information transferred from A.P.2453, Vol. I, to A.P.2453A has been revised, where necessary, to bring it up to date.

Removal of aircraft equipment

5. The following items of equipment should be removed before the aircraft is used for parachute operations:—

(i) Lower bracket for reconnaissance flares.

Fig. I.—View of fuselage interior, looking forward

(ii) Wire escape ladder.

(iii) Flame-float bracket on floor immediately forward of the parachute aperture.

Parachute aperture

6. This aperture, through which the parachuists drop, is circular, being an enlarged version of a hole already provided for a turret; the diameter is approximately 40 in. During take-off and flight to target the aperture is covered by two hinged doors, which are opened and latched to the sides of the fuselage when the parachute troops are ready to make their exit.

Door catches

7. The door catches are of a double-acting pattern, and provide a self locking attachment for the aperture doors when these are open or closed. Two catches are fitted to each door.

Windshield

8. The forward edge of the parachute aperture, on the underside of the aircraft, is fitted with a windshield to provide a region of comparatively calm air at the point where a parachutist leaves the aircraft. The rear edge of the aperture is fitted with a wooden bend to prevent chafing of the parachute strops.

Strong points *(fig. 2 and 3)*

9. A strong point for the attachment of parachute strops is fitted both on the port and the starboard side. There are two strong points and they are identical except for the securing brackets, which are "handed". (The starboard strong point only is illustrated in fig. 2 and 3.)

Fig. 2.—Strong point ready for attachment of strops

Strops

10. Ten strops are secured to the two strong points; they are supported, when in the stowed position, on two panels, see para. 13. The strops are of $1\frac{3}{4}$ in. wide, heavy, white, double webbing, and are fitted with press studs for attachment to the panels. One end of each strop carries a D-ring for attachment to a strong point, and the other end is fitted with a snap hook for attachment of the strop to the static line of a parachute. Strop No. 5 carries a tab for the cord which operates the container release switch. The distribution of the strops is as follows:—

Strop No.	Panel position	Length of strop	Strong point
1	Starboard. Aft	16 ft. 0 in.	Starboard
2	Starboard. Aft	16 ft. 0 in.	Starboard
3	Starboard. Forward	16 ft. 0 in.	Starboard
4	Port. Forward	16 ft. 0 in.	Port
5	Starboard. Forward	16 ft. 0 in.	Starboard
6	Port. Forward	16 ft. 0 in.	Port
7	Starboard. Forward	16 ft. 0 in.	Starboard
8	Port. Forward	16 ft. 0 in.	Port
9	Starboard. Forward	16 ft. 0 in.	Starboard
10	Port. Forward	16 ft. 0 in.	Port

Fig. 3.—Strong point with strops attached

11. The strops attached to the forward panel on the starboard side are grouped one above the other to pass under the hinges of the starboard aperture door. The strops attached to the forward panel on the port side are laid side by side under the hinges of the port aperture door.

12. For attachment to the panels each strop is folded and tied with webbing tabs having eyelets through which are passed double lengths of linen thread, Stores Ref. 15A/108, looped and knotted.

Note . . . All the strops are 16 ft. in length to ensure safe deployment of the parachutes at approximately 2 ft. aft of the tail wheel. It is therefore essential that only the correct strops are used.

Panels

13. Three khaki duck panels are secured by tapes to brackets on the fuselage frames. One port, and one starboard panel, each equipped for four strops, is fitted forward of the parachute aperture. One starboard panel

only, equipped for two strops, is fitted aft of the aperture.

Mattresses (fig. 4)

14. Six special mattresses, each measuring 5 ft. by 3 ft., are laid across the floor of the aircraft. Two of the mattresses (*A, B, see fig. 4*) are laced together and tied to the aircraft structure well forward of the parachute aperture; they then provide a non-slip surface for the parachute troops. The remaining four mattresses (*C, D, E, F*) are laid loosely on the floor for the comfort of the parachute troops during the flight to target, and are arranged as follows:—

(i) One mattress (*C*) adjacent to the fixed ones and immediately forward of the aperture.

(ii) One mattress (*D*) across the closed apterture doors.

(iii) Two mattresses (*E, F*), preferably laced together, placed aft of the aperture, the forward mattress partially covering the entrance door when this is shut.

15. When the parachute troops take up

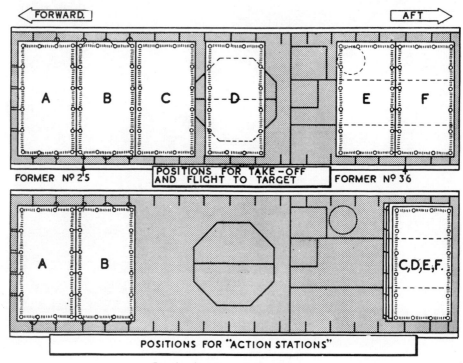

Fig. 4.—Arrangement of mattresses

"action stations" the two rear mattresses (E, F) are folded together and the remaining two loose ones are piled on top so that all the loose mattresses occupy a space 5 ft. by 3 ft. aft of the main entrance door.

Container release switch (fig. 5)

16. A Type "B" single-unit switch, Stores Ref. 5D/534, is fitted on the starboard side of the fuselage adjacent to the parachute aperture.

(a) Switch **OFF**

(b) Switch **ON**

Fig. 5.—Container release switch

This switch is electrically connected to the bomb selector, and when operated by a cord attached to strop No. 5, releases the containers from the bomb carriers. The operating cord terminates in a ring which is passed over the switch lever under a divided bridge piece when the switch is OFF. When No. 5 parachute troop makes his exit and his strop is pulled from its stowage, the switch is operated and the cord and ring are automatically released from the switch lever.

17. A piece of linen thread, Stores Ref. 15A/108, is whipped to a loop in the operating cord (as shown at (a) in fig. 5) and secured through the hole provided beneath the switch. This ensures that an accidental pull on the strop will stress or break the thread, but will not actuate the switch.

18. In some aircraft the release switch is fitted with a guard to assist in preventing accidental operation. (The guard is not, however, illustrated in fig. 5).

Parachuting signal lights (fig. 6)

19. The signal lights—one RED and one GREEN—are mounted inside the fuselage on the starboard side, adjacent to the parachute aperture. The two lights are wired to a switch in the pilot's cockpit, and indicate "action stations" and "drop" respectively.

Fig. 6.—Parachuting signal lights

Bomb selector and distributor

20. No special modification is required for the bomb selecting and distributing circuits when these are used for the purpose of releasing containers. A pre-selector, which is a standard fitting wired between the selector switchbox and the bomb release mechanism, enables each bomb station to be controlled by one of the sixteen selector switches. It is thus a simple matter to drop the containers in any order required. The necessary setting on the bomb distributor is 0·15 sec. between successive containers.

Dim-lighting installation

21. A standard dim-lighting installation can be provided. It consists of two lamps attached to the fuselage roof (one forward and one aft of the aperture), a resistance mounted on the port side of the fuselage, and a plug for connecting the installation to one of the normal roof lighting fitments. The wiring is attached throughout by means of "Bulldog" clips.

22. The dim-lighting system permits a gradual reduction in the illumination of the fuselage interior, so that the parachute troops can accustom their eyes to the outside darkness in a minimum of time when making descents during night operations.

Accessories

23. The following accessories may be required in the aircraft as part of the equipment for parachute operations:—

(i) Intercomm. helmet.

(ii) Thermos flask(s).

(iii) Rubber urine bottles.

(iv) A supply of paper "sick" bags.

Stores References

24. The following are the Stores References of the panels and strops:—

Stores Ref.	Nomenclature	No. off
15A/420	Panels	1 set
	Consisting of:—	
15A/459	Panel, port, forward	1
15A/461	Panel, starboard, forward	1
15A/462	Panel, starboard, aft	1
15A/419	Strops	1 set
	Consisting of:—	
15A/453	Strop, 16 ft.	10

7

Parachutist's Equipment

Fig. 1.—Three views of paratroop with parachute and personal equipment

CHAPTER 3

PERSONAL PARATROOP EQUIPMENT

General

1. The personal equipment of paratroops may be divided into four categories as follows:—

(i) Clothing

(ii) Parachute

(iii) Arms and ammunition

(iv) Provisions and toilet requisites

2. The information given in this chapter should be treated as representative only. Items of clothing and provisions may be varied according to the length and nature of an operation, and the arms and ammunition carried may be varied at the discretion of Brigade Commanders.

Clothing

3. A water-proof tunic is worn over the standard battle-dress. The purpose of the tunic is to prevent any entanglement of such items as ammunition pouches and respirator during the descent. The tunic may be either retained or discarded on landing.

4. In some instances it has been found convenient to rip out the lining sleeves of the tunic and stitch these inside the tunic to serve as pockets for hand grenades. There is at present no official ruling on this subject.

5. A close-fitting helmet, with camouflage net and chin strap, is worn by paratroops during descent and subsequent action. The helmet need not be worn during the flight to target.

6. Leather boots and anklets are worn by paratroops.

7. A spare pullover and a pair of socks is packed in the haversack with the paratroops provisions. .

Parachute

8. For paratroop operations the standard parachute is the 'X' type, Stores Ref. 15A/386 (standard canopy) and 15A/387 (Jacob canopy), which is fully described in A.P.1180A, Vol. I, Part 3. This is a static line parachute and carries a D ring for attachment to one of the strops and strong points in the paratroop aircraft.

9. On landing, the parachute harness is disconnected by twisting and sharply pressing the release disc which is located on the wearer's chest.

Arms and ammunition

10. Each paratroop wears over his battle-dress a belt to which is attached an assault respirator. If this respirator is worn at the back, two ammunition pouches may be carried towards the front of the belt. If, however, the respirator is worn at the right-hand side of the belt towards the front, the ammunition pouches must be attached to shoulder braces. The arms and ammunition carried vary with the category of the paratroops.

Rifleman

11. The following armament and defensive equipment is carried by a rifleman:—

(i) One light assault respirator, attached to belt.

(ii) Two pouches, each with two Bren gun magazines, attached either to belt or shoulder braces.

(iii) One needle bayonet and scabbard held in 'frog' on belt.

(iv) One bandolier with fifty rounds of rifle ammunition.

(v) Two hand grenades carried either in knee pockets of battle-dress or in tunic pockets, *see* para. 4.

(vi) One fighting knife, either in scabbard on hip or in pocket provided in battle-dress.

(vii) One toggle rope, for climbing, slung round shoulders.

(viii) One haversack. For contents *see* paras. 14 to 18.

Bren gunner

12. The following armament and defensive equipment is carried by a Bren gunner:—

(i) One light assault respirator, attached to belt.

(ii) One revolver carried at left-hand side.

(iii) One pouch with revolver ammunition carried at right-hand side.

(iv) Two pouches, each with two Bren gun magazines, attached to shoulder braces.

(v) Two hand grenades.

(vi) One fighting knife.

(vii) One toggle rope.

(viii) One haversack. For contents *see* paras. 14 to 18.

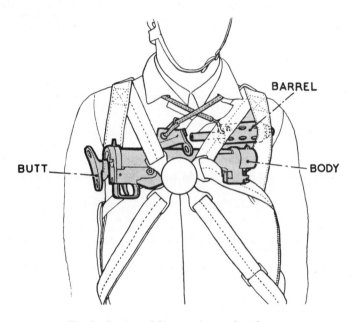

Fig. 2.—Stowage of Sten gun in parachute harness

Sten gunner

13. The following armament and defensive equipment is carried by a Sten gunner:—

(i) One light assault respirator, attached to belt.

(ii) One Sten gun. The barrel, body and butt are stowed separately in the parachute harness, *see* fig. 2.

(iii) One Sten bandolier containing seven magazines of twenty-eight rounds each.

(iv) One magazine either in pocket or tucked in parachute harness.

(v) Two hand grenades.

(vi) One fighting knife.

(vii) One toggle rope.

(viii) One haversack. For contents *see* paras. 14 to 18.

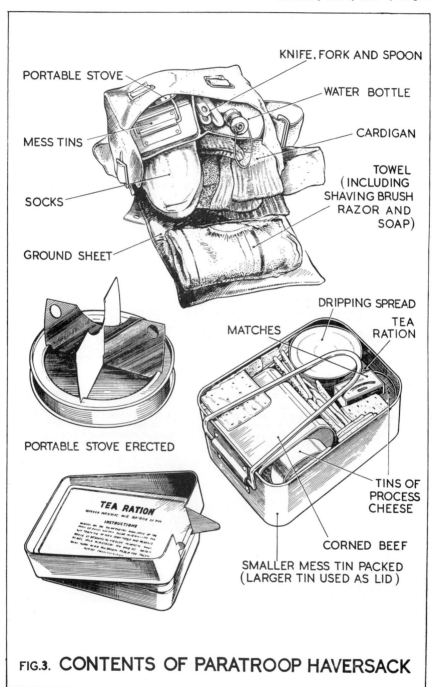

KNIFE, FORK AND SPOON

WATER BOTTLE

CARDIGAN

TOWEL
(INCLUDING
SHAVING BRUSH
RAZOR AND
SOAP)

PORTABLE STOVE

MESS TINS

SOCKS

GROUND SHEET

DRIPPING SPREAD

TEA
RATION

MATCHES

PORTABLE STOVE ERECTED

TEA RATION

INSTRUCTIONS

TINS OF
PROCESS
CHEESE

CORNED BEEF

SMALLER MESS TIN PACKED
(LARGER TIN USED AS LID)

FIG.3. CONTENTS OF PARATROOP HAVERSACK

Provisions and toilet requisites

14. A paratroop haversack is packed, for a typical operation, with the following items:—

One ration S.T.6 (4 lb. 4 oz.), *see* para. 16.

One knife.

One fork.

One spoon.

One solidified spirit burner.

One mess tin (two parts).

One water bottle.

One ground sheet or gas cape.

One pullover.

One pair of socks.

One towel.

Soap, shaving soap, shaving brush, razor, toothbrush and comb.

15. The system of packing these items in the haversack is illustrated in fig. 3.

Ration S.T.6

16. This ration is intended to cover a period up to forty-eight hours and comprises the following items:—

One 12 oz. tin of corned beef, with key.

One 2 oz. tin of dripping spread.

Two tins of processed cheese.

One tin of tea and dried milk.

One box of matches.

One tin containing service biscuits, sweet biscuits, chocolate, acid drops, and barley sugar.

17. The ration S.T.6 is issued to paratroops at their operational base where the separate articles should be packed tightly in the smaller mess tin, using broken biscuits to prevent any possibility of rattle which might reveal to the enemy the whereabouts of a paratroop. The method of packing is illustrated in fig. 3. The larger mess tin is used as a lid when packing is complete.

Solidified spirit burner

18. The burner is supplied in the form of a flat tin filled with $4\frac{1}{2}$ oz. of solidified spirit. To use the burner the lid is removed and the two tin vanes are sprung out from the lower lip of the tin. The vanes are pushed one into the other in the form of a cross and are then inserted in the tin to form a stand for the mess tin. A protection from draughts is essential. The flame is extinguished, after removing the vanes by a wire passed through the holes provided, simply by replacing the lid.

CHAPTER 4

PARATROOP SUPPLIES EQUIPMENT

General

1. Paratroop supplies are packed in containers or slung in harnesses and are usually dropped by means of parachutes from the bomb stations of paratroop-carrying aircraft   The selection of bomb stations in each type of aircraft is dealt with in Sect 2, Chap. 5 of this manual.

C.L.E. Mark I container (*see* figs. 1 and 3)

2. The C.L.E. Mark I container is fully described in A.P.1180A, Vol. I, Part 2, Sect. 1, Chap. 1. The container comprises a metal framework, faced with plywood, and is made in halves which are hinged along their length to make an approximate cylinder when closed.   It can be carried by and released from a 500 lb. or a Universal bomb carrier.   One end of the container (the forward end when loaded on an aircraft) is domed to form a percussion head and to house an identification lighting set when required.   The other end of the container provides stowage for the Mark I parachute and pack described in A.P.1180A, Vol. I, Part 2, Sect. 2, Chap. 1. The weights of the C.L.E. Mark I container and parachute are 103½ lb. nett and 350 lb. gross (max.).

Stores Ref. numbers

3. The Stores Ref. number of the C.L.E. Mark I container is 15C/89; that for the C.L.E. Mark I parachute is 15C/90–95, the serial numbers referring to different coloured canopies.

Packings for C.L.E. Mark I containers (*see* fig. 2)

4 Containers used for paratroop supplies equipment are packed by the paratroop section concerned who work from instructions issued by Airborne Division relative to a given operation. A series of Air Diagrams, Nos. A.D.2349 *et seq.*, has been issued to illustrate certain standard packing arrangements.   One of these diagrams is reproduced in miniature in fig. 2.   It should be noted that the aircraft numbers appearing in these diagrams are representative only and may vary with each operation.

C.L.E. Mark I.T. container (*see* fig. 1)

5. The C.L.E. Mark I.T. container is fully described in A.P.1180A, Vol. I, Part 2, Sect. 1, Chap. 1.   It is a replica of the Mark I container except in regard to the outer covering which is of metal instead of plywood.   The carrying capacity of this container and the type of parachute used are the same as for the Mark I container described in paras. 2 and 4.   The weights of the C.L.E. Mark I.T. container and parachute are 135½ lb. nett and 350 lb. gross (max.).

Stores Ref. number

6. The Stores Ref. number of the C.L.E. Mark I.T. container is 15C/119.

C.L.E. Mark III container (*see* fig. 1)

7. The C.L.E. Mark III container is fully described in A.P.1180A, Vol. I, Part 2, Sect. 1, Chap. 2.   It is generally similar to the Mark I and Mark I.T. containers and may be faced either with a plywood skin or metal covering.   Its length is 8 in. less than that of the Mark I, and, when closed, its cross section is exactly circular.   A percussion head with provision for an identification lighting set is fitted at one end of the container.   The other end provides stowage for the Mark I parachute and pack.   The weights of the C.L.E. Mark III container and parachute are 113½ lb. nett and 350 lb. gross (max.). A GROSS (MAX.) WEIGHT OF 400 LB. IS NOW PERMISSIBLE.

8. The Mark III container is intended to supersede the Mark I and Mark I.T. types for all packings except those requiring the additional length of the earlier types.

Stores Ref. number

9. The Stores Ref. number of the C.L.E. Mark III container is 15C/165.   In addition to the C.L.E. Mark I parachute, Stores Ref. 15C/90–95, the Type C parachute, Stores Ref. 15C/63, may also be used with the Mark III container.

Identification lighting (*see* fig. 3, sketch III)

10. The identification lighting equipment for Mark I, I.T. and III containers is mounted on a wooden baffle between the container body and the percussion head, and is for use when the containers are dropped at night.   The lighting equipment comprises a dry battery, 3 volt, Ever Ready No. 800, and four lamps with a switch that automatically completes the circuit when the percussion

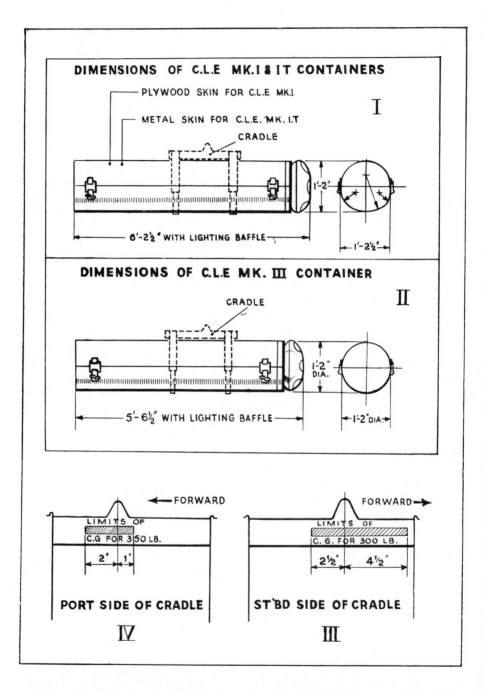

DIMENSIONS OF C.L.E MK.I & IT CONTAINERS

PLYWOOD SKIN FOR C.L.E MK.I

METAL SKIN FOR C.L.E. MK. I.T

CRADLE

I

1'-2"

6'-2½" WITH LIGHTING BAFFLE

1'-2½"

DIMENSIONS OF C.L.E MK. III CONTAINER

CRADLE

II

1'-2" DIA.

5'-6½" WITH LIGHTING BAFFLE

1'-2' DIA.

FORWARD

LIMITS OF
C.G FOR 350 LB.

2'   1'

PORT SIDE OF CRADLE

IV

FORWARD

LIMITS OF
C.G. FOR 300 LB.

2½'   4½"

ST'BD SIDE OF CRADLE

III

FIG. 1 C.L.E.MK.I., I T.& III.CONTAINERS

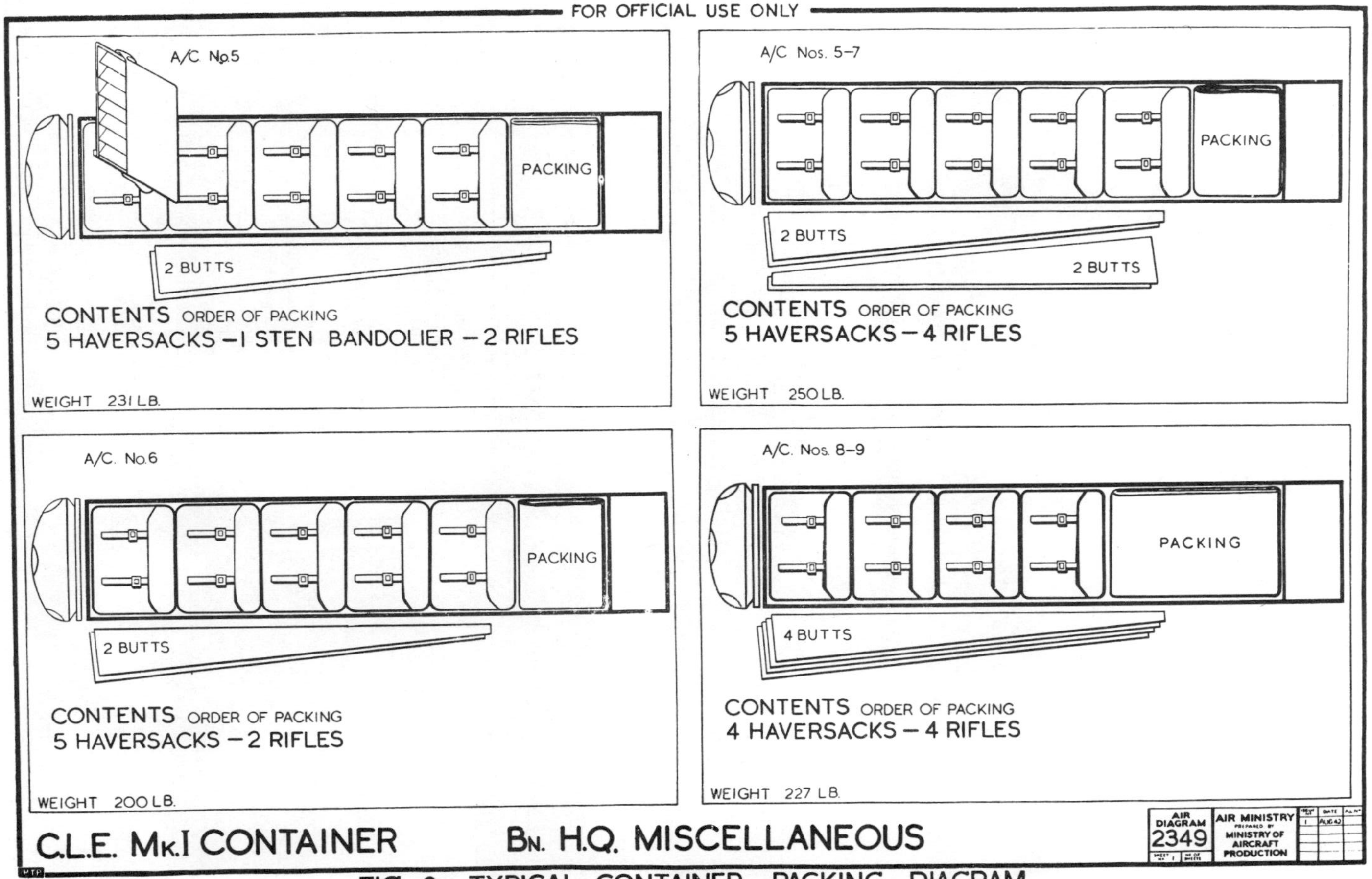

FOR OFFICIAL USE ONLY

A/C No5

PACKING

CONTENTS ORDER OF PACKING
5 HAVERSACKS – 1 STEN BANDOLIER – 2 RIFLES

2 BUTTS

WEIGHT 231 LB.

A/C Nos. 5-7

PACKING

2 BUTTS

2 BUTTS

CONTENTS ORDER OF PACKING
5 HAVERSACKS – 4 RIFLES

WEIGHT 250LB.

A/C No6

PACKING

CONTENTS ORDER OF PACKING
5 HAVERSACKS – 2 RIFLES

2 BUTTS

WEIGHT 200 LB.

A/C Nos 8-9

PACKING

4 BUTTS

CONTENTS ORDER OF PACKING
4 HAVERSACKS – 4 RIFLES

WEIGHT 227 LB

AIR DIAGRAM 2349
AIR MINISTRY
MINISTRY OF AIRCRAFT PRODUCTION

C.L.E. Mk.I CONTAINER   Bn. H.Q. MISCELLANEOUS

FIG. 2 TYPICAL CONTAINER PACKING DIAGRAM

209

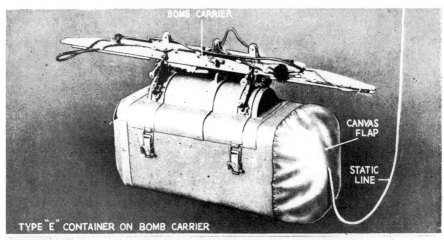

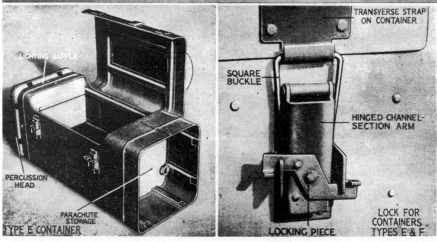

FIG. 4—TYPE E AND F CONTAINERS

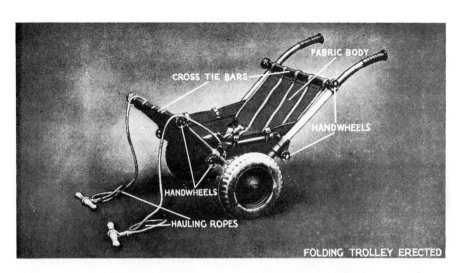

CROSS TIE BARS

FABRIC BODY

HANDWHEELS

HANDWHEELS

HAULING ROPES

FOLDING TROLLEY ERECTED

2 LIGHTING BULBS

CONTACT PLUNGER

2 LIGHTING BULBS

BATTERY BOX

STABILISING BRACKET

LIGHTING SWITCH BUMPER

TROLLEY CRADLE

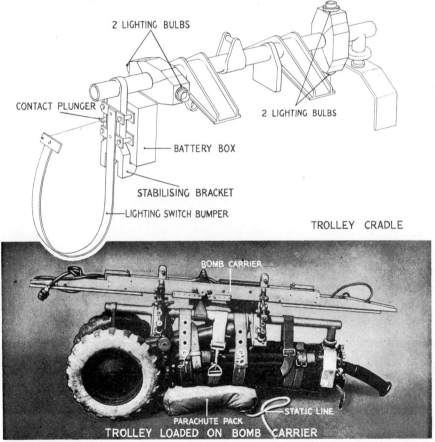

BOMB CARRIER

PARACHUTE PACK

STATIC LINE

TROLLEY LOADED ON BOMB CARRIER

FIG. 5.—TYPE D APPARATUS AND FOLDING TROLLEY

cradle (see A.P.1180A, Vol. I, Part 2, Sect. 1, Chap. 1) which incorporates the suspension hook bracket for attachment to the bomb carrier. Four men are normally required to handle a packed container.

Delayed opening device for parachute

23. A device is in course of development for establishing a short delay in the opening of the parachute after the container has been released from the bomb carrier. A description of this device will be issued as soon as it is approved for Service use.

Type E container (see fig. 4)

24. The type E container is fully described in A.P.1180A, Vol. I, Part 2, Sect. 1, Chap. 4. The container body is of metal, rectangular-shaped with longitudinal rounded edges. The top face is provided with a hinged lid carrying a suspension hook bracket for direct attachment to the bomb carrier. One end of the container (the aft end when loaded on an aircraft) carries a domed percussion head which is designed to house an identification lighting set when this is required. The other end of the container provides stowage for the C.L.E. Mark I parachute and pack described in A.P.1180A, Vol. I, Part 2, Sect. 2, Chap. 1.

Stores Ref. numbers

25. The Stores Ref. number of the Type E container is 15C/30; that for the C.L.E. Mark I parachute is 15C/90–95, the serial numbers referring to different coloured canopies.

Contents of type E container

26. The type E container is designed to house the No. 18 W/T.

Type F container (see fig. 4)

27. The type F container is fully described in A.P.1180A, Vol. I, Part 2, Sect. 1, Chap. 5. It is generally similar to the Type E container, but is several inches greater in length. A percussion head is fitted, and identification lighting may be used if required. Stowage is provided for the C.L.E. Mark I parachute and pack.

Stores Ref. numbers

28. The Stores Ref. number of the type F container is 15C/75; that for the C.L.E. Mark I parachute is 15C/90–95, the serial numbers referring to different coloured canopies.

Contents of type F container

29. The type F container is designed to house the Nos. 11, 19, 21 and 22 W/T sets.

Weights of types E and F containers

30. The empty and gross weights of these containers are as follows:—

(i)	Type E container empty (including parachute) ...	...	...	...	89 lb.
(ii)	Type E container with No. 18 W/T ...	...	...	...	190 lb.
(iii)	Type F container empty (including parachute) ...	...	...	...	lb.
(iv)	Type F container with No. 11 W/T ...	...	...	...	lb.
(v)	Type F container with No. 19 W/T ...	...	...	...	lb.
(vi)	Type F container with No. 21 W/T ...	...	...	...	lb.
(vii)	Type F container with No. 22 W/T ...	...	...	...	lb.

General notes

31. The types E and F containers are generally received from military sources with the supplies packed. The procedure for loading these containers on the bomb racks of paratroop-carrying aircraft is similar to that outlined in paras. 10 to 22 with the exception that no provision is made for adjusting the longitudinal position of the C.G. Three or four men are normally required to handle a packed W/T container. It should be noted that these containers are mounted on the Universal bomb carriers with their percussion heads aft in order to suit the non-adjustable crutches of these carriers.

FIG. 6—FOLDING BICYCLE ERECTED FOR USE AND FOLDED FOR DROPPING

213

Type D supplies dropping apparatus (*see* fig. 5)

32.   The type D apparatus is fully described in A.P.1180A, Vol. I, Part 2, Sect. 1, Chap. 6. It is designed to carry the folding trolley and comprises a special cradle with identification lighting, the switch for this being automatically operated on impact.   A type D parachute pack, as described in A.P.1180A, Vol. I, Part 2, Sect. 2, Chap. 3, is strapped on to the cradle.   It is opened, when the apparatus is released from the bomb rack, by means of a static line attached to a strong point on the aircraft.

Stores Ref. numbers

33.   The Stores Ref. number of the type D apparatus is 15C/55; that for the type D parachute is 15C/48–51, the serial numbers referring to different coloured canopies.

Folding trolley

34.   The folding trolley (*see* fig. 5) comprises two side frames, each with one wheel, and a fabric body incorporating four tie-bars with handwheels for quick attachment to lugs on the side frames.

Weight of type D apparatus and folding trolley

35.   The weights are as follows:—

(i)   Type D apparatus without trolley   ...   .   23 lb.

(ii) Type D apparatus with folding trolley ...   .   73 lb.

Type Q apparatus—folding bicycle (*see* fig. 6)

36.   The folding bicycle is fully described in A.P.1180A, Vol. I, Part 2, Sect. 1, Chap. 8.   The frame of the bicycle is elliptical and is hinged at two points.   The slackening of two wing-nuts enables the frame to be folded so that the two wheels lie side by side.   The wheels are lashed to the frame to prevent their turning and a type Q parachute with 12 ft. canopy, as described in A.P.1180A, Vol. I, Part 2, Sect. 2, Chap. 4, is attached to their circumference.   Any partial bending of the handlebars on landing can usually be corrected by hand.

Stores Ref. number

37.   The Stores Ref. number of the parachute is 15C/84

Weight of folding bicycle

38.   The weight of the folding bicycle and parachute is 32½ lb.

General note

39.   It is necessary to throw the bicycle vertically downwards through the door of the aircraft to prevent the parachute fouling the tail.   Tests were made by A.F.E.E. from a C.47. with satisfactory results.

Albemarle, modified container cradles

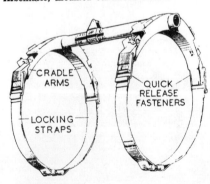

40.   The overall width of the normal cradle is too great to enable three containers to be carried side by side on the Albemarle aircraft.   The width is decreased sufficiently if the cradle arms are shortened and the metal locking straps lengthened to bring the quick release fasteners above the horizontal centre-line.

CRADLE ARMS

QUICK RELEASE FASTENERS

LOCKING STRAPS

ALBEMARLE   MODIFIED CRADLE
FIG. 7

This leaf issued with A.L. No. 17
May, 1946

AIR PUBLICATION 2453A
VOL. I PART 4 SECT. 2

EQUIPMENT ATTACHED TO PARACHUTISTS

LIST OF CONTENTS

LIST OF ILLUSTRATIONS

LIST OF APPENDICES

AIRBORNE KITBAG

General

1. This special kitbag, developed for the purpose of dropping equipment with parachute troops, is of conventional shape but opens down one side as well as across the top, and is fitted with a resilient base to withstand landing shocks. The kitbag may be used in a variety of ways as described in this chapter, and may be loaded with any equipment as long as the maximum permissible weight is not exceeded and the kitbag remains approximately cylindrical. Special loads which can be carried in the kitbag are dealt with in the Appendix to this chapter.

Description *(fig. 1, 2 and 3)*

2. The kitbag is approximately cylindrical, measuring about 30 in. in length and $14\frac{1}{2}$ in. in diameter. In addition to being open at one end, it is open down one side, the whole aperture being fitted with eyeletted holes and laced with cord. The base of the kitbag is padded to a depth of four inches and embodies a slot which accommodates the parachutist's foot when the kitbag is carried strapped to the leg.

3. A pair of leather straps about 11 in. apart are sewn to the kitbag. The buckle of each strap is fixed to a small leather tab which in turn is fitted to a leather flap by a pin-and-cone release, permitting both length adjustment and quick-release action. The leather flap carries the cones of the releases and is sewn to the valise along one side only.

4. The pins of the pin-and-cone releases are connected by a length of cord, one end of which is extended and tied to a suspension D-ring at the top of the kitbag. A cone-release cover is provided in the form of a canvas flap, similar in shape and size to the leather flap referred to in para. 3. This is sewn to the kitbag along one side. The cone-release cover, when closed, is fastened to the leather flap by three press-studs. Two slits in the cone-release

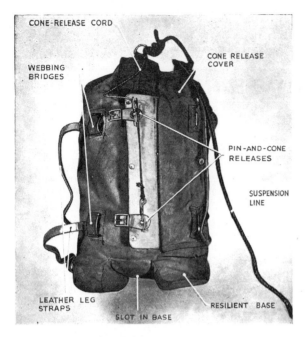

Fig. 1.—Side view of kitbag

Labels on Fig. 1:
CONE-RELEASE CORD
WEBBING BRIDGES
CONE RELEASE COVER
PIN-AND-CONE RELEASES
SUSPENSION LINE
LEATHER LEG STRAPS
SLOT IN BASE
RESILIENT BASE

6. A sleeve-type quick release, Part Number 478606, may be issued as part of the complete kitbag. This quick release, when closed, is a cylinder of about $\frac{3}{4}$ in. diameter and $2\frac{1}{2}$ in. long, at each end of which a D-ring is attached by a swivel joint. One D-ring is attached to a webbing loop which secures the quick release to the parachute harness, the harness leg strap passing through the webbing sleeve. To the the other D-ring is tied the suspension line of the kitbag. Should the parachutist wish to jettison the kitbag he takes the sleeve on the cylinder of the release in his right hand and pulls it upwards. This automatically releases the lower D-ring with its attached load.

Methods of use
Kitbag carried on the chest
(fig. 3 and 4)

7. Only kitbags loaded with items susceptible to damage are carried on the chest for descent

cover are so positioned that each buckle, with about an inch of its leather tab, can be passed through the cover. On the outside of the cone-release cover is sewn another piece of canvas to form a deep pocket which serves as the suspension line stowage (fig. 2).

5. The kitbag is strengthened at the top by canvas strips which secure a D-ring to either side of the top opening, as shown in fig. 2. When the kitbag is packed, these D-rings are drawn together and secured with the loose end of the suspension line, which consists of a 20 ft. length of cord with a spliced loop at one end. The anti-sear sleeve, which consists of a canvas sleeve about 6 in. long through which the suspension line passes, is on the suspension line, close to the point of attachment of the line to the D-rings (fig. 3).

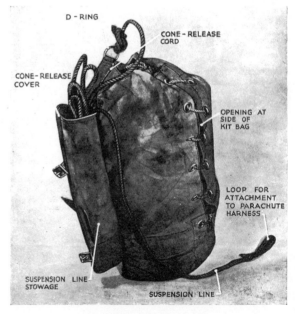

Labels on Fig. 2:
D - RING
CONE - RELEASE CORD
CONE-RELEASE COVER
OPENING AT SIDE OF KIT BAG
LOOP FOR ATTACHMENT TO PARACHUTE HARNESS
SUSPENSION LINE STOWAGE
SUSPENSION LINE

Fig. 2.—General view of kitbag

and landing, as this method increases slightly the risk of injury to the parachutist. Ensure that the kitbag has been prepared as shown in fig. 3, the following main points being noted:—

(i) The pin-and-cone releases for the leather leg straps are in the "fast" position and that the release cord emerges from the end of the release-cone cover towards the base of the kitbag, the loose end being tied to a convenient point on the kitbag.

(ii) The suspension line is coiled round the kitbag as shown in fig. 3 and the loose end temporarily attached to the lower leg strap.

(iii) The leg straps pass through the canvas bridges; this shortens their effective length.

8. The method of attaching the kitbag is as follows. Lay the kitbag across the chest with the padded end on the parachutist's right-hand side. Unbuckle the leg straps, pass them round behind the two upper chest straps of the parachute harness and re-buckle tightly. Unfasten the looped end of the suspension line which is attached to the lower leg strap, pull it tight, and attach it to the parachute-harness lower right leg strap. (Tying the suspension line in this way removes any possibility of the kitbag striking the parachutist in the face, should he somersault.)

9. When jumping with the kitbag on his chest the parachutist can either land with it still in this position, or release it to the full extent of the suspension line as soon as the parachute canopy has developed; this is done by pulling the pin release cord with the right hand and paying out the suspension line through the anti-sear sleeve, controlled by the left hand.

Fig. 4.—Kitbag attached to chest

Whether the kitbag is lowered on the suspension line or not, is determined by the store packed in it or by emergency.

Kitbag carried on the right leg (fig. 5)

10. Used in this way, the kitbag does not require to have the suspension line coiled round it. Before attaching the kitbag to the leg ensure that the pin-and-cone releases are in the "fast" position with the pin release cord emerging from the top end of the cone-release cover. Place the kitbag against the right leg so that the right foot fits into the slot provided in the base. Pass the straps through the canvas

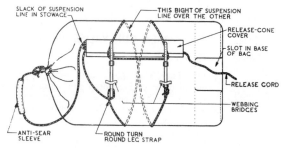

Fig. 3.—Kitbag loaded to 60 lb. ready for fitting on chest

SUSPENSION LINE
FIXED TO
PARACHUTE
HARNESS

FOOT IN SLOT

Fig. 5.—Kitbag attached to right leg

bridges and fasten them sufficiently tight to ensure that the kitbag does not slip downwards when the parachute canopy develops. Loop the end of the suspension line round the lower right leg strap of the parachute harness and slide the anti-sear sleeve close to the attachment of the suspension line to the D-rings. Fold the surplus line, tie with No. 8 thread, and place in the stowage on the cone-release cover. When jumping with a kitbag in this position, the right leg should be swung out of the aircraft parachute exit first and, to prevent somersaulting, the left leg brought up to it as soon as possible. As soon as the canopy has developed the parachutist should pull the pin-release cord with his right hand and allow the kitbag to descend to the full extent of the suspension line, controlling its rate of descent by the anti-sear sleeve held in the left hand.

Kitbag carried attached to both legs (for "sitting exit" only)

11. When making a "sitting exit" from an aircraft the kitbag may be attached to both legs. This method of attachment has little advantage over attachment to one leg except that the weight of the kitbag is borne by both legs instead of one when the canopy develops. When the kitbag is carried in this way, the leg straps do not pass through the bridges. The kitbag is placed on the right foot and the straps are passed round both legs and tightened. The loose end of the suspension line is attached to the lower right leg strap of the parachute harness in the same way as for single-leg attachment. Normal "sitting exit" jumping procedure is followed.

RIFLE VALISE

General

12. The rifle valise was originally intended for packing the No. 4 Lee-Enfield Service rifle prior to its stowage in containers or crates, and consisted of a simple felt sleeve. With the alterations described in para. 13 it is used when dropping rifles attached to parachutists. Appendix I to this chapter describes the various uses of the valise in both forms.

Description

13. The valise consists of a flat, felt sleeve about 44 in. long, 8 in. broad, and open at one end. An adjustable webbing belt, fitted with a pin-and-cone quick release, is sewn about 8 in. from the closed end. A webbing strap is sewn across the open end, and a fabric pocket is sewn to the edge of the valise for the stowage of the suspension line. This is a 20 ft. length of cord, looped at each end, which is used for securing the valise to the parachutist. A slit is provided in the sewn edge of the valise about 14 in. from the open end to enable one end of the suspension line to be secured to the contents of the valise.

BREN GUN VALISE MK. I

General

14. The Bren gun valise was originally intended for packing Bren guns prior to their stowage in containers or crates, and consists of a simple felt sleeve. It has become available as a protective cover for many articles of equipment carried by parachutists. Appendix I to this chapter describes specific uses of the valise.

Description

15. The valise is a flat, felt sleeve about 46 in. long with an average width of 9 in. It is closed and padded at one end, the other end being open and fitted with a padded flap. Rectangular, white, recognition patches are sometimes to be found sewn on the sides near the closed end of the sleeves.

Method of use

16. The valise is attached to a suspension line, and secured by quick-release straps.

BREN GUN VALISE, MK. II

General

17. When Bren guns are to be dropped with parachute troops they are packed in Bren gun valises strapped to the parachutists. The valise is always lowered on a suspension line during descent; this enables the parachutist to land unencumbered by the valise and ensures that the equipment is immediately available for use. In addition, when the ground cannot be seen, the slackening of the suspension line caused by the valise landing about a second before the parachutist lands, serves as a warning.

Description (fig. 6 and 7)

18. The valise consists of a flat felt sleeve about 46 in. long with an average width of 9 in. It is closed and padded at one end, the other being open across the bottom and for 8 in. or 9 in. up one side. The open end is closed by bringing the end flap round the bottom and securing it by means of a quick-release buckle. The upper loose corner of felt is tucked round and under the butt of the gun and the lower loose corner is brought round and over the end flap to which it is fastened by a quick-release buckle.

19. A canvas pocket is sewn to the front of the valise about 14 in. from the upper, or closed, end. This pocket is stitched along one side only, the open end being towards the top of the valise and is the stowage for the suspension line which is a twenty foot length of circular woven cord with a loop at each end. One loop of the suspension line is secured to the loop on the end of the length of webbing which runs almost the whole length of the

valise, terminating in the end flap quick-release buckle. The webbing loop is situated about 6 in. from the top of the valise and just above the webbing band which encircles the valise.

20. An anti-sear device which consists of a padded sleeve of webbing is provided on the suspension line to enable the parachutist to control the descent of the load without damage to his hands. A band is sewn to the sleeve to prevent it from slipping from his hand.

21. About 8 in. from the top of the valise an adjustable webbing belt is sewn to the back. This belt is fitted with a pin-and-cone release and is located so that the cone comes to one side of the back of the valise as shown in fig. 7.

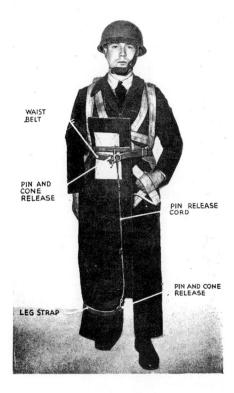

WAIST BELT

PIN AND CONE RELEASE

PIN RELEASE CORD

PIN AND CONE RELEASE

LEG STRAP

Fig. 6.—Bren gun valise Mk. II in jumping position

22. An adjustable webbing strap fitted with a pin-and-cone quick-release is sewn approximately four inches from the bottom of the valise. This strap is located on the back of the valise so that the cone comes to the side in the same way as the waist belt shown in fig. 7.

23. The pins of the pin-and-cone releases on the waist belt and ankle strap are joined by a length of $\frac{1}{4}$ in. webbing lanyard which has a

steel ring inserted about four inches from the upper end. When the pins are in position the lanyard is held in a straight line along the valise by two fabric loops.

Method of use

24. A full description of how to pack and carry the valise will be found in Appendix I to this chapter.

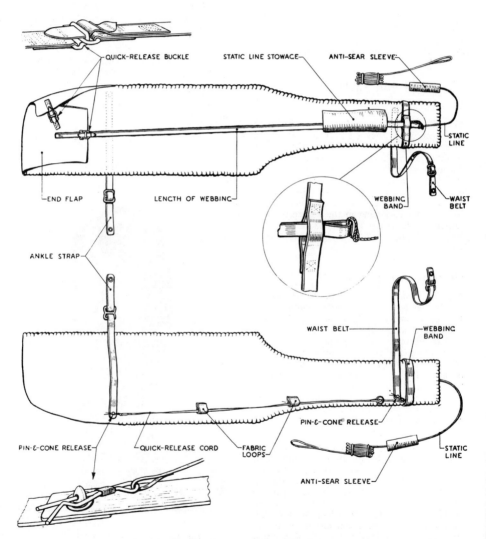

QUICK-RELEASE BUCKLE — STATIC LINE STOWAGE — ANTI-SEAR SLEEVE

STATIC LINE

END FLAP — LENGTH OF WEBBING — WEBBING BAND — WAIST BELT

ANKLE STRAP

WAIST BELT — WEBBING BAND

PIN-&-CONE RELEASE — QUICK-RELEASE CORD — FABRIC LOOPS — PIN-&-CONE RELEASE — STATIC LINE

ANTI-SEAR SLEEVE

Fig. 7.—Bren gun valise Mk. II

This leaf issued with A.L. No. 17
May, 1946

QUICK-RELEASE STRAPS

General

25. Equipment which is not to be carried by means of a special kitbag can be attached to a parachutist's harness by quick-release straps. The equipment is held securely in place by the straps until the parachute canopy has developed; the parachutist then pulls the dual release pin and lowers the equipment to the end of a 20 ft. suspension line. An anti-sear sleeve is provided to control the rate of descent of the load and to prevent the line from burning the man's hands.

Description (fig. 8)

26. (i) The device is shown in fig. 8, and consists of the pin-and-cone release straps from the following obsolete stores:—

　　　(a) Sten leg ammunition case (Army Stores Ref. AA. 5333)

　　　(b) 2 in. mortar leg case (Army Stores Ref. AA.5380)

　　　(c) 2 in. mortar bomb leg case (Army Stores Ref. AA.5381) each modified by increasing the length of the straps by 6 in.

(ii) Both straps are adjustable and are spaced about 6 in. apart by a length of webbing in which are the eyeletted holes for the quick-releases and the two short lengths of webbing with buckles. A dual-release pin holds both cones secure.

Method of use

27. The device is normally used for equipment carried on the chest. Methods of using it are described in Appendix I to this chapter.

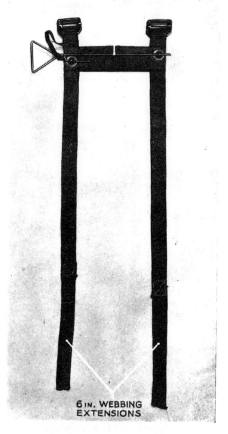

DUAL RELEASE PIN

6 IN. WEBBING EXTENSIONS

Fig. 8.—Pin-and-cone release

EQUIPMENT ATTACHED TO PARACHUTISTS

BREN GUN

General

1. When Bren guns are dropped attached to parachutists they must be packed in valises, Bren Gun Mk. II, a full description of which will be found in Chapter 1, para. 17 to 24. In all cases the load, which is attached to the parachutist by a suspension line, must be released to the full extent of the line during descent. Normal jumping procedure may be followed.

Method of packing and attaching to parachutist

2. Place the gun in the valise, muzzle foremost, and close the open end by securing the end flap with the quick-release buckle. Tuck the upper loose corner of felt round and under the butt and bring the lower loose corner round and over the end flap; fasten with the quick-release buckle. Rest the loaded valise on the parachutist's right foot with the suspension line stowage towards him, secure the ankle strap and waist belt with the pin-and-cone quick releases. Pass the parachute-harness lower right leg strap through the free loop on the suspension line, fold the slack line, secure with No. 8 thread (Stores Ref. 15A/108) and place in the stowage.

Note . . . The anti-sear sleeve must be located on the suspension line between its attachment to the valise and the stowage. Sufficient slack must be left to permit the parachutist to grip it comfortably at his side (*see fig. 6* in Chapter 1 of this Section).

SERVICE RIFLE

General

3. Parachutists may jump with service rifles so long as they are packed and carried as described below. In all instances the load must be released to the full extent of the suspension line during descent. Normal jumping procedure may be followed.

Method of packing and attaching to parachutist

4. Loop one end of the suspension line round the rifle below the upper sling-swivel; ensure that it passes between the sling and the barrel, and put the rifle into the valise, butt-end first. Thread the free end of the suspension line through the slit provided in the valise, fold and stow the remainder of the line in the pocket leaving 18 in. free for subsequent attachment to the parachute harness. Fasten the strap across the open end of the valise, ensuring at the same time that the muzzle protrudes from the side remote from the suspension-line stowage. Affix a webbing bayonet frog to the upper strap of the parachutist's right anklet. Place the muzzle in the bayonet frog and secure the belt round the parachutist's waist. Pass the parachute-harness right leg strap through the loop on the free end of the suspension line and re-assemble the parachute harness.

AIRBORNE BICYLE

General

5. Parachuting with the airborne bicycle from either Dakota or Stirling aircraft is simple and requires little equipment. The bicycle is suspended from the parachutist's body by a quick-release strap when jumping and is always released and lowered to the full extent of a 20 ft. suspension line during descent.

Preparation of bicycle

6. Fold the bicycle and push the pedals through into the stowed position. Lower the handlebars and raise the saddle so that the latter will receive most of the landing shock.

7. Strap both wheels together, securing them to the rear chain stays to prevent them from rotating (An Army-issue valise strap is most suitable for this). Tie one end of the 20 ft. suspension line to both the wheels in such a position that when the cycle is suspended by the line the saddle is lowermost. This is important to prevent damage to the handlebars on landing.

Method of attaching bicycle to parachutist (fig. I)

8. Commencing from the free end, plait the suspension line to ensure that it will pay out quickly and easily without forming loose coils likely to foul the cycle. Take the free end and tie it to the lower left leg strap of the parachute harness. Finally, suspend the bicycle from a quick-release strap passing round the back of the parachutist's neck.

Fig. I.—Airborne bicycle in jumping position

Method of jumping with airborne bicycle (fig. 2 and 3)

9. When making an exit from Dakota aircraft, hold the bicycle slightly forward and to the right-hand side, as shown in fig. 2. Take care to avoid fouling the forward edge of the door and catching the brake cable of the bicycle on

Fig. 2.—Jumping position from Dakota

Fig. 3.—Jumping position from Stirling

Note:—Parachutist to be slightly to the starboard side of the aircraft centre-line

the door jettison handle. Step well out to avoid being brushed along the side of the aircraft. As soon as the canopy has developed, release the bicycle by pulling the loose end of the quick-release strap.

10. When jumping from Stirling aircraft, hold the bicycle slightly forward and to the right-hand side, as shown in fig. 3. It is important to stand slightly to the starboard side of the aircraft centre-line to prevent the cycle from fouling the exit. As soon as the canopy has developed, release the bicycle by pulling the loose end of the quick-release strap. No anti-sear sleeve is required.

AIRBORNE STRETCHER

General

11. The airborne stretcher is strapped diagonally across the chest of the parachutist who jumps with it in this position. It must always be released to the full extent of the suspension line during descent.

Preparation of stretcher (fig. 4)

12. The stretcher is folded, and the handles are strapped to the frame by a pair of Army-issue valise straps. The suspension line,

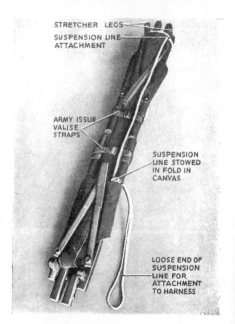

Fig. 4.—Airborne stretcher packed

which consists of a 20 ft. length of line, is tied to one end of the folded stretcher. To make this attachment secure, the line is passed once round each leg, as shown in fig. 4. The remainder of the line is folded and tucked into the canvas of the stretcher leaving about 18 in. of the loose end free for attachment to the parachutist.

Attachment of stretcher to para-chutist (fig. 5)

13. The quick-release device (described in Chapter 1, paras. 25 to 27) is placed against the chest and one strap is passed under the para-chute-harness upper right chest strap, the other strap being passed under the parachute-harness lower left chest strap. The stretcher is then held almost vertically against the parachutist's chest and the straps buckled round it. Finally, the loose end of the suspen-sion line is attached to the left leg strap of the parachute harness.

14. The stretcher is held almost vertical for jumping. As soon as the canopy has developed the stretcher is released by pulling the dual release pin of the pin-and-cone release device. It is not necessary to use an anti-sear sleeve

Fig. 5.—Airborne stretcher in jumping position

as this load weighs only 16 lb. Apart from the special points mentioned in this paragraph, standard jumping procedure is followed.

AIRBORNE-STRETCHER BUNDLES
General

15. Stretcher bundles consist of an airborne stretcher, together with all, or a combination, of the items listed in paragraph 16. Stretcher bundles may be carried either across the chest or packed in a kitbag attached to the right leg.

Preparation of bundle

16. The items which may be packed with the airborne stretcher are:—

Blankets	2
Sheets, ground	1
Splints, knee, Thomas	1
Splint, knee, bar, suspension ...	1
Splint, knee, stirrup	1
Bandage, flannelette	1
Pins, safety, $4\frac{1}{2}$ in.	3
Container, canvas, $3\frac{1}{2}$ gal. ...	1
Pick	1
Shovel	1

In addition, the following will be required for packing the above:—

Army-issue valise straps (or similar)	1 set
Quick-release straps	1 set
Suspension line, 20 ft.	1
Anti-sear sleeve	1
Airborne kitbag, if required ...	1
No. 8 linen thread, Stores Ref. 15A/108	As required
Cord for lashing ...	As required

17. Fold the stretcher and lash it to the Thomas splint so that one end protrudes through the leather-padded ring of the splint. Remove the head of the pick from the helve and secure it to the splint frame with cord. Next secure the helve to one side of the splint frame and the suspension bar to the other. Place the shovel pan on the leather-padded ring and secure the handle to the suspension bar with cord. Should the Thomas splint not be included, the above items must be securely lashed to the folded stretcher frame. Place the flannelette bandage, safety pins and stirrup in the canvas container, fold the container, and lash it to the shovel-side of the bundle. Finally wrap the folded blankets, covered by the ground sheet, round the bundle and secure the whole at each end with an Army valise strap.

Attachment of bundle to parachutist

18. There are two approved methods for attaching stretcher bundles to parachutists. They are:—

(i) Attach one end of the suspension line to the leather-padded ring of the splint, or if the splint is not included in the bundle, round both legs of the stretcher at one end. The procedure is then the same as for the airborne stretcher described in para. 13 and 14 of this Appendix, except that an anti-sear sleeve must be used.

(ii) Place the bundle, with the leather padded ring of the splint downwards, in an airborne kitbag and attach it to the right leg as described in para. 10 of Chapter 1.

MEDIUM MACHINE GUN

General

19. The medium machine gun is dropped with parachute troops as two separate parachutists' loads. One load consists of the machine-gun barrel complete with action and is carried in a Bren Gun Valise Mk. I, across the parachutist's chest while the other load consists of the tripod in an airborne kitbag.

Machine-gun barrel, complete with action

Method of packing (fig. 6)

20. The barrel is placed muzzle-first in a Bren Gun Valise Mk. I and is bound round

PIN-AND-CONE RELEASE DEVICE

ATTACHMENT OF 20 ft. ROPE TO HARNESS

Fig. 7.—M.M.G. in jumping position

with the suspension line of a rifle valise. A 20 ft. rope is used as a suspension line for the barrel, and is secured at the end containing the butt, passing under the line binding. The slack line is folded and tied with linen thread (Stores Ref. 15A/108), about 18 in. of the free end being left for attachment to the parachutist. An anti-sear sleeve is slipped on the line between its attachment to the load and the stowage.

Method of attachment to parachutist (fig. 7)

21. The straps of a pin-and-cone release device are passed one behind each of the upper chest straps of the parachutist's harness. The packed machine gun barrel is then laid across the chest, with the butt end to the parachutist's right-hand side, and buckled tightly. The loose end of the suspension line (a 20 ft. rope) is looped round the right leg strap of the parachute harness.

Jumping procedure (fig. 8)

22. To prevent fouling the sides of the aircraft parachute exit when jumping the load is held

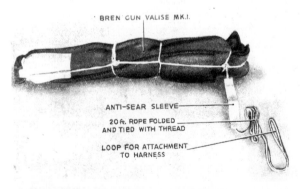

BREN GUN VALISE MK.I.

ANTI-SEAR SLEEVE

20 ft. ROPE FOLDED AND TIED WITH THREAD

LOOP FOR ATTACHMENT TO HARNESS

Fig. 6.—M.M.G. (C/W action) packed in Bren gun valise Mk. I

almost vertically, as shown in fig. 7. After his exit from the aircraft the parachutist need no longer hold the load which should, of its own accord, take up a horizontal position. As soon as the parachute canopy has developed, the load should be released by holding the anti-sear sleeve in the right hand and pulling away the dual release-pin from the quick release strap with the left hand. The load is then allowed to descend slowly to the full extent of the suspension line, but under special circumstances the parachutist may land with the load still strapped across his chest.

Machine gun tripod
Method of packing

23. As the tripod is both heavy and angular it must be well padded and packed in an airborne kitbag. It should be folded and inserted in the kitbag with its legs uppermost. One leg will remain protruding from the bag, and therefore must be particularly well padded.

Method of attachment to parachutist, and jumping technique

24. The load may be attached

to the parachutist's legs or across his chest. No special jumping technique is required but, due to the shape of the load, it must always be lowered to the full extent of the suspension line during descent. Full details of method of attachment will be found in para. 7–11 of Chapter 1 (to which this is an Appendix).

3 in. MORTAR

General

25. The 3 in. mortar is carried as two separate parachutists' loads when dropped with parachute troops. One load consists of the barrel, which is packed in a rifle valise and strapped to one parachutist's chest, and the other, the base plate, is carried by another parachutist in an airborne kitbag. 15 lb. of additional equipment may be carried in the kitbag bringing the load up to 60 lb. Both loads must be released to the full extent of the suspension line during descent.

Barrel

Method of packing (fig. 9)

26. The barrel is placed in a rifle valise, and another valise (modified by cutting to 14 in. in length) is put over the muzzle end. The whole assembly is then bound up with a rifle-valise suspension line. A 20 ft. rope is attached by making a bowline loop at one end and tying the short end to the valise, as shown in fig. 9. The remainder of the 20 ft. rope is folded and secured with No. 8 linen thread (Stores Ref. 15A/108). Ensure that there is an anti-sear sleeve on the suspension line between its attachment to the load and the line in the stowage.

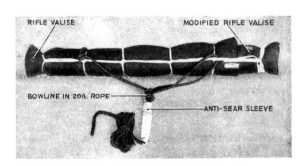

Fig. 9.—Mortar barrel packed

Method of attachment to the parachutist (fig. 10)

27. The straps of a pin-and-cone release device are passed behind the parachute-harness straps, one behind the right upper chest strap and the other behind the left leg strap. The packed barrel is placed against the chest in an almost vertical position and is strapped tightly. The loose end of the 20 ft. rope is tied to the parachutist's right leg strap.

Jumping procedure

28. The load is held almost vertically for jumping as shown in fig. 10. As soon as the parachute canopy has developed, the load should be released by holding the anti-sear sleeve in the right hand and pulling the dual release-pin away with the left hand. The rate of descent of the load is controlled by the anti-sear sleeve.

Base plate

Method of packing

29. The base plate is padded and packed in an airborne kitbag. As the base plate weighs only 45 lb. an additional 15 lb. of equipment may be packed into the bag.

Attachment to parachutist and jumping procedure

30. The load may be carried as a normal kitbag load, as described in Chap. 1, para. 10.

Note . . . The load must be released on the 20 ft. line during descent.

P.I.A.T.

General

31. The P.I.A.T. may be dropped (as one load) attached to a parachutist. It does not need any protective covering when it is packed for dropping as described in para. 32. It is lowered on a 20 ft. suspension line during descent, but under special circumstances the parachutist may land with it still strapped across his chest.

Method of preparation

32. The action is cocked and the monopod removed and replaced in the projectile support. The clamp of the monopod is passed through

Fig. 10.—Mortar barrel in jumping position

the aperture which the adapter normally fills. The lower sling is removed and the upper sling is attached to the butt end and passed round the foresight bracket, up the left-hand side of the weapon, round the monopod base plate, back down the right-hand side of the weapon, and is finally attached to the forward swivel attachment of the lower sling. The sling is then tightened to hold the monopod firmly in the projectile support. The 20 ft. suspension line is attached to the weapon at the clamp groove; the remainder of the line is folded and secured with linen thread, Stores Ref. 15A/108. Ensure that there is an anti-sear sleeve on the suspension line between its point of attachment to the load and the folded line.

Method of attachment to parachutist (fig. 11 and 12)

33. The straps of the pin-and-cone release device are passed behind the upper chest straps of the parachute harness. The weapon is placed against the parachutist's chest and the straps are fastened round it, one before and one behind the trigger guard. The loose end of the suspension line is attached to the right leg strap.

Note . . . The spigot-guide tube stopper must be in place to prevent the ingress of dirt.

Jumping procedure

34. When jumping, the P.I.A.T. must be held firmly against the body in the position shown in fig. 11. As soon as the parachute canopy has developed, the weapon is released by holding the anti-sear sleeve in the right hand and pulling the dual release pin away with the left hand. The rate of descent of the weapon is controlled by the anti-sear sleeve held in the right hand. The parachutist may, if necessary, land with the load on his chest, in which case it should be held in a horizontal position for landing (fig. 12).

Fig. 11.—P.I.A.T. in jumping position

Fig. 12.—P.I.A.T. in landing position

8

Towing of Glider-Borne Forces and Equipment, 1942/3

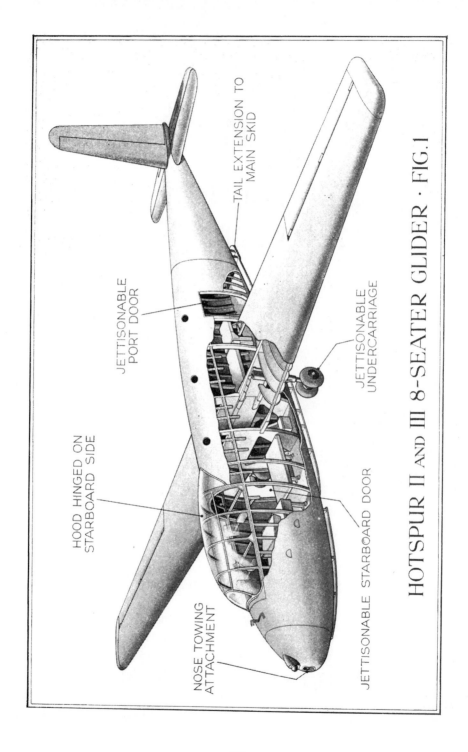

TAIL EXTENSION TO MAIN SKID

JETTISONABLE PORT DOOR

JETTISONABLE UNDERCARRIAGE

HOOD HINGED ON STARBOARD SIDE

JETTISONABLE STARBOARD DOOR

NOSE TOWING ATTACHMENT

HOTSPUR II AND III 8-SEATER GLIDER · FIG.1

CHAPTER 2

GLIDERS

General

1. Each type of glider employed for the carriage of troops and equipment is fully described in the relevant glider handbook to which reference is made in the following pages. The purpose of this chapter is to epitomise the leading particulars of each glider and to draw attention to the provision for towing, the seating accommodation for troops, the method of stowing military equipment, and other features directly concerning airborne forces.

2. Reference should be made to Sect. 4, Chap. 6 of this manual, and to Sect. 4 of the glider handbooks for C.G. and loading data of the gliders here described.

Hotspur II and III

Description (*see* fig. 1)

3. The Hotspur II is fully described in A.P.2092A, Vol. I. The Hotspur III is the version of the Hotspur II incorporating the most recent modifications.

4. The Hotspur is an eight-seater, mid-wing, monoplane glider, largely of monocoque construction and adapted for nose towing. The principal dimensions are as follows:—

Overall length	...	...	...	...	39 ft. 3½ in.
Span (normal)	...	...	...	...	45 ft. 11 in.
Overall height	...	...	...	...	10 ft. 10 in.
Fuselage height	...	...	...	...	5 ft. 6 in.
Fuselage width	...	...	...	...	3 ft. 6 in.

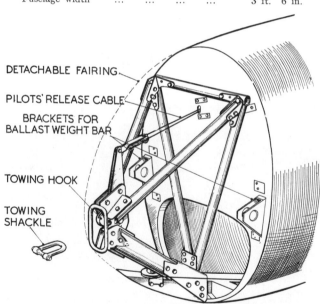

DETACHABLE FAIRING

PILOTS' RELEASE CABLE

BRACKETS FOR
BALLAST WEIGHT BAR

TOWING HOOK

TOWING
SHACKLE

Fig. 2.—Hotspur tow release mechanism

Controls

5. The flying controls are in duplicate for the first and second pilots whose seats are arranged in tandem. In addition to the flying controls, dual tow release knobs are mounted on the left-hand side of the instrument panel in each cockpit, and a lever for jettisoning the undercarriage is mounted on the right-hand side, accessible to both pilots.

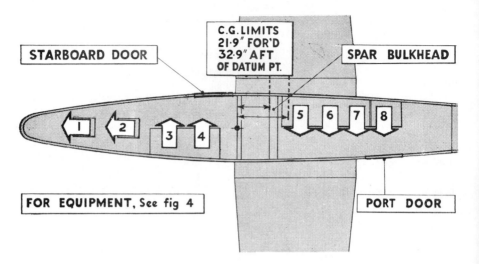

Fig. 3.—Seating diagram—Hotspur II and III

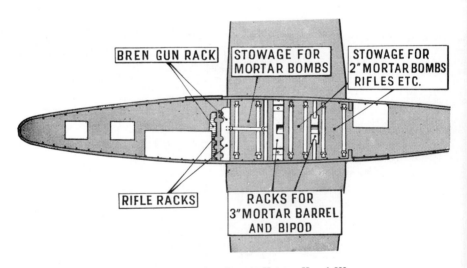

Fig. 4.—Stowage of equipment—Hotspur II and III

Tow release mechanism (*see* fig. 2)

6. The tow release mechanism is of the G.A.L. type and is situated in the nose of the glider. The mechanism comprises a single claw which is maintained in the closed position by a tension spring and toggle. The claw is controlled by a cable from the pilots' cockpits. To insert the cable shackle it is necessary to open the claw by means of the pilot's control. When the shackle is inserted and the pilot's control is released the tension spring causes the claw to grip the shackle. To release the glider from the towing cable the claw is opened by pulling back either one of the dual-control knobs in the cockpits. Details of the tow release mechanism are given in A.P.1492B, Vol. I, Sect. 2, Chap. 3.

Jettisonable undercarriage

7. The undercarriage comprises two separate cantilever shock-absorber struts, each with twin wheels and jettisonable after take-off. Normally each undercarriage leg is held in its housing by a supporting cable which resists the action of an ejector spring. When the jettison control lever is operated the supporting cables are released, allowing the undercarriage legs to leave their housings assisted by the action of the ejector springs.

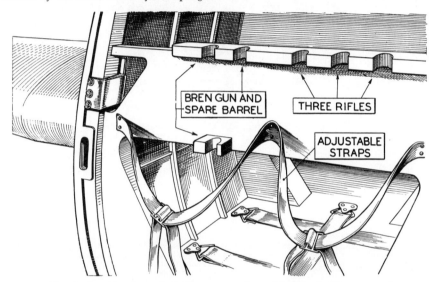

Fig. 5.—Provision for equipment stowage at forward bulkhead and centre section

Landing skid

8. When the undercarriage has been jettisoned the glider lands on a two-piece ash skid which is secured to the underside of the fuselage by metal attachment plates vulcanised to rubber blocks. The main skid is extended far enough aft to serve also as a tail skid.

Glider equipment

9. The normal equipment of the Hotspur II and III includes torches, vacuum flasks, a map case, four urine bottles and a storage battery for navigation and signalling lamps.

Accommodation for troops (*see* fig. 3)

10. The fuselage is divided by two bulkheads into forward and aft compartments. Each compartment has a removable door for entry and exit, the door for the forward compartment being situated on the starboard side immediately in front of the wing, and that for the aft compartment on the port side just behind the wing. Each door is held in position by two spigots on its leading edge and a bolt-type lock on its rear edge, and, when removed, may either be jettisoned or stowed within the fuselage. Seats are provided for two pilots and two troops in the forward compartment, and for four troops in the aft compartment of the glider.

Safety harness

11. Each pilot is provided with Sutton safety harness, Mark V, as described in A.P.1182, Vol. I, Part 2, Chap. 2. The troops, all of whom face inboard, are provided with quick-release straps which give protection against landing shocks.

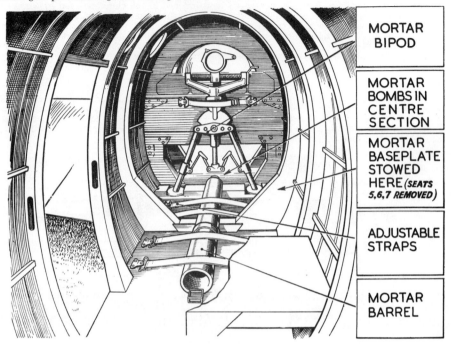

MORTAR
BIPOD

MORTAR
BOMBS IN
CENTRE
SECTION

MORTAR
BASEPLATE
STOWED
HERE *(SEATS
5,6,7 REMOVED)*

ADJUSTABLE
STRAPS

MORTAR
BARREL

Fig. 6.—3 in. Mortar stowage—seats 5, 6 and 7 removed

Stowage of military equipment (*see* fig. 4)

12. On some Hotspurs a rack is provided, on the leading edge of the forward bulkhead, to accommodate three rifles, one Bren gun, and one spare Bren gun barrel. Adjustable straps secure these items in position (*see* fig. 5).

13. The floor of the centre section of the glider, between the two bulkheads, is used for the stowage of small items such as mortar bombs. Six adjustable straps are provided to secure such items.

14. In order to accommodate a 3 in. mortar barrel, bipod and baseplate, the seat for troops Nos. 5, 6 and 7 is removed and two wooden cradles are fitted between formers on the floor of the aft compartment (*see* fig. 6). Adjustable straps are provided on the floor of some Hotspurs and on the spar bulkhead for securing these and smaller items in position.

Horsa I

Description (*see* fig. 7)

15. The Horsa I is fully described in A.P.2097A, Vol. I. It is nominally a twenty-eight seater, high-wing, monoplane glider with a fuselage of circular section constructed in three semi-monocoque portions. Towing is effected from two points underneath the wing, at the outer ends of the centre plane main spar. The principal dimensions are as follows:—

Overall length	...	...	...	...	67 ft. 0 in.	
Span ...	...	...	...	...	...	88 ft. 0 in.
Overall height (to top of rudder)				...	19 ft. 6 in.	
Fuselage diameter	...	....	...	...	7 ft. 6¼ in.	

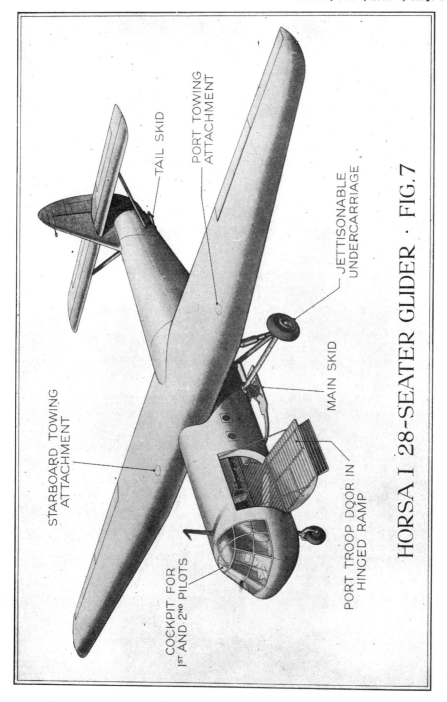

STARBOARD TOWING
ATTACHMENT

TAIL SKID

PORT TOWING
ATTACHMENT

JETTISONABLE
UNDERCARRIAGE

MAIN SKID

COCKPIT FOR
1ST AND 2ND PILOTS

PORT TROOP DOOR IN
HINGED RAMP

HORSA I 28-SEATER GLIDER · FIG.7

Controls

16. The flying controls are in duplicate for the first and second pilots whose seats are arranged side by side in the nose of the glider. In addition to the flying controls a red lever operating the tow release mechanism is mounted at the top of the control pedestal, and a jettison release control lever for the undercarriage is mounted to starboard of the flap lever.

Tow release mechanism

17. The tow release mechanism is of the No. 6A plug and socket type. Duplicate fittings are attached to the extremities of the centre plane main spar. The mechanism comprises a retracting hook which is maintained in the closed position by a return spring, lever and link. The hook is controlled by a trigger operated from the lever in the pilots' cockpit. To insert the towing hook plug, attached to the towing cable, it is necessary to open the retracting hook by means of the pilot's control. When the plug is inserted and the pilot's control is released, the return spring causes the retracting hook to grip the towing hook plug. To release the glider from the towing cable, the retracting hooks are opened simultaneously by means of the pilot's control. Full details of the tow release mechanism are given in A.P.1492B, Vol. I, Sect. 2, Chap. 2.

Jettisonable undercarriage

18. The main undercarriage comprises two separate triangular frames of tubular construction which pivot on brackets attached to the fuselage. The shocks are absorbed by the rubber blocks in two shock struts, one of which is interposed between each tubular structure and a bracket on each centre plane. When the jettison control is operated the shock struts are disengaged at both ends and the tubular wheel-carrying structures disengage at the inner pivoting joints.

Nose wheel

19. A castoring nose wheel with a rubber shock absorber is fitted to the Horsa and is used for take-off and for landing whether or not the undercarriage has been jettisoned.

Main skid

20. A wooden, metal-faced skid with a rubber shock-absorber mounting is attached to the underside of the fuselage.

Tail skid

21. A tail skid is provided and, in addition, a tail prop for use when the glider is being loaded.

Glider equipment

22. The normal equipment of the Horsa I includes torches, vacuum flasks, a map case, sanitary tubes and one sanitary container, a 12-volt accumulator for lighting services, hatches for the operation of unmounted Bren guns, T.R.9D radio equipment and one parachute flare.

Accommodation for troops (see fig. 8)

23. The central cabin extends from the pilots' cockpit to a bulkhead about six feet aft of the wing. Access to the pilots' cockpit is obtained from the central cabin through folding doors. The forward end of the cabin is equipped with a large door in the port side. This door is hinged along its lower edge and, when open, forms a ramp by means of which bulky equipment may be loaded or unloaded from the glider. A sliding door in the combined door and ramp is provided for the use of troops, and a second sliding door is provided at the rear of the central cabin just aft of the starboard wing. Seats are provided in the central cabin for twenty-six troops, and, in the pilots' cockpit, for a first and second pilot sitting side by side.

24. An alternative loading of twenty-nine troops in addition to the first and second pilots is permissible in circumstances where the troops are lightly equipped. For this purpose an additional seat for three troops is fitted on the starboard side of the central cabin, opposite the forward entrance door.

Safety harness

25. The two pilots are provided with Sutton safety harness, Mark V, as described in A.P.118,2 Vol 1, Part 2, Chap. 2. The troops are provided with quick-release straps which give protection against landing shocks.

Carriage of military equipment

26. Certain items of military equipment which may be carried in the Horsa will be found listed in the C.G. statement in A.P.2097A, Sect. 4. A system of loading for heavy equipment is now being developed which includes the use of steel channels for the stowage of wheeled items. Information on this subject will be published by amendment action as soon as it becomes available.

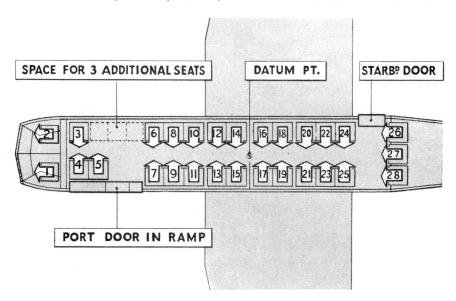

Fig. 8.—Seating diagram—Horsa I

THE HAMILCAR I GLIDER

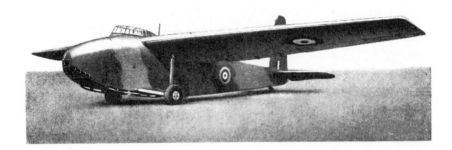

LOADING AND LASHING IN THE HAMILCAR I GLIDER

Description

1—The Hamilcar I is fully described in Air Publication 2219A, Vol. I. It is a high wing cantilever monoplane transport glider capable of carrying military loads. A bifurcated tow cable (described in A.P.1492B, Vol. I, Sect. 1) is attached to release devices on the underside of the mainplane centre section. The principal dimensions of the glider are as follows:—

	ft.	in.
Overall length	68	1
Span	110	0
Overall height to top of rudder —on "ferrying" or "operational" undercarriage (tail down)	20	3
Overall height to top of rudder —on "ferrying" undercarriage (fuselage datum horizontal) ...	27	0
Overall height to top of rudder —on "operational" undercarriage (fuselage datum horizontal)	26	6
Overall height to top of rudder —on landing skids (fuselage datum horizontal)	24	4
Fuselage width	9	3

Controls

2—The pilot's cockpit is situated above, and is completely separated from, the cabin. Two pilots are seated in tandem, and the flying controls are duplicated. A tow cable release lever and an emergency release are provided on the left of each pilot's seat. The "operational" undercarriage can be jettisoned by either pilot by means of a lever on his right.

3—The towing and release mechanism consists of two Malcolm plug and socket units, one on each extremity of the mainplane centre section. The units are operated by means of a lever adjacent to each pilot's seat. Details of the tow release units are given in A.P.1492B, Vol. I, Sect. 2, Chap. 2.

Undercarriage

4—It is possible to fit either an "operational" or a "ferrying" undercarriage. The "operational" undercarriage consists of two wheels mounted on a single beam axle; the unit is jettisonable and fits into crutches mounted on the underside of the fuselage.

5—The "ferrying" undercarriage is non-jettisonable. It is composed of port and star-

This leaf issued with A.L. No. 3
OCTOBER, 1944

LOADING AND LASHING IN THE HAMILCAR I GLIDER

board axle and drag strut units with a shock absorber strut attached to the outboard ends of each. The wheel is carried at the junction of the axle, drag and shock absorber struts. The upper end of the shock absorber strut is located in a ball joint housing on the underside of the mainplane centre section. A modification has made it possible for the shock absorber struts to be deflated, thus lowering the glider on to its skids for loading and unloading operations.

Landing skids

6—Two pairs of landing skids, attached at their forward ends to frames No. 1 and 11, run under each bottom longeron. They are supported for the remainder of their length by solid rubber blocks between them and the longerons.

Tail wheel unit

7—The tail wheel unit is of the fixed self-centring type and incorporates a Vickers shock-absorber strut.

Glider equipment (fig. 1 and 2)

8—Torches are stowed on the port side of the cockpit. On the starboard side are map cases, one each for the pilot and co-pilot. Type "A" safety harness is attached to a rail at the back of each seat.

9—In the cabin are provided vacuum flasks, a sanitary tube, torches, first-aid packs, and a stowage bag for the controls locking gear. For demolition purposes two axes, a hand saw and a pair of shears are provided. Three fire extinguishers are normally stowed in the cabin, but additional extinguishers are required for certain loads, as laid down in Appendix I to this Chapter.

10—Safety harness for the crews of vehicles etc. is fitted either in the vehicles comprising the cargo or in the cabin of the glider itself, according to the requirements of the load carried (see Appendix I to this Chapter).

Intercommunication

11—Telephonic communication is provided between the pilots and the personnel in the cabin, and also between the glider and its tug aircraft. There is a call light system at the pilots' positions and in the cabin. A radio transmitter can be fitted to work in conjunction with the intercommunication system.

Cabin lighting

12—Four lamps are fitted in the cabin for use in night operations. The brilliance of the light emitted can be adjusted by a rheostat mounted in a control panel near the entrance door on the port side.

Crating

13—

	Length ft. in.	Width ft. in.	Height ft. in.	Weight ton cwt.
Front fuselage				
Crate No. 1	36 0½	11 4	13 2	7 0
Centre section				
Crate No. 2	35 0½	17 5	7 2	7 0
Mainplane				
Crate No. 3	40 0½	17 6½	7 8	7 13
Rear fuselage				
Crate No. 4	32 11½	10 8	8 6	3 12

Cabin dimensions (fig. 6 and 7)

14—A dimensional view of the glider's cabin is shown in fig. 6. It can be used for checking whether or not a proposed cargo can be accommodated.

Nose door (fig. 3 and 4)

15—The nose door is of semi-monocoque wooden construction, with a louvre on either side for ventilating purposes. The two main hinges are mounted on the starboard side. The lock is mounted on the forward face of front fuselage frame No. 1, on the port side, and can be operated manually from inside or outside the glider, or automatically by a vehicle in the cabin. Situated at the top starboard corner of the door, on the inside, is a cable-operated push-rod assembly, actuated either manually, or in the case of certain wheeled equipment, automatically. The door can be jettisoned from the inside in an emergency by means of a lever on the starboard side. A picketing ring in the bottom port corner of the door frame enables the door to be retained in the open position when the glider is on the ground.

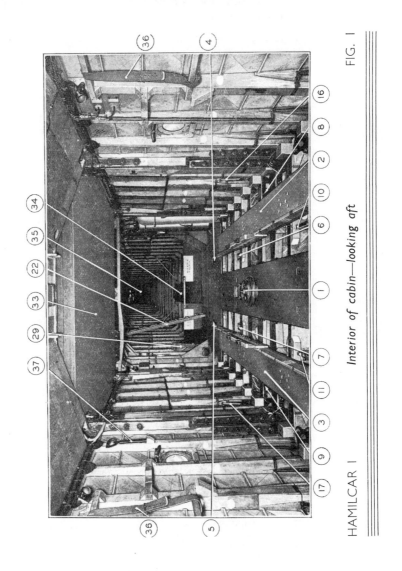

FIG. I

Interior of cabin—looking aft

HAMILCAR I

This leaf issued with A.L. No. 3
OCTOBER, 1944

AIR PUBLICATION 2453D
Vol. I Part 3 Sect. 3 Chap. I

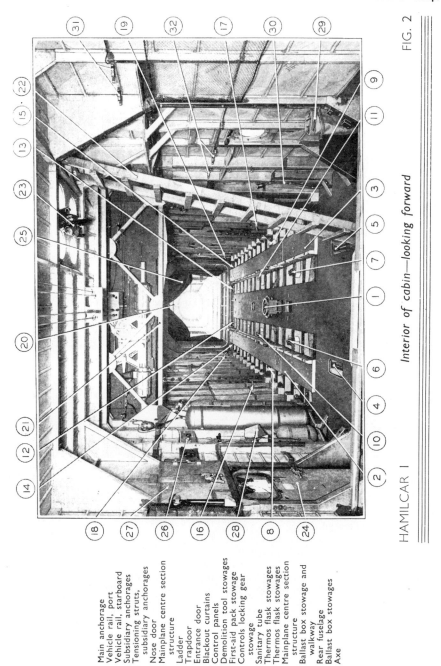

FIG. 2

HAMILCAR I   Interior of cabin—looking forward

1. Main anchorage
2. Vehicle rail, port
3. Vehicle rail, starboard
4/15. Subsidiary anchorages
16/19. Tensioning struts,
    subsidiary anchorages
20. Nose door
21. Mainplane centre section
    structure
22. Ladder
23. Trapdoor
24. Entrance door
25. Blackout curtains
26. Control panels
27. Demolition tool stowages
28. First-aid pack stowage
29. Controls locking gear
    stowage
30. Sanitary tube
31. Thermos flask stowages
32. Thermos flask stowages
33. Mainplane centre section
    structure
34. Ballast box stowage and
    walkway
35. Rear fuselage
36. Ballast box stowages
37. Axe

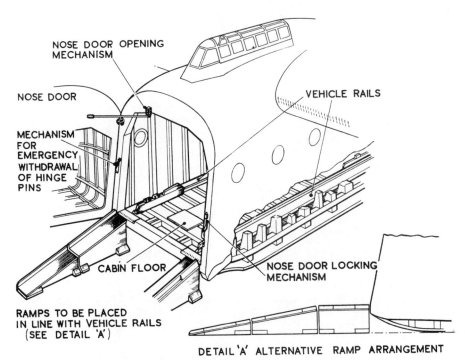

NOSE DOOR OPENING MECHANISM

NOSE DOOR

MECHANISM FOR EMERGENCY WITHDRAWAL OF HINGE PINS

VEHICLE RAILS

CABIN FLOOR

NOSE DOOR LOCKING MECHANISM

RAMPS TO BE PLACED IN LINE WITH VEHICLE RAILS (SEE DETAIL 'A')

DETAIL 'A' ALTERNATIVE RAMP ARRANGEMENT

HAMILCAR I   *Aircraft prepared for loading and unloading*   FIG. 3

Accommodation of cargo crew

16—Personnel accommodated in the cabin are provided with seats in the vehicles comprising the cargo or on seats in the cabin itself, according to the nature of the load.

Accommodation of cargo

17—All cargo must be carried in the cabin, the structure of which is designed to support the loads.

18—Cargo is loaded into the glider through the nose door and is supported in the glider by two "vehicle.rails". The rails provide a base on which to lash equipment comprising the cargo. They are of wooden construction with vertical curbs on the inside edges to prevent excessive lateral movement of vehicles. The rails rest on the bottom members of the front fuselage frames and each is located by bolts passing vertically through the bottom members of the front fuselage frames No. 3, 6, 9, 12, 13, 14, and 16. The positions of the rails relative to the centre line of the glider can be adjusted to accommodate the items of equipment comprising the cargo.

19—The lashing equipment for certain loads includes subsidiary structures to ensure security of the cargo while the aircraft is in flight. (These structures are items of lashing equipment and are not part of the glider. Their construction and method of use are described in Appendix I to this Chapter.)

This leaf issued with A.L. No. 3
OCTOBER, 1944

AIR PUBLICATION 2453D
Vol. I Part 3 Sect. 3 Chap. I

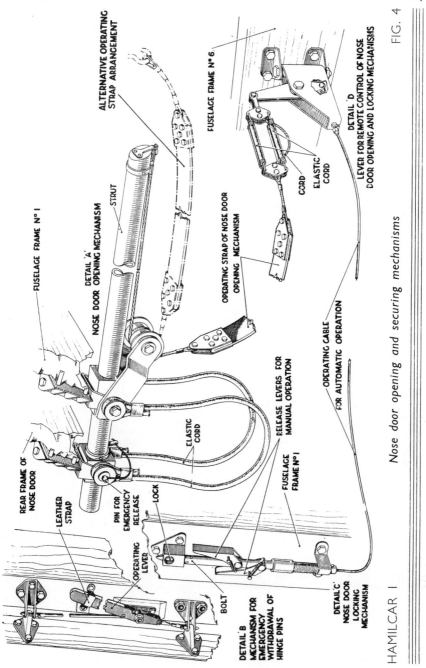

FIG. 4

HAMILCAR I   Nose door opening and securing mechanisms

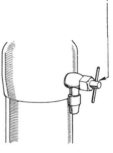

UNSCREW TO RELEASE FLUID

VALVE AT TOP OF
OLEO STRUT

RELEASE OF FLUID FROM SHOCK ABSORBER
STRUT: POSITION OF OPERATOR

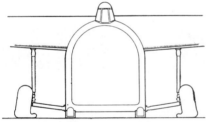

COLLAPSED UNDERCARRIAGE ON AIRCRAFT
WITH EARLY "FERRYING" UNDERCARRIAGE
MODIFICATION

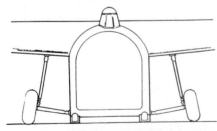

COLLAPSED UNDERCARRIAGE ON AIRCRAFT
WITH LATER "FERRYING" UNDERCARRIAGE
MODIFICATION

HAMILCAR I   FIG 5

*Method of collapsing "ferrying"
undercarriage*

Cargo stations

20—To facilitate reference to any particular position in the cabin, cargo loading stations are marked at 1 ft. intervals on the port and starboard sides from the nose to 30 ft. aft.

Cargo lashing

21—The main anchorage (fig. 1 and 2) whereby loads are anchored in the cabin of the glider, is attached to a beam running between front fuselage frames No. 11 to 15. It consists of a nest of pulleys comprising a large pulley flanked by two smaller pulleys, and carried on a steel arm which is free to move vertically upward about a pivot point attached to a bracket. The methods of using the pulleys in various combinations are governed by the different loading cases.

22—Fourteen subsidiary anchorages are provided, twelve in the structure of the cabin floor and two at the bottom of fuselage frame No. 27 in the rear fuselage.

Precautions to be observed when loading and unloading

23—The Hamilcar I is of wooden construction and will not withstand stresses resulting from the incorrect embarkation and lashing of heavy cargo. A check should be carried out to ensure that fouling cannot occur during the process of loading or unloading. In operational emergency, however, damage during the process of unloading is permitted.

This leaf issued with A.L. No. 3
OCTOBER, 1944

AIR PUBLICATION 2453D
Vol. I   Part 3   Sect. 3   Chap. I

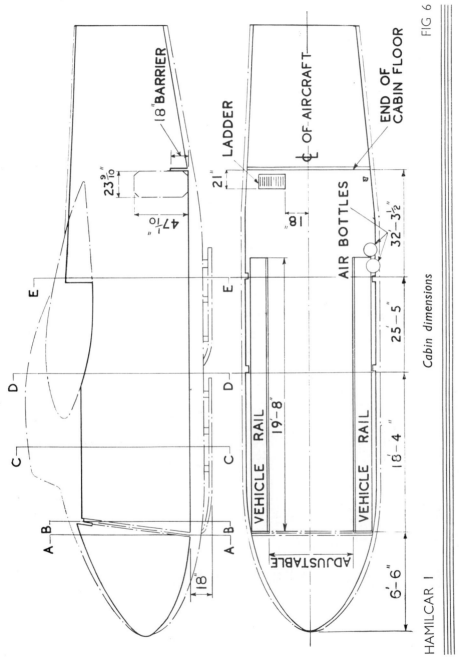

FIG 6

Cabin dimensions

HAMILCAR I

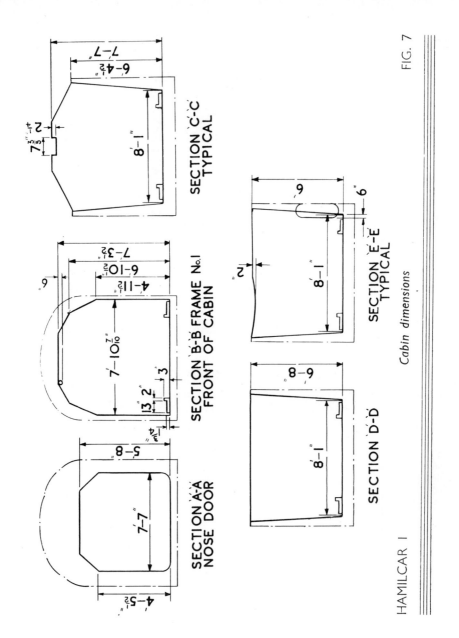

SECTION A-A
NOSE DOOR

SECTION B-B FRAME No.1
FRONT OF CABIN

SECTION C-C
TYPICAL

SECTION D-D

SECTION E-E
TYPICAL

HAMILCAR I

Cabin dimensions

FIG. 7

248

This leaf issued with A.L. No. 3
OCTOBER, 1944

AIR PUBLICATION 2453D
Vol. I   Part 3   Sect. 3   Chap. I

LOADING AND LASHING IN THE HAMILCAR I GLIDER

24—When heavy towed equipment is embarked or disembarked it should be attached to a rope of suitable strength which passes round a strong point, such as the main anchorage. This will permit full control of the weight, but to avoid possible injury, personnel should stand clear during the lowering of heavy equipment down the ramps.

Preparations for loading (fig. 3)

25—For the loading of heavy equipment the glider should rest on its skids, and the wooden ramps or a ramp of sandbags should be used to assist in embarkation.

Note—Para. 32 describes the drill for collapsing the modified "ferrying" undercarriage, before the commencement of loading operations.

26—If the glider is fitted with an "operational" undercarriage, this must be removed before the aircraft can rest on its skids.

27—The ground handling is described in A.P.2219A, Vol. I, Sect. 4, Chap. 2.

Preparations for unloading

28—The glider should rest on its skids for unloading operations involving heavy equipment, unless operational requirements and the nature of the load dictate otherwise. The wooden ramps or a ramp of sandbags can be used for unloading heavy equipment, but ramps are not required for the unloading of some lighter cargoes.

Note—Para. 32 lays down the drill for collapsing the modified "ferrying" undercarriage, which is usually necessary when unloading.

29—If the aircraft is fitted with an "operational" undercarriage (which is jettisoned after take-off) a skid landing will have been made, and the glider will already be in the right attitude for unloading without the necessity for ground handling.

Drill before take-off; collapsible "ferrying" undercarriage

30—The undercarriage can be identified by the fact that the shock absorber legs are not fitted with fairings. An alteration in the attachment of the shock absorber legs on certain gliders has made it possible to collapse the under-

carriage without deflation of the tyres, whilst in other cases tyre deflation for this purpose is essential.

31—If deflation of the tyres is necessary for the lowering of the glider on to its skids after landing, the following drill should be carried out before flight:—

  (i) Inflate the tyres to 50 lb. per sq. in. pressure.

  (ii) Remove the Schrader valve from each tyre and screw on the special valve cap (Part No. D49/U355.)

  Note—It is important that the special[1] valve cap should be tightened up by hand only, and that each cap should not be used more than once. The process of removing the Schrader valve and substituting a special valve cap for the one originally fitted should be carried out just before take-off, as it is possible for the special cap to develop a slow leak.

Drill after landing; collapsible "ferrying" undercarriage

32—When the aircraft comes to rest, members of the crew should proceed as follows:—

  (i) Unscrew and remove the valve cap on each tyre, permitting the air to escape.

  (ii) Partially unscrew the relief valve at the top of each oleo strut, permitting the hydraulic fluid to escape. A man can stand on the tyre to unscrew the valve, but should not place himself in front of it, otherwise he will be in the path of the escaping fluid.

  (iii) Regulate the flow of fluid from the shock-absorber strut, making certain that fouling between the strut and the tyre does not occur until the tyre is sufficiently deflated to permit full collapse of the undercarriage. (The time required to lower the glider is from two to three minutes.)

If deflation of the undercarriage tyres is unnecessary, for the reason given in para. 30 of this Chapter, only the operation detailed in (ii) of this paragraph is required to lower the glider.

Exhaust gas extractors

33—It is of the utmost importance that the extractors should be used whenever internal combustion engines are "run up" in the cabin of the glider, and a check should be carried out to ensure that they are fitted correctly and functioning properly. (Exhaust gas extractors form part of the standard Hamilcar I glider equipment. Their application is described in Appendix I to this Chapter.)

Ballast boxes

34—Ballast is required with certain loads to maintain the C.G. of the glider within the specified limits. Collapsible boxes for containing ballast are fully described in A.P.2219A, Vol. I, Sect. 4, Chap. 2. There are three of these boxes, constructed of wood, which are secured in position by standard Hamilcar I lashing gear, and can be stowed in the cabin when not required.

CHAPTER 3

TOWING EQUIPMENT ON TUGS

General

1. The glider towing equipment fitted to tug aircraft comprises a towing and release unit and a pilot's towing release lever. In some instances the towing and release unit is mounted rigidly on the structure of the tug; in others a hinged towing bridle is used to carry the standard unit. For operational purposes provision is made for line intercomm. between the tug and glider.

Towing and release units

2. The standard towing and release units, No. 4 and No. 6A, are described in Sect. 4, Chap. 4 of this manual. Both units incorporate an indicator rod which shows when the retracting claws are properly closed on the towing plug.

3. The No. 6A unit, which is used on all but the smallest tugs, can be operated for attachment of the towing plug by means of a small lever mounted on an extension of the cam spindle. The lever serves also as a positive indicator of the position of the retracting claws.

4. If the towing and release unit is removed from the tail of a tug aircraft, and the aircraft is to be flown for other purposes before the unit is replaced, a blank disc should be bolted over the hole in the towing mounting to exclude water and grit.

Pilot's towing release lever

5. Various types of remote control for the towing and release units are fitted to aircraft used as tugs. These controls are described and illustrated in subsequent paragraphs under the aircraft type names.

Intercomm.

6 Communication between the pilots of a glider and its tug is possible either by radio or by line intercomm. For operational purposes, however, radio communication is unsuitable.

7. At the time of going to press the type of terminal suitable for breaking contact when the glider is released from its tug is still undergoing development. The plug and socket illustrated in the accompanying figs. 3 to 6 should be regarded as experimental only.

Engine cooling

8. In some instances modifications are necessary to prevent engine overheating on glider tugs. Considerations of engine temperature limit the the use of certain tug/glider combinations to British winter conditions (see Sect. 4, Chap. 5 of this manual). Further modifications, releasing tug/glider combinations for use in temperate climates are issued from time to time.

Handling technique for tugs

9. The technique for handling aircraft used as glider tugs is described in appendices to the Pilot's Notes for the glider in any tug/glider combination; it is not included in the aeroplane hand-books. Sect. 4, Chap. 7 of this manual gives references to the relevant Pilot's Notes.

Master II (see fig. 1)

Modification numbers

10. The adaptation of the Master II for glider towing is covered by Mods. Nos. 450, 617, 623, and 647.

Towing and release unit

11. The Master II is equipped with the No. 4 towing and release unit incorporating a single retracting claw. There is no indicator lever by means of which the claw may be operated from the tail of the aircraft, and the lever in the pilot's cockpit must therefore be used for attachment of the towing plug as well as for release. The sternpost of the Master is strengthened to take the stresses involved in glider towing.

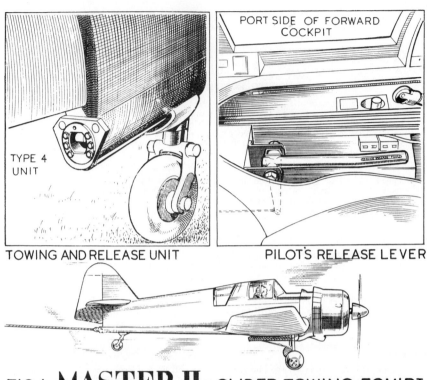

TYPE 4
UNIT

TOWING AND RELEASE UNIT

PORT SIDE OF FORWARD
COCKPIT

PILOT'S RELEASE LEVER

FIG.1 **MASTER II** GLIDER TOWING EQUIP^T

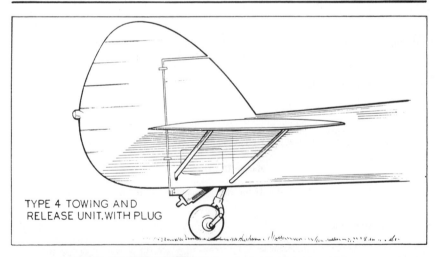

TYPE 4 TOWING AND
RELEASE UNIT. WITH PLUG

FIG.2 **HECTOR** GLIDER TOWING EQUIP^T

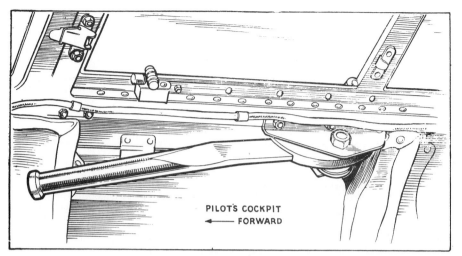

PILOT'S TOWING RELEASE LEVER

PILOT'S COCKPIT ← FORWARD

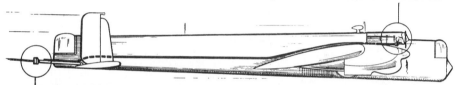

TOWING AND RELEASE UNIT

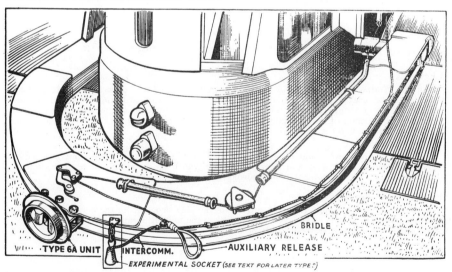

TYPE 6A UNIT — INTERCOMM. — AUXILIARY RELEASE — BRIDLE
EXPERIMENTAL SOCKET (SEE TEXT FOR LATER TYPE.)

FIG. 3 WHITLEY V GLIDER TOWING EQUIP^T

253

Pilot's towing release lever

12. A lever is mounted at the port side of the front cockpit on the forward edge of the rear spar for the purpose of operating the towing and release unit. An upward pull on the lever opens the retracting claw and releases the towing plug. Tension springs mounted in the tail of the aircraft cause the lever to return automatically, when released, to a horizontal position with the claw closed. The lever is connected to the towing and release unit by means of a wire cable running just inside the port fuselage wall.

Rearward vision mirror

13. A mirror is mounted at the top centre of the front windscreen in order that the relationship of the glider to the tug and, subsequently, the release of the glider, may be under the observation of the tug pilot.

Engine cooling

14. For the purpose of glider towing the Master II may be equipped only with the Mercury 30 engine and with the De Havilland 3-bladed, 20 deg. pitch range, variable-pitch propeller with spinner. Engine intake ducts, outlet cowl and oil coolers must be fitted in accordance with Mod. No. 623, otherwise serious overheating may result.

Rudder trimming tab

15. The rudder trimming tab is non-servo in operation and has no initial offset.

Non-aerobatic limitation

16. A notice on the port side of the instrument panel of the modified Master II states that straight flying only is permissible.

Hector (*see* fig. 2)

Modification number

17. The adaptation of the Hector for glider towing is covered by Mod. No. 637.

Towing and release unit

18. The Hector is fitted with a No. 4 towing and release unit which can be operated only from the pilot's lever in the front cockpit.

Whitley V (*see* fig. 3)

Modification numbers

19. The adaptation of the Whitley V for glider towing is covered by Mods. Nos. 522, 524, 661, and 664.

Towing bridle

20. The Whitley V is equipped with a towing bridle attached to a cross shaft which projects at each side of the fuselage just forward of the rear turret. The starboard arm of the bridle carries the conduit of the operating cable for the release unit which is mounted at the rearmost extremity of the bridle. For details of the restriction of movement of the gun turret see the relevant appendix to the Pilots' Notes for the glider.   A.L.10

Towing and release unit

21. The No. 6A towing and release unit is used on the Whitley V. This unit incorporates two retracting claws and a strap and lever by means of which the claws may be operated from the tail of the aircraft for attachment of the towing plug.

Pilot's towing release lever

22. A lever is mounted on the starboard side of the pilot's cockpit for the purpose of operating the towing and release unit. The lever is connected to the unit by means of a cable in a tubular conduit running along the starboard side of the fuselage.

Wellington III (*see* fig. 4)

Modification numbers

23. The adaptation of the Wellington III for glider towing is covered by Alteration No. P.1035 and Bristol Mod. RE 46.

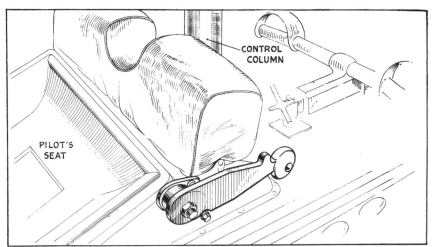

PILOT'S TOWING RELEASE LEVER

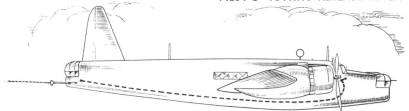

TOWING AND RELEASE UNIT (TYPE 6A)

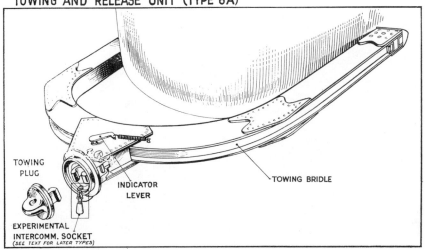

FIG. 4 WELLINGTON III GLIDER TOWING EQUIPMENT

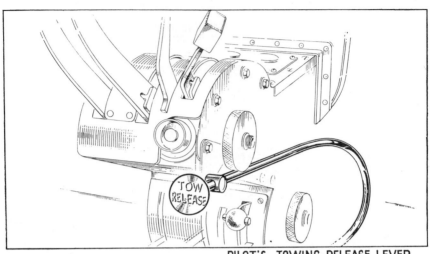

PILOT'S TOWING RELEASE LEVER

TOWING AND RELEASE UNIT (TYPE 6A)

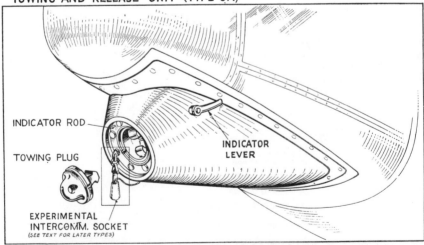

INDICATOR ROD

TOWING PLUG

INDICATOR LEVER

EXPERIMENTAL
INTERCOMM. SOCKET
(SEE TEXT FOR LATER TYPES)

FIG.5 ALBEMARLE I GLIDER TOWING EQUIPMENT

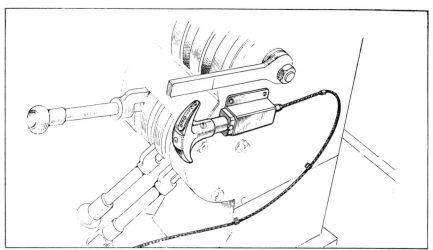

PILOT'S TOWING RELEASE LEVER

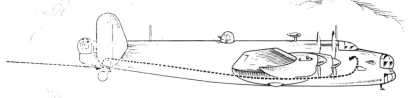

TOWING AND RELEASE UNIT (TYPE 6A)

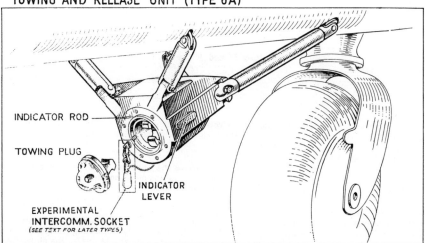

INDICATOR ROD

TOWING PLUG

INDICATOR LEVER

EXPERIMENTAL
INTERCOMM. SOCKET
(SEE TEXT FOR LATER TYPES)

FIG. 6 HALIFAX II & V GLIDER TOWING EQUIPMENT

Towing bridle

24. The Wellington III is equipped with a towing bridle similar to that used for the Whitley V. For details of the restriction of movement of the gun turret see the relevant appendix to the Pilots' Notes for the glider. A.L.10

Towing and release unit

25. The No. 6A towing and release unit is used on the Wellington III. This unit incorporates two retracting claws and a lever by means of which the claws may be operated from the tail of the aircraft for attachment of the towing plug.

Pilot's towing release lever

26. A lever is mounted on the starboard side of the pilot's seat for the purpose of operating the towing and release unit. The lever is connected to the unit by means of a cable and conduit.

Engine cooling

27. Bristol Mod RE 46 incorporates the necessary engine modifications to prevent overheating during glider towing operations under the conditions of release of approved tug/glider combinations.

Albemarle I (see fig. 5)

Modification numbers

28. The adaptation of the Albemarle I for glider towing is covered by Mods. Nos. AN 218, AN 261, AN 297, and Mod. 365.

Alteration to frame

29. This alteration provides for a strengthened rear frame with an additional tubular structure to carry the towing and release unit.

Towing and release unit

30. The No. 6A towing and release unit is fitted into the rear of the tubular structure at the tail of the Albemarle. This unit incorporates two retracting claws and a lever by means of which the claws may be operated from the tail of the aircraft for attachment of the towing plug.

Pilot's towing release control

31. The pilot's towing release control is attached to the starboard side of the control column. It comprises a tubular conduit, bell-mouthed to receive the boss of the control knob. The control knob is pulled to release the glider towing plug from the retracting claws. A pull of 45 lb. is the maximum permissible. The control knob is connected to the release unit by means of a cable and conduit.

Halifax II and V (see fig. 6)

Modification numbers

32. The adaptation of the Halifax II and V for glider towing is covered by Mods. 104 and 194 and by Alteration 5110.

Outrigger

33. A system of bracing tubes, known collectively as an outrigger, is attached to the underside of the tail of the Halifax fuselage to carry the glider towing and release unit.

Towing and release unit

34. The No. 6A towing and release unit is fitted to the outrigger at the tail of the Halifax. This unit incorporates two retracting claws and a lever by means of which the claws may be operated from the tail of the aircraft for attachment of the towing plug.

Pilot's towing release lever

35. The pilot's towing release control is attached to the starboard side of the throttle box. The control comprises a pilot's handgrip and a Bowden cable assembly connecting it with the towing and release unit. The handgrip is pulled to open the retracting claws and release the glider towing plug.

Propellers

36. In order to obtain the required performance for Halifax/Horsa and Halifax/Hamilcar tug/glider combinations, the Halifax must be equipped with propellers of 12 ft. 9 in. or 13 ft. diameter.

CHAPTER 4

TOWING EQUIPMENT

LIST OF CONTENTS

LIST OF ILLUSTRATIONS

CHAPTER 4

TOWING EQUIPMENT

General

1. Glider towing equipment is fully described in A.P.1492B, to which reference should be made for descriptive and maintenance details of the items summarized in the following paragraphs. Glider towing equipment comprises towing and release units, towing cables and accessories, inter-comm. systems, and ground equipment.

G.A.L. towing and release unit

2. This unit is incorporated in Hotspur gliders only, and is illustrated in Sect. 4, Chap. 2 of this manual. It is fully described in A.P.1492B, Vol. I, Sect. 2, Chap. 3.

No. 4 towing and release unit *(see fig. 1)*

3. This unit is used on the smaller tug aircraft. It comprises a towing hook plug and a socket incorporating a release mechanism with a single retracting claw. The socket is provided with an outer flange for attachment by eight bolts to the aircraft mounting. An indicator pin projects from the flange and moves outwards when the retracting claw closes on the towing hook plug. In some instances the pin may have been filed to lie flush with the flange when the retracting claw is open. A control attachment arm is provided for the operation of the unit by cable from the pilot's cockpit, and return springs cause the retracting claw to close when the pilot's control is released. *See* A.P.1492B, Vol. I, Sect. 2, Chap. 1.

No. 6A towing and release unit *(see fig. 2)*

4. This unit is used on the larger tug aircraft and on the larger gliders. It comprises a towing hook plug and a socket incorporating a release mechanism with double retracting claws. The socket is provided with an outer flange for bolting to the aircraft mounting plate. An indicator pin projects from the flange and moves outwards when the retracting claws close on the towing hook plug. In some instances the pin may have been filed to lie flush with the flange when the retracting claws are open. The control cable from the pilot's cockpit actuates a lever on the cam spindle of the mechanism, thereby opening the retracting claws. No return spring is incorporated in the mechanism and the claws are closed by the action of an external spring in association with a lever on the cam spindle. *See* A.P.1492B, Vol. I, Sect. 2, Chap. 2.

Indicator lever

5. In most instances the No. 6A towing and release unit carries an indicator lever on an extension of the cam spindle. This lever is a positive indicator of the position of the retracting claws and is also used for opening the claws in order to attach the towing hook plug. The different types of lever in use are described in the chapters of this manual referring to the various gliders and tugs.

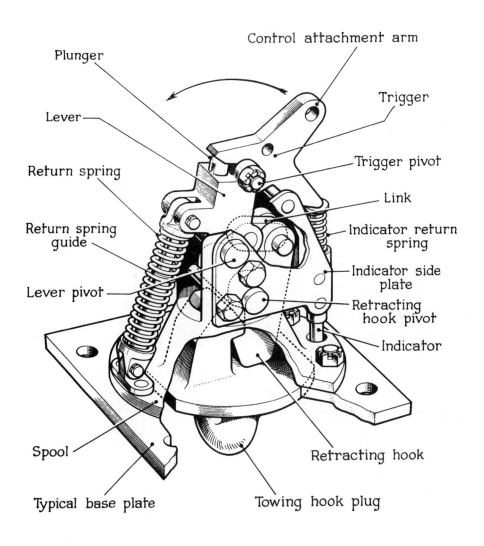

Plunger

Control attachment arm

Trigger

Lever

Trigger pivot

Return spring

Link

Return spring guide

Indicator return spring

Lever pivot

Indicator side plate

Retracting hook pivot

Indicator

Spool

Retracting hook

Typical base plate

Towing hook plug

FIG.1. TOWING HOOK PLUG AND SOCKET No. 4.

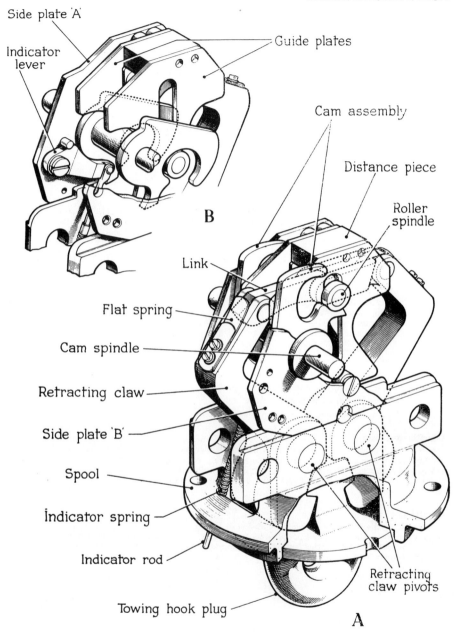

Side plate 'A'

Indicator lever

Guide plates

Cam assembly

Distance piece

Roller spindle

Link

Flat spring

Cam spindle

Retracting claw

Side plate 'B'

Spool

Indicator spring

Indicator rod

Towing hook plug

Retracting claw pivots

B

A

FIG. 2 TOWING HOOK PLUG AND SOCKET No. 6A.

This Chapter issued with A.L. No. 9
(Superseding Chapter 5 issued with A.L. No. 4)
June, 1943

AIR PUBLICATION 2453
Volume I
Section 4

CHAPTER 5

TUG/GLIDER COMBINATIONS

LIST OF CONTENTS

General

1. Tug/glider combinations affecting the gliders Hotspur I, II and III, Horsa I, Hamilcar I and Hadrian I are included in this chapter in the form of tables. Each glider, with the exception of the Hadrian is included in tables "a", "b" and "c" for ferrying, training and operational use respectively. In the case of the Hadrian I these conditions are contained in one table.

2. Handling details for these combinations are given in appendices to the Pilot's Notes for the relevant gliders (*see* Sect. 4, Chap. 7).

Radius of operations

3. A practical radius of 250 miles (tug returning alone) is at present envisaged for glider borne operations. This practical radius is 75 per cent of the "still-air" value, the safety margin being intended to allow for reasonable errors of pilotage, a reasonable time over target, the effect of moderate winds and other minor deviations from optimum flying conditions.

4. The fuel carried for the practical radius of 250 miles has, therefore, to be determined on the following basis:—

   (i)   335 miles flight with glider in tow, plus

  (ii)   335 miles flight tug returning alone, plus

 (iii)   Fuel for taxying and take-off, plus

 (iv)   Fuel used for climb in excess of that required for level flight.

Climatic conditions

5. The climatic conditions under which tug/glider combinations can be successfully operated are limited by considerations of engine temperature. According to the modifications made to keep engine temperature within safe limits, tug/glider combinations are released for (1) British winter conditions (Oct. to March inclusive); (ii) Temperate climates; or (iii) Temperate and Tropical climates.

General note

6. Since the Hector is obsolescent and is in limited use as a tug for training purposes only, it is not covered by the Hotspur Pilot's Notes appendices. For this reason additional data is included for this aircraft. All the other tug/glider combinations listed in this Chapter are detailed in the relevant Pilot's Notes in regard to engine limitations, flying speed limitations, and performance.

HOTSPUR I, II and III

Table (a). Ferrying conditions

	Conditions of approval	Tug loading (Non-essential equipment includes guns, ammunition, pyrotechnics, etc.)	Fuel and oil	Glider loading See Sect. 4, Chap. 6	Practical range	Take-off (a) Ground run (b) Gross distance to clear a height of 50 ft.
Hector Hotspur II or III	1		As for training			
Master II Hotspur II or III	2		As for training			
Master II Two Hotspurs I or II	3		As for training			
Whitley V Two Hotspurs	4		As for operational			
Wellington Ic Hotspur	5		As for training			
Wellington Ic (Light tug) Two Hotspurs (Light gliders)	6	Temperate climates	23,000 lb. Crew of three. 1,250 lb. of non-essential equipment stripped	300 gals. fuel Capacity oil	2,200 lb. each. Crew of two. Wheel u/carriages may be retained	240 miles	(a) 800 yds. (b) 1,500 yds.
Harvard II Hotspur I or II	7		As for operational			

263

HORSA I

Table (a). Ferrying Conditions

		Conditions of approval	Tug loading (Non-essentail equipment includes guns, ammunition, pyrotechnics, etc.)	Fuel and oil	Glider loading See Sect. 4, Chap. 6	Practical range	Take-off (a) Ground run (b) Gross distance to clear a height of 50 ft.
1	Whitley V (Light tug) Horsa I (Light glider)	Temperate climates	23,000 lb. Crew of three. 1,100 lb. of non-essential equipment stripped	300 gals. fuel 54 gals. oil	9,000 lb. Crew of two. Wheel u/carriage may be retained	240 miles	(a) 950 yds. (b) 1,700 yds.
2	Halifax II or V (Light tug) Horsa I (Light glider)	Temperate climates	Halifax Mk. II, 42,500 lb., Mk. V, 43,000 lb. Crew of three. 1,400 lb. non-essential equipment stripped	600 gals. fuel Capacity oil	9,000 lb. Crew of two. Wheel u/carriage may be retained	305 miles	(a) 660 yds. (b) 1,200 yds.
3	Albemarle I (Light tug) Horsa I (Light glider)	Temperate climates	27,000 lb. Crew of three. 1,400 lb. non-essential equipment stripped. 250 lb. ballast attached to joint 29. Hercules engines must have completed	400 gals. fuel (wing tanks) Capacity oil 20 hours non-tugging flight	9,000 lb. Crew of two. Wheel u/carriage be retained	345 miles	(a) 1,000 yds. (b) 1,300 yds.
4	Wellington III (Light tug) Horsa I (Light glider)	Temperate climates	25,500 lb. Crew of three. 1,400 lb. of non-essential equipment stripped	360 gals. fuel Capacity oil	9,000 lb. Crew of two. Wheel u/carriage may be retained	300 miles	(a) 800 yds. (b) 1,350 yds.
5	Lancaster I (Light tug) Horsa I (Light glider)	Temperate climates	42,000 lb. Crew of three. 2,000 lb. of non-essential equipment stripped	500 gals. fuel Capacity oil	9,000 lb. Crew of two. Wheel u/carriage may be retained	270 miles	(a) 620 yds. (b) 940 yds.
6	Dakota (C47 and C53) Horsa I		Not yet approved				
7	Stirling Horsa I		Not yet approved				

HAMILCAR I

Table (a). Ferrying conditions

		Conditions of approval	Tug loading (Non-essential equipment includes guns, ammunition, pyrotechnics, etc.)	Fuel and oil	Glider loading See Sect. 4, Chap. 6	Practical range	Take-off (a) Ground run (b) Gross distance to clear a height of 50 ft.
Halifax II or V Hamilcar I	1			As for training			
Lancaster I (Light tug) Hamilcar I (Light glider)	2	Temperate climates	42,000 lb. Crew of three. Stripped of 2,000 lb. of non-essential equipment	500 gals. fuel Capacity oil	23,000 lb. Crew of two. Minimum ballast. Ferrying u/carriage may be retained	225 miles	(a) 1,130 yds. (b) 2,000 yds.

HOTSPUR I, II and III

Table (b). Training Conditions

		Conditions of approval	Tug loading (Non-essential equipment includes guns, ammunition, pyrotechnics, etc.)	Fuel and oil	Glider loading See Sect. 4, Chap. 6	Practical range	Take-off (a) Ground run (b) Gross distance to clear a height of 50 ft.
Hector Hotspur II or III	1	Temperate climates	5,200 lb.		3,600 lb.		(a) 530 yds. Recommended take-off speed 75 m.p.h. tug I.A.S.
Master II Hotspur II or III	2	Temperate climates, Mercury 30 engine	5,350 lb.		3,635 lb.		(b) 1,020 yds.
Master II (Heavy tug) Two Hotspurs (Light gliders)	3	Temperate climates, Mercury 30 engine	5,400 lb. Crew of two	70 gals. fuel Capacity oil	2,200 lb. each. Crew of two. Wheel u/carriage may be retained	180 miles	(a) 950 yds. (b) 1,550 yds.
Whitley V Two Hotspurs	4		As for operational				
Wellington Ic (Light tug) Hotspur (Heavy glider)	5	Temperate climates	23,000 lb. Crew of three. 1,250 lb. of non-essential equipment removed	300 gals. fuel Capacity oil	3,600 lb. Wheel u/carriage may be retained. Operationally equipped	375 miles	(a) 720 yds. (b) 1,300 yds.
Wellington Ic (Light tug) Two Hotspurs (Light gliders)	6	Temperate climates	23,000 lb. Crew of three. Stripped of 1,250 lb. non-essential equipment	300 gals. fuel Capacity oil	2,200 lb. each. Crew of two. Wheel u/carriages may be retained	240 miles	(a) 800 yds. (b) 1,500 yds.
Harvard II Hotspur I or II	7		As for operational				

Climb:—800 ft./min. at 93 m.p.h. tug I.A.S. optimum

HORSA I

Table (b). Training Conditions

		Conditions of approval	Tug loading (Non-essential equipment includes guns, ammunition, pyrotechnics, etc.)	Fuel and oil	Glider loading *See* Sect. 4, Chap. 6	Practical range	Take-off (a) Ground run (b) Gross distance to clear a height of 50 ft.
Whitley V (Light tug) Horsa I (Heavy glider)	1	Temperate climates	23,000 lb. Crew of three. Stripped of 1,100 lb. non-essential equipment	300 gals. fuel 54 gals. oil	15,250 lb. Wheel u/carriage may be retained. Operationally equipped	225 miles	(a) 1,075 yds. (b) 1,930 yds.
Halifax II or V (Light tug) Horsa I (Heavy glider)	2	Temperate climates	Halifax II 42,500 lb. Halifax V 43,000 lb. Crew of three. Stripped of 1,400 lb. non-essential equipment	600 gals. fuel Capacity oil	15,250 lb. Wheel u/carriage may be retained. Operationally equipped	300 miles	(a) 770 yds. (b) 1,400 yds.
Albemarle I (Light tug) Horsa I (Heavy glider)	3	Temperate climates	27,000 lb. Crew of three. Stripped of 1,400 lb. of non-essential equipment. 250 lb. ballast attached to joint 29 Hercules engines must have completed 20 hours non-tugging flight	400 gals. fuel (in wing tanks) Capacity oil	15,250 lb. Wheel u/carriage may be retained. Operationally equipped	340 miles	(a) 1,200 yds. (b) 1,700 yds.
Wellington III (Light tug) Horsa I (Heavy gliders)	4	Temperate climates	25,500 lb. Crew of three. Stripped of 1,400 lb. non-essential equipment	360 gals. fuel Capacity oil	15,250 lb. Wheel u/carriage may be retained. Operationally equipped	275 miles	(a) 1,000 yds. (b) 1,700 yds.
Lancaster I (Light tug) Horsa I (Heavy glider)	5	Temperate climates	42,000 lb. Crew of three. Stripped of 2,000 lb. non-essential equipment	500 gals. fuel Capacity oil	15,250 lb. Wheel u/carriage may be retained. Operationally equipped	270 miles	(a) 720 yds. (b) 1,120 yds.
Dakota (C47 and C53) Horsa I	6			Not yet approved			
Stirling Horsa I	7			Not yet approved			

HAMILCAR I

Table (b). Training conditions

		Conditions of approval	Tug loading (Non-essential equipment includes guns, ammunition, pyrotechnics, etc.)	Fuel and oil	Glider loading *See* Sect. 4, Chap. 6		Practical range	Take-off (a) Ground run (b) Gross distance to clear a height of 50 ft.
Halifax II or V (Light tug) **Hamilcar I** (Heavy glider)	1	Temperate climates	Halifax II 42,500 lb. Halifax V 43,000 lb. Crew of three. Stripped of 1,400 lb. of non-essential equipment	600 gals. fuel 72 gals. oil	36,000 lb. U/carriage retained. Operationally equipped		250 miles	(a) 1,450 yds. (b) 2,600 yds.
Lancaster I (Light tug) **Hamilcar I** (Heavy glider)	2	Temperate climates	42,000 lb. Crew of three. Stripped of 2,000 lb. non-essential equipment	500 gals. fuel Capacity oil	36,000 lb. Operationally equipped. Ferry u/carriage may be retained		210 miles	(a) 1,140 yds. (b) 2,200 yds.

HOTSPUR I, II and III

Table (e) Operational Conditions

	Conditions of approval	Tug loading	Fuel and oil	Glider loading *See* Sect. 4, Chap. 6	Range and radius (Tug returning singly) U/carriage dropped	retained	Take-off (a) Ground run (b) Gross distance to clear a height of 50 ft.	Operational height
Hector **Hotspur II or III** — 1			Not approved					
Master II **Hotspur II or III** — 2			Not approved					
Master II **Two Hotspurs** — 3			Not approved					
Whitley V (Heavy tug) **Two Hotspurs** (Heavy gliders) — 4	Temperate climates	26,000 lb. Operationally equipped less bombs and racks.	520 gals. fuel Capacity oil	3,600 lb. Operationally equipped	Range 520 miles Radius 320 miles	Range 480 miles Radius 305 miles	(a) 1,000 yds. (b) 1,800 yds.	10,000 ft.
Wellington IC (Heavy tug) **Hotspur** (Heavy glider) — 5	Temperate climates	25,300 lb. Operationally equipped less bombs and racks	450 gals. fuel Capacity oil	3,600 lb. Operationally equipped		Range 490 miles Radius 300 miles	(a) 850 yds. (b) 1,550 yds.	8,000 ft.
Wellington IC **Two Hotspurs** — 6			Not approved					
Harvard II (Heavy tug) **Hotspur I or II** (Heavy glider) — 7	Temperate climates	5,300 lb. Crew of two All ballast removed	Capacity fuel Capacity oil	3,600 lb. Operationally equipped		Range 270 miles Radius 178 miles	(a) 850 yds. (b) 1,500 yds.	7,500 ft.

HORSA I

Table (e) Operational Conditions

		Conditions of approval	Tug loading	Fuel and oil	Glider loading *See Sect. 4, Chap. 6*	Range and radius (Tug returning singly) U/carriage dropped	Range and radius (Tug returning singly) U/carriage retained	Take-off (a) Ground run (b) Gross distance to clear a height of 50 ft.	Operational height
Whitley V	1			Not approved					
Horsa I									
Halifax II or V (Heavy tug)	2	Temperate climates	Halifax II 47,000 lb. Halifax V 47,500 lb. Operationally equipped except for bombs	960 gals. fuel 72 gals. oil		Range 525 miles Radius 300 miles	Range 480 miles Radius 270 miles	(a) 900 yds. (b) 1,900 yds.	10,000 ft.
Horsa I (Heavy glider)					Operationally equipped				
Albemarle I (Heavy tug)	3	Temperate climates	31,200 lb. Operationally equipped except for bombs and racks. Hercules engines must have completed 20 hours non-tugging flight	770 gals. fuel Capacity oil			Range 415 miles Radius 310 miles	(a) 1,400 yds. (b) 2,000 yds.	6,000 ft.
Horsa I (Heavy glider)					Operationally equipped				
Wellington III (Heavy tug)	4	Temperate climates	28,300 lb. Operationally equipped except for bombs	530 gals. fuel Capacity oil		Range 424 miles Radius 271 miles	Range 405 miles Radius 260 miles	(a) 1,650 yds. (b) 2,400 yds.	7,000 ft.
Horsa I (Heavy glider)					Operationally equipped				
Lancaster I (Heavy tug)	5	Temperate climates	47,000 lb. Operationally equipped except for bombs and racks	800 gals. fuel 70 gals. oil		Range 410 miles Radius 272 miles	Range 370 miles Radius 250 miles	(a) 900 yds. (b) 1,450 yds.	10,000 ft.
Horsa I (Heavy glider)					Operationally equipped				
Dakota (C47 and C53) Horsa I	6			Not yet approved					
Stirling Horsa I	7			Not yet approved					

HAMILCAR I

Table (c) Operational Conditions

		Conditions of approval	Tug loading	Fuel and oil	Glider loading See Sect. 4, Chap. 6	Range and radius (Tug returning singly) U/carriage dropped	Range and radius (Tug returning singly) retained	Take-off (a) Ground run (b) Gross distance to clear a height of 50 ft.	Operational height
Halifax II or V (Heavy tug)	1	Temperate climates	Halifax II 48,000 lb. Halifax V 48,500 lb. Operationally equipped minus bombs	1,090 gals. fuel 72 gals. oil	36,000 lb.	Range 395 miles Radius ⁓60 miles	Range 375 miles Radius 250 miles	(a) 1,700 yds. (b) 3,100 yds.	5,000 ft.
Hamilcar I (Heavy glider)					Operationally equipped				
Lancaster I (Heavy tug)	2	Temperate climates	48,000 lb. Operationally equipped except for bombs and racks	950 gals. fuel 70 gals. oil	36,000 lb.	Range 410 miles Radius 290 miles	Range 370 miles Radius 250 miles	(a) 1,500 yds. (b) 2,600 yds.	8,000 ft.
Hamilcar I (Heavy glider)					Operationally equipped				

HADRIAN I

Tables (a), (b) and (c) Ferrying, Training and Operational Conditions

	Conditions of approval		Tug loading	Fuel and oil	Glider loading See Sect. 4, Chap. 6	Range and radius (Tug returning singly) U/carriage dropped	retained	Take-off (a) Ground run (b) Gross distance to clear a height of 50 ft.	Operational height
Hudson III (Heavy tug) **Hadrian I** (Heavy glider)	Temperate and tropical climates	1	18,000 lb. Operationally equipped except for bombs and racks. Steel ballast ring and aperture cover fitted in place of dorsal turret	536 gals. fuel Capacity oil	7,500 lb. Operationally equipped		Range 520 statute miles Radius 350 statute miles	(a) 1,000 yds. (b) 1,700 yds.	10,000 ft.
Halifax II or V (Heavy tug) **Hadrian I** (Heavy glider)	Temperate climates	2	Halifax II 47,000 lb. Halifax V 47,500 lb. Operationally equipped except for bombs	960 gals. fuel Capacity oil	7,500 lb. Operationally equipped Wheel u/carriage may be retained	Performance superior to that obtained with the Halifax II or V/Horsa I combination			
Albemarle (Heavy tug) **Hadrian I** (Heavy glider)	Temperate climates	3	31,200 lb. Operationally equipped except for bombs and racks	770 gals. fuel Capacity oil	7,500 lb. Operationally equipped Wheel u/carriage may be retained	Performance superior to that obtained with the Albemarle I/Horsa I combination			
Wellington III (Heavy tug) **Hadrian I** (Heavy glider)	Temperate climates	4	28,300 lb. Operationally equipped except for bombs	530 gals. fuel Capacity oil	7,500 lb. Operationally equipped Wheel u/carriage may be retained	Performance superior to that obtained with the Wellington III/Horsa I combination			
Lancaster I (Heavy tug) **Hadrian I** (Heavy glider)	Temperate climates	5	47,000 lb. Operationally equipped except for bombs and racks	800 gals. fuel 70 gals. oil	7,500 lb. Operationally equipped Wheel u/carriage may be retained	Performance superior to that obtained with the Lancaster I/Horsa I combination			

CHAPTER 6

GLIDER LOADINGS

General

1. The object of the information contained in this chapter is to enable simple calculations to be made to ensure that the C.G. position for a glider loaded with troops and equipment is within the allowed limits.

2. General instructions for the use of Loading and C.G. Diagrams are contained in Vol. I, Sect. 4 of the glider handbooks and will not be repeated here.

Moisture absorption

3. Gliders, being principally of wooden construction, are subject to considerable moisture absorption which may cause a variation in tare weight, under extreme atmospheric changes, of as much as 15%. A variation in tare weight of plus or minus 3% due to this cause is quite usual.

4. Tare weights given in the following tables must be regarded as typical examples only. These figures are constantly undergoing revision, and reference should be made to the relevant glider handbook, Vol. I, Sect. 4, for the correct information in regard to the aircraft concerned.

Hotspur II and III

Loading and C.G. diagram (*see* fig. 1)

5. This diagram furnishes a typical example of a Hotspur II with a load of eight troops and light equipment. The first and second pilots are included as troops Nos. 1 and 2. An additional loading table in fig. 1 sets out the weights of certain heavy items and their positions relative to the datum point of the aircraft. In order to compile a loading table from this data, reference should be made to the series of military loadings given in para. 6.

Military loadings

6. The following alternative loadings have been scheduled for the Hotspur II and III:

"A" load

Seat No.	Personnel			Equipment
1	Pilot	...	...	Pilot's equipment.
2	Coy. Comd.	...	...	Pistol, 21 rounds; sig. pistol, 12 rounds.
3	C.S.M.	.	...	... Sten gun, 5 magazines.
4	Signaller ...	...	...	Rifle, bayonet, 50 rounds S.A.A.
5	Signaller	.	...	... Pistol, 21 rounds, 18 set.
6	Batman ...	...	...	Sten gun, 5 magazines.
7	L/Cpl. Clerk	...	...	Rifle, bayonet, 50 rounds, 38 set.
8	Nursing Ordly. (R.A.M.C.)			Pistol, 21 rounds.

"A 1" load

Seat No.	Personnel			Equipment
1	Pilot	...	...	Pilot's equipment.
2	2nd i/c Coy.	...	...	Pistol, 21 rounds.
3	Batman ...	...	...	Rifle, bayonet, 50 rounds S.A.A.
4	Cpl. Signals	...	...	Rifle, bayonet, 50 rounds S.A.A. 38 set.
5	Signaller ...	...	...	Pistol, 21 rounds, 18 set.
6	Nursing Ordly. (R.A.M.C.)			Pistol, 21 rounds.
7	Storeman	...	...	Rifle, bayonet, 50 rounds S.A.A.
8	C.Q.M.S. ...	...	...	Rifle, bayonet, 50 rounds S.A.A.

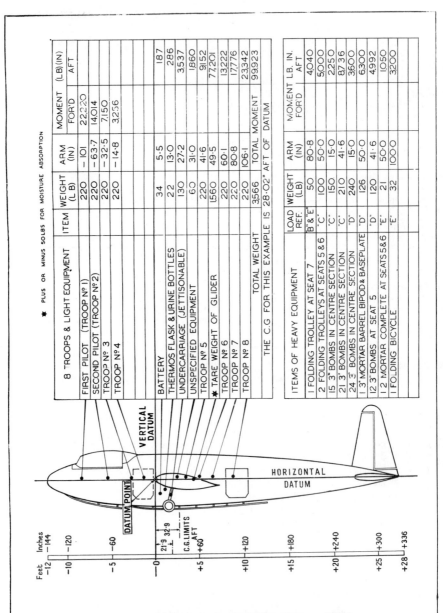

* PLUS OR MINUS 50 LBS FOR MOISTURE ABSORPTION

8 TROOPS & LIGHT EQUIPMENT	ITEM	WEIGHT (LB)	ARM (IN)	MOMENT (LB)(IN) FOR'D	MOMENT (LB)(IN) AFT
FIRST PILOT (TROOP N° 1)		220	– 101	22,220	
SECOND PILOT (TROOP N° 2)		220	– 63·7	14,014	
TROOP N° 3		220	– 32·5	7,150	
TROOP N° 4		220	– 14·8	3,256	
BATTERY		34	5·5		187
THERMOS FLASK & URINE BOTTLES		22	13·0		286
UNDERCARRIAGE (JETTISONABLE)		130	27·2		3537
UNSPECIFIED EQUIPMENT		60	31·0		1860
TROOP N° 5		220	41·6		9152
★ TARE WEIGHT OF GLIDER		1560	49·5		77,201
TROOP N° 6		220	60·1		13,222
TROOP N° 7		220	80·8		17,776
TROOP N° 8		220	106·1		23,342
TOTAL WEIGHT		3566	TOTAL MOMENT		99,923

THE C.G. FOR THIS EXAMPLE IS 28·02" AFT OF DATUM

ITEMS OF HEAVY EQUIPMENT	LOAD REF.	WEIGHT (LB)	ARM (IN)	MOMENT LB. IN. FOR'D	MOMENT LB. IN. AFT
1 FOLDING TROLLEY AT SEAT 7	"B" & "E"	50	80·8		4,040
2 FOLDING TROLLEYS AT SEATS 5 & 6	"C"	100	50·0		5,000
15 3" BOMBS IN CENTRE SECTION	"C"	150	15·0		2,250
21 3" BOMBS IN CENTRE SECTION	"C"	210	41·6		8,736
24 3" BOMBS IN CENTRE SECTION	"D"	240	15·0		3,600
1 3" MORTAR BARREL BIPOD & BASEPLATE	"D"	126	50·0		6,300
12 3" BOMBS AT SEAT 5	"D"	120	41·6		4,992
1 2" MORTAR COMPLETE AT SEATS 5 & 6	"E"	21	50·0		1,050
1 FOLDING BICYCLE	"E"	32	100·0		3,200

VERTICAL DATUM

HORIZONTAL DATUM

DATUM POINT

21'9 32·9
C.G. LIMITS AFT

Feet Inches
–12   –144
–10   –120
      –60
–5
0
+5   +60
+10   +120
+15   +180
+20   +240
+25   +300
+28   +336

FIG. 1 **HOTSPUR II & III**

LOADING AND C.G. DIAGRAM – TROOP TRANSPORT

"A 2" load

Seat No.	Personnel	Equipment
1	Pilot	Pilot's equipment.
2	Sec. Comd.	Sten gun, 5 mags., 2 Bren mags.
3	Deputy Comd.	Rifle, 50 rounds S.A.A., 2 Bren mags.
4	Bren gunner	Bren gun, 3 mags., 50 rounds S.A.A.
5	No. 1 rifleman	Rifle, 50 rounds S.A.A., 2 Bren mags.
6	No. 2 rifleman	Rifle, 50 rounds S.A.A., 2 Bren mags.
7	No. 3 rifleman	Rifle, 50 rounds S.A.A., 2 Bren mags.
8	Smokeman	E.Y. Rifle, 50 rounds S.A.A., 2 Bren mags., 4 "77" grenades.

"B" load

Seat No.	Personnel	Equipment
1	Pilot	Pilot's equipment.
2	Sup. Sec. Comd. ...	Rifle, bayonet, 50 rounds S.A.A.
3	Sup. Sec. No. 1 ...	Pistol, 21 rounds, 45 L.M.G. mags.
4	Sup. Sec. No. 2 ...	Pistol, 21 rounds, 45 L.M.G. mags.
5	Sup. Sec. No. 3 ...	Rifle, bayonet, 50 rounds S.A.A., tripod, 5 mags.
6	Nil	Nil.
7	Nil	1 folding trolley, 32 mags.
8	Sup. Sec. No. 4 ...	Rifle, bayonet, 50 rounds S.A.A., tripod, 5 mags.

"C" load

Seat No.	Personnel	Equipment
1	Pilot	Pilot's equipment.
2	Mortar Sgt.	Rifle, bayonet, 50 rounds.
3	No. 4 on mortar ...	Rifle, bayonet, 50 rounds.
4	Nil	15 mortar bombs in centre section.
5	Nil	21 mortar bombs round this seat. 2 folding trolleys.
6	Nil	
7	Nil	
8	No. 4 on mortar ...	Rifle, bayonet, 50 rounds.

"D" load

Seat No.	Personnel	Equipment
1	Pilot	Pilot's equipment.
2	Det. Comd.	Rifle, bayonet, 50 rounds S.A.A.
3	No. 1 on mortar ...	Pistol, 21 rounds.
4	No. 2 on mortar ...	Pistol, 21 rounds.
5	Nil. Seat removed	24 mortar bombs in centre section.
6	Nil. Seat removed	3 in. mortar barrel, bipod and baseplate. 12 mortar bombs.
7	Nil. Seat removed ...	
8	No. 3 on mortar ...	Pistol. 21 rounds.

"E" load

Seat No.	Personnel	Equipment
1	Pilot	Pilot's equipment.
2	Subaltern ... ...:	Pistol, 21 rounds, ·45 signal pistol, 12 signal cartridges.
3	No. 1 on mortar ...	Pistol, 21 rounds, ·45.
4	Nil	
5	Batman	Sten gun, 5 mags. 2 in. mortar and bombs under this seat.
6	Nil	
7	Nil	Folding trolley (38 set).
8	No. 2 on mortar ...	Rifle, 50 rounds, ·303, bicycle.

"F" load

Seat No.	Personnel	Equipment
1	Pilot	Pilot's equipment.
2	Sec. Comd.	Rifle, telescopic sights, 50 rounds S.A.A., 2 Bren mags., etc.
3	Bren gunner	Bren gun, 3 mags., 50 rounds S.A.A.
4	Nil	
5	Pl. Sgt.	E.Y. rifle, grenade discharger, 2 "68" grenades, 50 rounds S.A.A.
6	Rifleman	Rifle, 50 rounds S.A.A., 2 Bren mags.
7	Nil	
8	Sniper	Rifle, telescopic sights, 50 rounds S.A.A., 2 Bren mags.

Distribution of light loads

7.   The Hotspur may be required to carry less than its maximum load of eight troops (including pilots) without the addition of any of the items of equipment scheduled above.   In such instances the distribution of the troops should be as follows:—

Eight troops only	Seats 1, 2, 3, 4, 5, 6, 7, 8
Seven troops only	Seats 1, 2, 3, 4, 5, 6, 7 –
Six troops only	Seats 1, 2, 3, – 5, 6, – 8
Five troops only	Seats 1, 2, – 4, 5, 6, – –
Four troops only	Seats 1, 2, – 4, – – 7, –
Three troops only	Seats 1, 2, – – – – – 8

9

Supplies Dropping and Transport, 1943

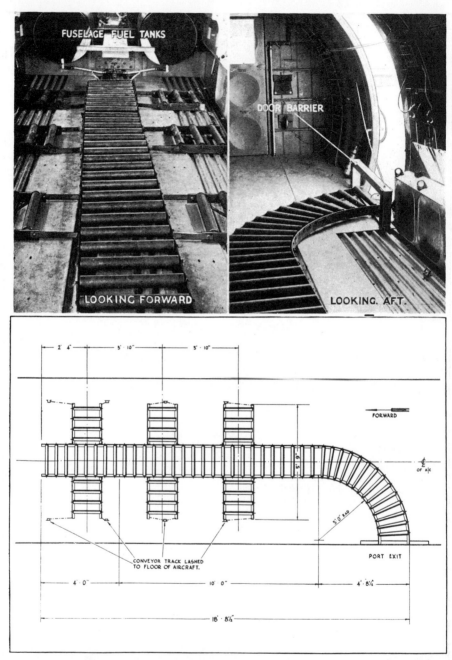

FUSELAGE FUEL TANKS

DOOR BARRIER

LOOKING FORWARD

LOOKING. AFT.

FORWARD

2' · 4" 5' · 10" 3' · 10"

5' · 6"

CONVEYOR TRACK LASHED
TO FLOOR OF AIRCRAFT.

3' 0" RAD

PORT EXIT

4' · 0" 10' · 0" 4' · 8½"

18' · 8½"

FIG. 1 DAKOTA I ROLLER RUNWAY

CHAPTER 2

AIRCRAFT FOR SUPPLEMENTARY SUPPLIES DROPPING AND FOR SUPPLIES TRANSPORT

General

1. The equipment necessary for converting an aircraft for supplementary supplies dropping differs from that necessary for converting the same aircraft for supplementary supplies transport. For this reason the aircraft installations described in the following paragraphs are divided into the two separate categories:—

DAKOTA I (C.47)—SUPPLIES DROPPING

Description

2. The Dakota I is a twin-engined transport aircraft suitable for the carriage and dropping of wicker panniers loaded with supplies. A.F.E.E. report No. P/39 describes in detail the results of trials of the aircraft for this purpose. Information relating to the use of the Dakota I for supplies dropping by means of wicker panniers may be divided into four main groups.

Aircraft equipment required

Modifications

3. No modifications are required to the Dakota I aircraft. All the equipment described in subsequent paragraphs can easily be installed by squadrons.

Installation of roller runway (see fig. 1)

4. A roller runway, including a 90° bend, is placed centrally in the fuselage with the curved section leading to the transport door. In addition, three short lengths of roller runway are fixed on either side of and at right-angles to the straight portion of the main runway.

Door barrier

5. A door barrier in the form of a transverse bar, hinged at one end to the curved section of the runway, is installed to prevent the panniers tumbling out through the door at "action stations". No. 1 of the despatching crew raises the barrier at the appropriate time by means of a rope attached to its free end.

Safety rope

6. For the safety of the despatching crew a piece of rope is fixed across the door at such a height that the panniers can pass underneath it without interference.

Strong point attachment

7. The American overhead static line cable normally fitted to the Dakota I is used for the despatch of panniers. This cable is used in preference to the fixed type of strong point in order to allow the points of attachment of the static lines to move along the fuselage as the panniers are moved along the roller runway towards the door.

8. The static line of the parachute for a single pannier (and that of the parachute for the top pannier of a pair) terminates in a snap hook which is slipped over the static line cable.

Loading of panniers into the aircraft

Wicker panniers (see fig. 2)

9. Wicker panniers for supplies dropping are described in Sect. 5, Chap. 3 of this manual. Each pannier is strapped in a modified Mark VI harness and is equipped with its own parachute and static line. Where two panniers are loaded in the aircraft one on top of the other for despatch by the "daisy chain" method, the static line of the parachute for the lower pannier is 5 ft. 6 in. in length, and is attached to the leather strap at the end of the top pannier; the static line of the parachute for the upper pannier is 15 ft. 6 in. in length, and terminates in a snap hook for attachment to the static line cable of the aircraft.

Modified Mark VI harness

10. This is described and illustrated in Sect. 5, Chap. 3 of this manual.

LOOKING FORWARD

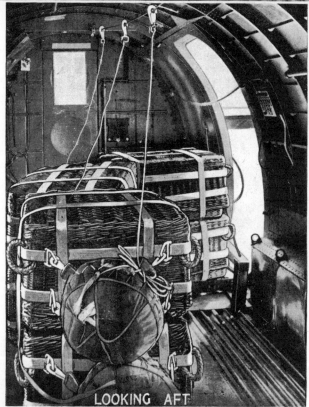

LOOKING AFT

FIG 2 **DAKOTA I** ARRANGEMENT OF PANNIERS

Ties between panniers for despatch by "daisy chain"

11. The four ties between the two panniers making up a pair are described and illustrated in Sect. 5, Chap. 2 of this manual.

Lashing of panniers

12. Fig. 3 illustrates the positions of panniers at take-off for loads of thirteen and fifteen panniers. Each side pair of panniers is lashed with rope to lugs on the side of the aircraft, to prevent lateral movement.

Preventer tackle

13. To prevent movement of the panniers down the fuselage at take-off, each row of panniers is lashed with a specially designed preventer tackle anchored to side lugs on the aircraft. The preventer tackle is illustrated in fig. 2 and in Sect. 5, Chap, 3, fig. 4.

Wooden stops

14. Wooden stops are used, between the rollers of the runway, to hold the panniers in position after removal of the rope lashings prior to assuming "action stations". When the panniers are at "action stations" with the leading one resting against the door barrier, the stops should be removed.

Despatch of panniers

Despatching crew

15. Four men are necessary for despatching wicker panniers from the Dakota I.

16. The positions of the despatching crew at take-off and at action stations are illustrated in fig. 3.

Signal lights

17. Signal lights are part of the equipment of the Dakota I and are used for communication between the pilot of the aircraft and the despatching crew. "Action stations" is indicated by a pre-arranged signal.

18. On the "red" signal No. 1 of the despatching crew raises the door barrier and the crew prepare to despatch the panniers.

19. On the "green" signal the panniers are despatched as described in para. 21.

"Daisy chain" method of despatch

20. The dropping of panniers in pairs by the "daisy chain" method is effected in order to reduce the time necessary for despatch. By this method the static line for the lower pannier is attached to a strap on the upper pannier while the static line for the upper pannier is attached to the aircraft static line cable. The opening of the upper parachute causes a jerk which breaks the four ties between the panniers allowing the lower pannier to fall freely until its static line is opened by the resistance of the upper pannier. The two panniers, with their open parachutes, reach the ground as independent units.

Despatching drill

21. The following is a summary of the despatching drill for a load of fifteen panniers in two sticks:—

(i) *Approach to target.*—At a pre-arranged signal from the pilot the crew unlash the first stick of panniers and move them slowly to "action stations". The aft panniers should be moved first. No. 1 connects the static line snap hooks of the top panniers in each pair to the overhead static line cable. The crew take up the positions shown in fig. 3 (15 panniers—action stations).

(ii) *"Red" signal.*—No. 1 raises the door barrier. The crew prepare for despatch of panniers.

(iii) *"Green" signal.*—No. 2, with his back braced against the starboard side of the aircraft, pushes with his feet against the bottom pannier of each pair in order to send them through the door. No. 1 guides the panniers through the door. Nos. 3 and 4 move the remaining pairs of the stick down the roller runway, taking care to see that the static line snap hooks are free to slide down the static line cable.

(iv) The second stick is despatched in the same way.

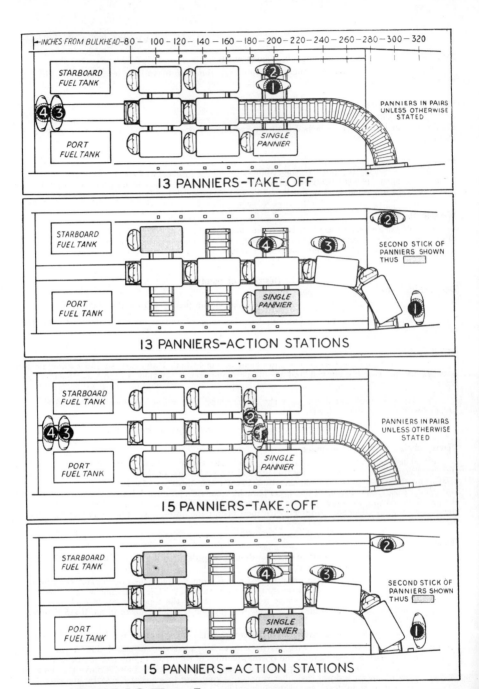

FIG. 3 DAKOTA I POSITIONS OF PANNIERS AND CREW

Length of stick

22.   The following are the lengths of stick based on test drops of wicker panniers:—

Case	No. of panniers	No. of runs	1st stick on 1st run		2nd stick on 2nd run		Minimum time between sticks
			No. of panniers	Stick length in yds.	No. of panniers	Stick length in yds.	
A	15	2	5 pairs	400	2 pairs + 1 single	190	3 min.
A	15	2	4 pairs	260	3 pairs + 1 single	260	4 min.
B	13	2	5 pairs	400	1 pair + 1 single	170	2 min.
B	13	2	4 pairs	260	2 pairs + 1 single	190	3 min.
B	13	2	3 pairs + 1 single	260	3 pairs	190	3 min.

23.   It will be noticed that the time taken to despatch a single pannier is assumed to be the same as that for a pair, with the result that the stick length for an odd number of panniers is approximately the same as that of the next higher even number.

CHAPTER 3

SUPPLIES DROPPING APPARATUS

LIST OF CONTENTS

LIST OF ILLUSTRATIONS

CHAPTER 3

SUPPLIES DROPPING APPARATUS

General

.1.   The apparatus described in this chapter is intended for use in supplementary supplies dropping operations as distinct from the dropping of supplies with a paratroop section.   In most instances the apparatus used for supplementary supplies dropping is different from that used for paratroop supplies, but, where the same apparatus is used, reference is made to the descriptions included in Sect. 2, Chap. 4, of this manual.

Mark VB apparatus

2. . The Mark VB apparatus is fully described in A.P.1180A, Vol. I, Part 1, Sect. 1.   The apparatus is made up of three portions, a hemispherical percussion cap forming the nose, a cylindrical container in one piece for the supplies, and a bucket in which the parachute is housed. The container can be adapted to carry either a liquid load, a load of ammunition, or a load of food or other supplies. The whole apparatus may be slung from a 500 lb. bomb carrier, or from either type of Universal bomb carrier.

Stores Ref. number

3.   The Stores Ref. number for the Mark VB apparatus complete with parachute is 15B/29.

Capacity of container

4.   The container is in the form of a cylinder, 31 in. long and 12½ in. in external diameter.   It has a volume, for supplies, of 2·07 cu. ft., which allows for the carriage of 11¼ gallons of liquid.   The open end of the container is fitted with a lid incorporating a filler cap.   For the carriage of liquids the lid is sweated in position, but for solid supplies the lid is loosely fitted.   It should be noted that solid and liquid supplies may not be carried in the container at the same time.

Weight of Mark VB apparatus

5.   The weight of the Mark VB container is as follows:—

    (i)   Mark VB container, empty, with temperate parachute,   41 lb.

    (ii) Mark VB container, empty, with tropical parachute,   46 lb.

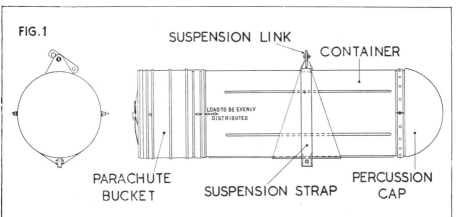

FIG.1

SUSPENSION LINK

CONTAINER

LOAD TO BE EVENLY DISTRIBUTED

PARACHUTE BUCKET

SUSPENSION STRAP

PERCUSSION CAP

MK.VB SUPPLIES DROPPING APPARATUS

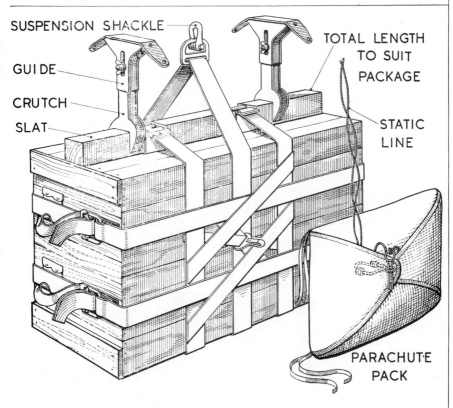

SUSPENSION SHACKLE

GUIDE

CRUTCH

SLAT

TOTAL LENGTH TO SUIT PACKAGE

STATIC LINE

PARACHUTE PACK

FIG.2 MK. VI HARNESS AND PARACHUTE

Mark VI apparatus

6.   The Mark VI apparatus is fully described in A.P.1180A, Vol. I, Part 1, Sect. 2.   It is also known as the "pack and harness" apparatus and comprises a webbing harness in which the package of supplies is wrapped as in a parcel, and a parachute in a pack is attached to the harness. The apparatus may be slung from a 500 lb. bomb carrier, or from either type of Universal bomb carrier.

7.   A modified form of the Mark VI apparatus is used in conjunction with the wicker panniers described in para. 15 of this chapter.

Stores Ref. number

8.   The Stores Ref. number for the Mark VI apparatus complete with parachute is 15B/39.

Weight of Mark VI apparatus

9.   The weight of the Mark VI apparatus is as follows:—

    (i)   Mark VI apparatus, unladen, with temperate parachute, $18\frac{1}{2}$ lb.
    (ii)   Mark VI apparatus, unladen, with tropical parachute, $23\frac{1}{2}$ lb.

C.L.E. Mark III container

10.   This container is briefly described and illustrated in Sect. 2, Chap. 4 of this manual.   It is fully described in A.P.1180A, Vol. I, Part 2 Sect. 1, Chap. 2.

Camouflet set carrier (*see* fig. 3)

11.   This apparatus is fully described in A.P.1180A, Vol. I, Part 2, Sect. 1, Chap. 7.   It comprises a special cradle (a modification of that used for the folding trolley and described in Sect. 2, Chap. 4 of this manual) in conjunction with a type D parachute pack as described in A.P.1180A, Vol. I, Part 2, Sect. 2, Chap. 3.

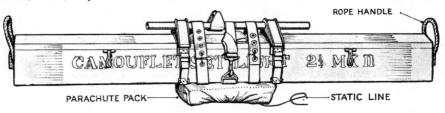

ROPE HANDLE

PARACHUTE PACK

STATIC LINE

CAMOUFLET SET AND CARRIER

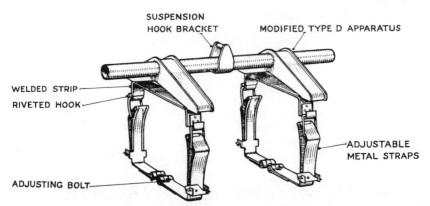

SUSPENSION HOOK BRACKET

MODIFIED TYPE D APPARATUS

WELDED STRIP

RIVETED HOOK

ADJUSTABLE METAL STRAPS

ADJUSTING BOLT

Fig. 3.—Camouflet Set and Carrier.

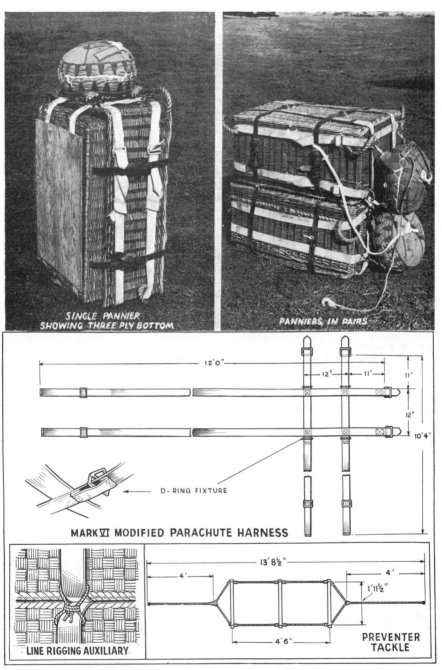

SINGLE PANNIER SHOWING THREE PLY BOTTOM

PANNIERS IN PAIRS

12'0"

12" 11"

11"

12"

10'4"

D-RING FIXTURE

MARK VI MODIFIED PARACHUTE HARNESS

LINE RIGGING AUXILIARY

13'8½"

4'

4'

1'11½"

4'6"

PREVENTER TACKLE

FIG. 4 WICKER PANNIERS AND HARNESS

Stores Ref. numbers

12. The Stores Ref. number of the camouflet set carrier has not yet been allocated; that for the type D parachute is 15C/47–54, the serial numbers referring to different coloured canopies.

Camouflet set, 2¼ in., Mark II

13. The camouflet set is used for drilling holes in hard ground for laying explosives and land mines. It is packed in a wooden box measuring 5 ft. 10 in. × 6½ in. × 6½ in. A rope handle is fitted to each end of the box. The box is held in the carrier by means of two adjustable metal straps (modifications of those used for the C.L.E. Mark I container cradle described in Sect. 2, Chap. 4 of this manual), and the parachute pack is strapped on to the underside of the box.

Weight of camouflet set and carrier

14. The gross weight of the camouflet set, carrier and parachute, is 122 lb.

Wicker panniers (*See* fig. 4)

15. Wicker panniers are made in the form of two rectangular hampers telescoping one into the other, and are fully described in A.P.1180A, Vol. I, Part 2, Sect. 1, Chap. 9. The closed dimensions of the pannier are 36 in. × 20 in. × 16 in., but the last dimension can be increased up to 30 in. by expanding the pannier. A piece of 5-plywood is wired to the base of a single pannier or a pair of panniers to enable the speed of despatch to be increased.

Modified Mark VI harness (*see* fig. 4)

16. Each pannier, whether for despatch singly or in pairs, is secured in a modified form of the Mark VI harness, which is used in conjunction with a parachute suitable to the load carried.

Parachutes for wicker panniers

17. For loads up to 100 lb. a type D parachute is suitable; for loads of 100 to 300 lb. a C.L.E. Mark I parachute should be used.

Stores Ref. numbers

18. The Stores Ref. number for the wicker pannier has not yet been allocated; that for the Mark VI harness *before modification* and without parachute is 15B/41; that for the type D parachute is 15C/47–54; that for the C.L.E. Mark I parachute is 15C/70, 90–96, the serial numbers referring to different coloured canopies.

Despatch of panniers by "daisy chain" method

19. By the "daisy chain" method, two panniers, placed one on top of the other are tied together by four single ties made of 100 lb. silk cord (Stores Ref. 15A/95), the ties being made between the leather straps on the panniers, two ties at each side, *see* fig. 4.

20. A C.L.E. Mark I parachute is attached to the end of each pannier, the static line of the bottom parachute (5 ft. 6 in. in length) being attached to the leather strap at the parachute end of the top pannier. The static line of the top parachute (15 ft. 6 in. in length) is attached to a snap hook which is hooked on the static line cable of the aircraft (Dakota I).

21. The two panniers fall as one object until the partial development of the top parachute causes a jerk which breaks the four ties between the panniers; the bottom pannier, falling away, has its static line pulled by the top pannier.

Weight of pannier

22. The weight of the pannier is as follows:—

(i)	Weight of pannier, empty, with harness and parachute …	50 lb.
(ii)	Gross weight of loaded pannier … … … …	350 lb.

General note

23. The installation on the Dakota I for the despatch of panniers is described and illustrated in Sect. 5, Chap. 2 of this manual.

Folding bicycle

24. The folding bicycle and parachute are briefly described in Sect. 2, Chap. 4 of this manual, and are fully described in A.P.1180A, Vol. I, Part 2, Sect. 1, Chap. 8.